Peninnah's World

Peninnah's World

A Jewish Life in Stories

Caren Schnur Neile

Foreword by Dan Ben-Amos

[handwritten inscription:] 10/21 For Stephanie with love and admiration, *[signature]*

Hamilton Books

Lanham • Boulder • New York • Toronto • London

Published by Hamilton Books
An imprint of The Rowman & Littlefield Publishing Group, Inc.
4501 Forbes Boulevard, Suite 200, Lanham, Maryland 20706
Hamilton Books Acquisitions Department (301) 459-3366

6 Tinworth Street, London SE11 5AL, United Kingdom

British Library Cataloguing in Publication Information Available

Library of Congress Cataloging-in-Publication Data Available

Names: Neile, Caren S. author.
Title: Peninnah's world : a Jewish life in stories / Caren Schnur Neile.
Description: Lanham : Hamilton Books, an imprint of Rowman & Littlefield, [2021] |
    Includes bibliographical references. | Summary: "Peninnah's World is the biography-
    in-stories of the iconic Jewish storyteller and folklorist Peninnah Schram. In vivid
    scenes, it dramatizes Schram's trajectory from brilliant daughter of Orthodox immi-
    grant parents in New London, Connecticut, to acclaimed performer, teacher, scholar
    and colleague of luminaries including Elie Wiesel, Isaac Bashevis Singer, and Molly
    Picon"—Provided by publisher.
Identifiers: LCCN 2021037510 (print) | LCCN 2021037511 (ebook) | ISBN
    9780761872917 (paperback) | ISBN 9780761872924 (epub)
Subjects: LCSH: Schram, Peninnah | Storytellers—United States—Biography. | Women
    storytellers—United States—Biography. | Jewish folk literature—History and criti-
    cism.
Classification: LCC GR55.S37 N45 2021 (print) | LCC GR55.S37 (ebook) | DDC
    398.2092 [B]—dc23
LC record available at https://lccn.loc.gov/2021037510
LC ebook record available at https://lccn.loc.gov/2021037511

♾TM The paper used in this publication meets the minimum requirements of American
National Standard for Information Sciences Permanence of Paper for Printed Library
Materials, ANSI/NISO Z39.48-1992.

For Jennifer and Chris Bourdain, with love and gratitude, always.

Contents

Foreword

Peninnah Schram is one of the initiators of the storytelling revival in contemporary Jewish culture. Storytelling is universal, but with the rise of print, radio and film, oral storytelling declined and slowly faded away from the public sphere of modern life. Quite likely in private quarters, storytelling has retained some of its vitality, but even there, parental book-reading has often replaced oral narration. As story-rich as Jewish culture is, it has not escaped that cultural turn.

Jewish culture evidences oral storytelling in its earliest literate document, the Hebrew Bible. In response to the Angel of God urging to lead his people in a war against the oppressing Midianites, Gideon son of Joash said: "Where are all His wonderous deeds about which our fathers told us?" (Judges 6:13). In the book of Psalms there are some further allusions to historical stories fathers tell their children (Psalms 44:2; 75:2; 78:3). Mothers are not storytellers in the Hebrew Bible.

The literature of the following historical period is distinguished nominally by its orality, *torah she-be-al-peh*, "Oral Torah." In addition to laws and religious regulations, the Talmud and the Midrash are replete with narratives of a broad generic range, from myths to jokes, projecting a dynamic storytelling in diverse contexts. While in the late antiquity, the transition from orality to literacy was rabbinically controlled, in the Middle Ages, with the increased rate of literacy, capable individuals wrote down popular tales that circulated orally in Jewish communities.

A fourth period of vital storytelling swept through the Pale of Settlement in East-European communities, thematically revolving around the miraculous and magical acts and the mystical experiences and revelations of the Hasidic holy men, the *rebbes*, In the nineteenth century, the Hasidic storytelling tradition transformed from orality to popular literature that circulated in Jewish communities and later, in the twentieth century, had a literary revival of its own, circulating in translation in urban Jewish European communities and in intellectual Jewish circles.

Finally, most recently, scholarly publications transferred to literacy the stories Jews told orally in the entire geographical and linguistic breadth of Asian, African and European Diaspora communities. Jewish scholars have recorded these tales, motivated not by their search for the exotic Other, but rather by their recognizing in them their lost brothers. The University of Haifa became the home of the central deposit of folktale manuscripts, The Israel Folktale Archives (IFA) named in honor of

Dov Noy (1920–2013), who founded it 1955. In her books and storytelling performances, Peninnah draws extensively on these tales, thereby introducing contemporary American Jewry to the ethnic tapestry of the modern gathering of exiles in Israeli society. With amazing erudition, Peninnah Schram draws upon all those Jewish literary resources both as a scholar and as a performing storyteller. As a scholar, in a series of narrative anthologies, she demonstrates that stories and storytelling, more effectively than laws and regulations, project the fundamental humanistic values and ideals that constitute the Jewish ways of life. Throughout Jewish history, narratives have taught compassion, generosity, and the preservation of human dignity and Jewish identity. In her research, teaching and storytelling, Peninnah Schram presents the Jewish narrative tradition as a manifestation of Jewish identity not only in the past, but also as applicable to contemporary culture.

As an artist, Peninnah Schram has taken Jewish storytelling out of its historical religious contexts and introduced it to the general education system and community life of modern Jewish society. Wisely, in her Jewish storytelling revival, she has not claimed ethnographic authenticity, nor has she sought to dramatize storytelling in staged traditional contexts. She shifts storytelling from either imaginary or informed ethnic or historic storytelling situations onto the stage of contemporary life and its contexts. Her storytelling has its own aesthetic integrity, introducing traditional folktales into modern society through performance. The classical transitions of storytelling from oral to literate cultural contexts were accomplished through print. Peninnah achieves this goal through performance, in community halls, in storytelling festivals, and in academic teaching. She does not assume the role of an actor playing the part of a storyteller. Rather she *is* the storyteller, enlisting all the professional means of mimicry, gesture and verbal modulation. Surely, her storytelling is entertaining, but this is an entertainment with morals for contemporary Jewish society.

—Dan Ben-Amos

The Storyteller

by Peretz Kaminsky (For Peninnah Schram)

talk
tell
use words

You tell stories
with your eyes
with your shoulders
your hands
You tell with your silences
tell without telling
in the spaces between words

You tell about madness
but you are not mad
and about rage
but you are not angry
and about dying
as though death is a story

We listen
to the words
to the silences
listen to your voice
and look at your face
at your moving lips
at your eyes
at your eyes opening and closing

Unnumbered whispers
Countless voices whispering
with eyes closed
with lips moving
in cadences
in rhythmic repetitions
in arpeggios

Flowing softly
opening meaning

the words in the whispers
    become prayers
    become stories
    become silence

There is imagination to fly in
There is truth to find
There are definitions to specify
There is terror to live through
There are stories to shape
There are dead to remember

There is the phoenix
Rising rising on the smoke
    . . . from the ashes
    . . . from the sparks
    in the story

The listeners become the phoenix
    with new hands and feet
    with new legs and arms
    with the entire catalogue
        of bones and functions
        that walk across the spaces
        and the times of memory
    become fertile once again

And the storyteller sings and sighs
    "The sand of time is flowing out
    of the mysteries we sing about"
after silences and searches
the storyteller sings and gells
    "The footprints that we leave behind
    become the treasures others find"

We make rituals of words
    there is imagination
    there is truth
    there are definitions
    there is terror
    there are the dead
    there is meaning

And there is the notion
that only the homeless can cherish
    that our footprints sink into an ocean of sand
    and that they never will perish

You talk

tell
use words
eyes
You tell with your eyes
with your shoulders
your hands
and with your silences

Acknowledgments

It takes a universe to publish a book. My brightest stars are Randi and Richard Jones for their unflagging and above-and-beyond support of me and of my work. A big thank-you also to Marc Kaminsky for allowing me to print his brilliant father's brilliant unpublished poem "The Storyteller," which he wrote and dedicated to Peninnah Schram in 1987. My sincere gratitude to Dan Ben-Amos for his important foreword. Thank you also to my dear, talented fellow writers and editors Angelika Kofler and Leslie Ross, for reading and commenting on early drafts. Without the belief in my work on the part of Brooke Bures of Hamilton Books, there would be no book, and for that I will always be grateful. I have adored and admired Peninnah Schram since the day we met, and that feeling has only grown throughout this amazing process. This gift to you has been a privilege for me. And finally, my thanks to Tom Neile, for everything.

Introduction

Telling the Human Story

This is the biography of a performance storyteller that, like the most compelling stories, dramatizes incidents of its subject's life in order to promote connection with, and understanding of, the events and emotions it contains. It is also a book about a scholar of storytelling, so it seeks to challenge us to consider the stories that are told and retold, and why.

My journey to this biography has taken twenty years. In 2001, I contacted the prominent storyteller and scholar Peninnah Schram out of the blue to ask her to serve on my doctoral dissertation committee. That was a little unusual. What was a lot more unusual was the fact that she immediately said yes.

Professor Schram taught storytelling, among other things, at a different academic institution from mine, in a different state. All she knew about me was that we were members of the same professional organization, the National Storytelling Network, that she had heard me speak, and that my research involved storytelling. At the time, she was sixty-six years old, an age at which many people are scaling back their work, if not retiring altogether. Yet Schram was still performing and teaching on a regular basis, and a great deal of her scholarship was still ahead of her. Nevertheless she said yes, yes, yes.

So I owe her, certainly. But that is not why I came to write this book—although, as we Jews say on Passover, *dayenu*. That would have been enough.

Peninnah Manchester Schram is among the world's preeminent scholars of Jewish folk narrative, having authored or co-authored fourteen books and numerous academic articles and chapters on the subject. She taught at Iona College and Yeshiva University (YU), and is currently Professor Emerita at YU's Stern College for Women. She is also a world-renowned performer of Jewish folk narratives. Among her numerous awards and honors is the Covenant Foundation's prestigious Covenant Award for Outstanding Jewish Educator, the National Jewish Book Award from the Jewish Book Council, and the Lifetime Achievement Award, among others, from the National Storytelling Network.

Whenever I perform Jewish stories in South Florida, moreover, someone from the audience invariably asks me if I know her. They usually go on to wax eloquent about a performance of hers they attended five or ten or twenty years earlier. So Schram is an icon in my field, certainly. But that is not why I wrote this book, either.

I wrote this book because I believe what Professor Schram believes. That the traditions and values of a people matter. That the past not only has something to teach us, but also that it is always with us. That the stories of our ancestors—whether in the form of folk narrative or family memorate—are crucial to our understanding of who we are, where we have been and where we are going—so crucial, in fact, that they deserve study and analysis in the highest echelons of academia. And, perhaps most importantly, that these stories must continue to be shared with future generations and among ourselves.

In the dedication to her anthology *Jewish Stories One Generation Tells Another*, Schram wrote of her parents that their "voices resonate in my *neshome* [soul]. They taught me what stories to tell" (1987, v). On one level, the sentiment reflects the collection's title and subject matter, and fittingly, the author dedicates the work to her children. But the phrase also situates her within a lineage of storytellers—making a clear distinction between wholly original artistic creation and the retelling of folk narrative, which by definition has been received either vertically from elders or horizontally from peers, prior to taking on the speech patterns and other unique creative elements of the individual teller. As opposed to those writers of fiction who suffer from the oft-cited "anxiety of influence," that is, those who strive to emerge from the shadows of their literary forebears, Schram sets her work squarely in the realm of the human, tribal and familial. In her "My Storyteller's Prayer" that appears in this book, she refers to "the collective wisdom of our people" embedded in the tales she tells, recognizing that the goal of storytelling is infinitely more than entertainment—although that matters, too. She is well aware that these stories are nothing less than the lifeblood of her Jewish heritage.

Some rabbis have held that Judaism rests on three equal pillars: the Torah, or the Five Books of Moses, ancient rabbinical commentaries on the Torah (Talmud), and *aggadah*, lore. According to traditional Jewish belief, the Torah was dictated to Moses by God, while the Talmud is the transcript of discussion and debate among rabbis through the centuries that was finally committed to text more than a millennium ago. Aggadah, meanwhile, is a non-legalistic component of the Jewish oral tradition that includes tales.

Thus orality is paramount in Judaism, beginning with the Biblical description of what may well have been the first speech act: "Let there be light." The Jewish oral tradition was employed not only by rabbis and teachers, but also, particularly in Europe, by *maggidim*—literally tellers—storytellers who, along with peddlers, traveled from town to town hawking their wares. When, in the chapter "What Joe Wants," the young Peninnah gazes over at the books beside her bed, these are compilations of the sort of tales that traveled with maggidim and were taught by rabbis and teachers. They comprise the stories of her people, and thus they not only serve to make the young teen feel strong, but also have served to strengthen her forebears.

Along with my assertion that Schram is connecting to the lifeblood of her people, however, I should note that a good amount of this lifeblood business is unconscious. When we tell stories about ourselves—which occurs both in ordinary human intercourse and, increasingly, onstage, particularly through the phenomenon of storytelling slams—we replicate, usually without a second thought, motifs and tale types (elements and plot patterns) that we have heard since childhood, demonstrating storytelling's connection to the (universal) collective unconscious. More specifically, when Schram wrote her storyteller's prayer, she had no idea that a prominent Chasidic rabbi from Poland had done a similar exercise two centuries earlier. When I collect single-panel cartoons that reference fairy tales, I cannot know how much thought the artists gave to the fact that a joke about Rapunzel transmits a folk narrative tradition, and when sportswriters refer to a "Cinderella story," they undoubtedly do so simply because it's shorthand for a certain narrative pattern with which most of their readers are familiar. Along these lines, there is an old *Star Trek: Next Generation* episode called "Darmok," in which an alien civilization communicates purely through allusions to its foundational myths. A great idea, that, because it illuminates something we humans do all the time. Shared referents are communication aids, certainly. But they also connect us to those who transmitted the tales before us and those who will do so after.

THE HUMAN STORY

Peninnah Schram's narratives connect her to her Jewish ancestors, but she is also a New Yorker, having spent most of her adult life in the city. Thus her world is one of delis and synagogues, the Lower East Side and the 92nd Street YWHA, Stern College for Women, Isaac Bashevis Singer and Molly Picon. Moreover while *Peninnah's World* celebrates that specific world, or that of New London, Connecticut, where she grew up, with the Mohican and Griswold hotels and nearby Jewish-owned farms, it is equally intended to inspire readers to remember, celebrate and share the stories and personalities that comprise their own worlds.

One of the saddest things I hear in the course of my professional life is "I have no stories," followed by "I am not a storyteller." According to the late communication scholar Walter Fisher, to be human is to be *homo narrans*, a storytelling animal, distinct from other animals in our ability to understand our lives not only as a series of stories, but also as a single, overarching story. Unfortunately, I have often found that the most unwilling storytellers are often quite well educated, yet feel unable in a way they likely never were as children to exercise this wholly human skill.

Consider the term "life story." Any life contains its formidable characters, memorable settings, and both bearable and unbearable conflicts that lead to transformations that its protagonist never saw coming. Any life is worth imagining, visualizing, reliving and sharing in a way that readers or listeners feel as though they had been present when the events took place. How else will we truly understand each other? Yet many of us, when faced with the question "Who are you?" are as likely as not to respond with a resume, a shopping list of data. *I've been there. I've done that.*

It is also important to note that not only is storytelling a human enterprise *par excellence*, but also that human stories overlap. Although particular variants, or versions, of folk narrative derive from specific cultures, the same general tale types, motifs and themes, the same symbols and archetypes, appear throughout the world. Case in point: In 1893, the English Folklore Society released a volume of 345 variants of Cinderella, collected by Marian Roalfe Cox, and since then many more have been discovered. Among these, "Rhodopis" (Egyptian), "Aschenputtel" (German) and "Yeh-Hsien" (Chinese) may at first glance appear to be very different stories, but they all roughly conform to what is known to folklorists as Tale Type ATU 501A. What does the fact that we respond to the same story throughout history and around the globe tell us about human beings? In short, that we humans are more alike than we are different.

If that is the case, is it then too much to hope that not only will the life stories in *Peninnah's World* inspire readers to tell their own, but that they will also cause them to reframe and reshape the stories in this book, to retell them for years to come in their own words and with their own perspectives, just as Schram and other storytellers do with folk narrative? If so, then the storyteller will become not only the story, as she has in these pages, but she will also become, like the stories she tells, immortal. Which seems to me a fitting legacy indeed.

The great poet of New York Walt Whitman wrote, "I contain multitudes." It is my intent, as well as my fervent wish, that Peninnah Schram's biography-in-stories will remind its readers that indeed, so do we all.

Maybe I should have called it *Peninnah's Worlds*.

About the Stories

The twenty-five story/chapters in this book are based on extensive interviews I conducted in person and over the telephone with Professor Schram between December 2019 and November 2020, as well as on some of her writings. I have divided them into three sections. "In the Beginning" chronicles Schram's early years as a cantor's daughter in New London, Connecticut. We meet her parents and her older brother Joe, and we see how her earliest experiences shaped the woman she became, with a love of Jewish folklore and performance, a striving for scholastic success, a strong love of *Yiddishkayt*, and, above all, a passion for faith, friendship and family. The next section, "A Woman of the World," presents Schram's years of coming into her own as a woman, wife and mother. The section ends with the loss of her beloved husband Irving, precipitating dramatic choice and equally dramatic change. The final section, "A Woman of Valor," follows the storyteller's entry into both academia and storytelling, coming to terms with the deaths of her parents, her second marriage, acclamation and awards, her retirement from Stern College, and a glimpse of what lies beyond.

Peninnah does not perform narratives from her life, neither did she tell me the stories as I have dramatized them. Based on the extensive details she provided, I was able to create scenes for which she then asked me to make adjustments for accuracy, with comments such as, "My mother would never have used that expression," or "Actually his name was. . . ." or "The sofa was maroon, not blue." In this way, I was able to turn a treasure trove of data into images that, I hope, are memorable. In so doing, I have employed a method I have used when ghostwriting memoirs for clients, which I have described as follows:

> This memoir is the result of an intensely creative collaboration between those who experienced the events it describes and one who attempted to bring their stories and their loved ones back to life on the page. All conversations are presented according to the authors' best recollections and represent their effort to recreate what was actually said. (Unnumbered page)

As I complete this book, Peninnah Schram is nearly eighty-seven years old, and she has barely altered her hectic performance and writing schedule, even during a pandemic. At this rate, *Peninnah's World* may be just the first of multiple volumes of her life. I wonder if she will ask me to record the ensuing chapters of her astonishing and inspiring life in stories. Because if she does, I will answer yes. *Yes, yes, yes.*

WORKS CITED

Cox, Marian Rolfe, 1893. *Cinderella: Three Hundred and Forty-Five Variants of Cinderella,* Catskin *and,* Cap O' Rushes, *Abstracted and Tabulated with a Discussion of Medieval Analogues and Notes.* London, UK: Folklore Society.

Menosky, Joe, 1981. "Darmok." *Star Trek: The Next Generation,* Season 5, episode 2. Winrich Kolbe, director.

Schram, Peninnah, 1987. *Jewish Stories One Generation Tells Another.* Lanham, Maryland: Jason Aronson. Rowman and Littlefield.

Walker, Fay, Rosen, Rosen, with Caren S. Neile, 2002. *Hidden: A Sister and Brother in Nazi Poland.* Madison: University of Wisconsin Press.

Timeline

1934 Peninnah Pearl Manchester born December 28

1952 Graduated Williams Memorial Institute

1956 Graduated University of Connecticut

1958 Met Irving Schram, traveled in Europe for nine weeks, married

1960 Moved to Paris

1961 First trip to Israel

1963 Birth of daughter Rebecca

1964 Launching of Theater à la Carte

1965 Birth of son Mordechai

1967 Death of Irving Schram, began teaching at Iona College

1968 Completed Columbia University graduate program

1969 Started teaching at Stern College for Women, began volunteering at the Jewish Braille Institute

1970 Father Samuel Manchester died

1973 Began 92nd St. Y storytelling

1973 Began first WEVD radio storytelling series

1974 Taught first storytelling class at Stern College

1974 Remarried

1978 Mother Dora Manchester died

1984 Organized the Jewish Storytelling Center/CAJE

1984 Organized first Jewish Storytelling Festival

1985 Featured first time at National Storytelling Festival

1986 Publication of first book

1990 Start of collaboration with Gerard Edery

1994 First grandchild born, organized Jewish storytelling festival

1995 Received Covenant Foundation Award

1996 Organized third storytelling festival

2015 Retirement

I

1934–1952: In the Beginning . . .

ONE

The Pearl

In the first hour of December 28, 1934, Dora Markman Manchester, nine months pregnant, was jarred from a fitful sleep.

"*Chazzen!*" she cried out to her husband. Even in moments of crisis or excitement, she could never forget that she had married a distinguished man of God.

Samuel was fully awake in an instant. "What is it, Dvorele?" Is it time?"

"Get the girl to come for Joe! I'm feeling the water we should go to the hospital!"

Their firstborn Joe, age two-and-a-half, bore a well-deserved reputation as a little hellion. When his usual babysitter, a local teenager named Elizabeth from a good Russian Orthodox family, received the call to come stay with him, she murmured a faint prayer that he would be fast asleep when she arrived.

While he waited for the young woman, Cantor Samuel Manchester paced in the general vicinity of the front door. He had too much *shpilkes* to sit, so helpless did he feel at his inability, until the babysitter arrived, either to make his wife more comfortable or to take her the mile and a half to Lawrence Memorial Hospital, which had opened in New London about twenty years earlier. There was no problem, of course: his mother-in-law was upstairs with Dora, and he knew that Elizabeth would arrive soon. While he paced, he thought about his beloved wife, how he had fallen in love with her five years earlier—the very moment he set eyes on the dark-haired beauty from White Russia, who had fortuitously attended a wedding he was conducting in New York City. She had been living with her parents in Harlem, and at the time of the wedding, his day job had been just twenty-five miles away in Bayonne, New Jersey. (What if, God forbid, he had still been employed in Holyoke or Fall River,

3

Massachusetts, or even Utica or Troy in New York State—all so much further from the city!) In the ten months between their meeting and their own wedding, Samuel, already a widower past fifty with five grown children, had penned numerous letters in Yiddish in his ornate handwriting, addressed to the much younger Miss Dora Markman. The first was in the mail not twenty-four hours after they met.

"I bless the day (or better to say the evening) when I met you, when we made the introductions," he began. He went on to describe how taken he had been by her bohemian style, with the flowing, flower-print dress and the large gold hoops hanging from her delicate ears.

Now Elizabeth would arrive any minute, and he would drive his beautiful wife to give birth to their second baby and, God willing, all would be well with mother and child. He hated the fact that his parents, long dead back in Lithuania, would never meet Dora or their children. His firstborn was the namesake of his own father, Yosef Hovchovich, a chazzen, *shochet* and *mohel* as he himself had become.

Samuel thought of his handsome, dignified father; he pictured the *Shabbes* walks they took together back home by the banks of the Nieman River, and the precious letters he had sent to America from the Old Country that began with such stunning traditional honorifics, so rare for a father to use to address his own child: "To my beloved son, my friend, man of great wisdom, well known in all areas, expert ritual slaughterer and verifier of *kashrut* and God-fearing man, chazzen and fine composer. . . ." "To my beloved son, my friend, as cherished as my own soul, ritual slaughterer and verifier of kashrut and well-known chazzen and man of great wisdom and fine composer. . . ." With a smile he pictured the few added lines written by his mother Perel, wishing him well and telling him how much she loved him.

They were both gone from this world, the wise man of God who had been his mentor, and the loving mother who had been his bastion of strength, who had taught him how to love. Maybe this was why he had married again, at his relatively advanced age. When his first wife Chana died, his children were old enough to fend for themselves. But he wanted *mishpacha* around him. What was life for a Jew, or anybody else for that matter, without family?

In the midst of his musings, the doorbell sounded, and Samuel strode over and reached for the knob.

"Hello, Reverend Manchester," the young girl at the door said primly. "Is Joe asleep?"

Grinning beneath his dark moustache, he let her pass into the hallway. "Yes, Elizabeth, you should have an easy night. Come, take a seat." As she made her way to the sofa, he approached the bookshelf on the opposite wall and pulled down the family *Tanach* from the rows of sacred volumes.

Elizabeth watched him leaf through the pages and then stop and draw down his finger to a certain spot. Then he walked over to her and showed her exactly where he was pointing.

"If the baby is a girl," he told the babysitter, "this is the name I'm going to give her. It's how my mother was called in Habrew. A beautiful name, don't you think?" She nodded. He reached down for a slip of paper, set it at the page he had chosen, and replaced the book on the shelf. Then he climbed the stairs and reappeared a few minutes later, gripping his weary-looking wife by the hand and waist, pausing with her at every step. At the door, he picked up the suitcase she had packed in preparation.

"*Gott tzu dankn,*" Dora whispered between contractions. "Thank God you're here, Elizabeth."

"Good luck, Mrs. Manchester," she replied.

Samuel turned to the babysitter. "Stay close by the phone, just in case I need to call."

Several hours later, the telephone rang. Elizabeth, who had been dozing, jumped an inch or two off the couch before reaching for it.

"Hello?"

"Elizabeth, everything is okay?"

"Yes, Reverend. Joseph is fast asleep."

"Good. Do me a kindness please to go over to the place in the Bible that I showed you, and remind me how to spell the name."

The girl didn't hesitate. She returned to the telephone with the book and read out the spelling. "P-E-N-I-N-N-A-H."

"That's it. Thank you, Elizabeth."

"So it's a girl, Reverend Manchester?" she asked shyly. "Congratulations!"

"Thank you very much. Yes, a beautiful little girl."

His voice was so quiet that Elizabeth thought perhaps mother and daughter were sleeping close by. She knew she should let him get back to them, but she had been wondering something since she arrived.

"Does the name have a meaning, sir?" she asked.

"Yes," Samuel replied. "It means 'pearl' in Hebrew. And her middle name is Pearl in English. My mother was Perel, which is 'pearl' in Yiddish."

The teen nodded, although there was no one to see. For no apparent reason, she added, "You must really miss your parents, Reverend."

He took a breath. He was not a young man. He had been on this earth more than half a century, and now had two beautiful families of his own. And yet.

"More than you can imagine, Elizabeth," he said. "More than you can imagine."

TWO

The Elijah Story

Shul, *kiddush* and lunch were long over. Samuel Manchester leaned back in the large maroon armchair in the living room, as he did every *Shabbes* afternoon. His eyes were closed, the long fingers of his right hand were lightly clasped around the Yiddish newspaper balanced on the armrest, and he was snoring softly. When five-year-old Peninnah scrambled onto his lap, he woke with a start. The child shimmied into a comfortable position, which she knew from long experience.

He lifted his wire-rimmed glasses to rub his eyes. When he spoke, his voice was dusky with sleep.

"*Nove bransiche, ehre plansiche, pastechl, katchke, tzuganke, goldene kepele!* What can I do for you?"

Soldier recruit, little airplane, little shepherd, goose, gypsy, golden head: that was his usual greeting for her, running the pet names together in a singsong, with a smile that covered the landscape of his entire face, from his dark goatee clear up to his hairline.

"Pa, tell me a story," she said, leaning her head against his chest.

"And which story would that be?"

"The Elijah story when he whistles!"

"*Nu?*" he teased, tickling her under the chin. "Why always the Elijah story? Why not, Deborah, or Judith?"

Her brow furrowed. "But Elijah is my favorite! Please, Papa. You can tell those stories tomorrow, okay?"

"I will remember that," he said, playfully wagging his finger. "But lucky for you, Elijah happens to be my favorite, too."

"I know," she whispered. "Elijah the Prophet."

The clock on the piano chimed four as her father adjusted the pillow behind him and settled more deeply into the chair.

"Eliyahu *ha Navi*, the Prophet," he began. "Sometimes he disguises himself as an old man, at other times a handsome horseman, or a beggar, who wanders from place to place. This way, people don't know who he is, you see?" He paused, reaching around her to pull his handkerchief from his pocket to wipe his nose.

"Papa!" she pleaded. "Say how he watches people!"

"Yes, yes, *mein goldene keppele*. He watches them to see how they act with each other, and how they speak to each other. Are they kind? Are they generous? Are they honest? He watches and witnesses, this Elijah. And most importantly," he said, tapping the tip of her nose, "he remembers."

The child wriggled with delight.

"One day," he said, "Elijah is walking down the street of a small village in the disguise of a poor man. He comes to a broken down cottage. Its shutters lost their hinges, and the roof is full of holes. But still, there is something he likes about this little cottage. So he says to himself, 'I'm going to stay here and rest awhile.'"

Peninnah's eyelids lower, but only with pleasure, like those of a cat in mid-purr.

"The poor couple that live in this hut, they have nothing. Can you imagine that? No radio, no piano, not even what to make *latkes* for Chanukah. But they invite him in anyway, give him water to wash, and ask him to share some herring and black bread for supper.

"'It's all we have,' the man tells Elijah, 'but we are happy to share it with a guest.'"

"Like Ma says," the little girl piped up.

"What is that, my little gypsy?"

"Ma always says when company comes, it feels more like a banquet."

Her father chuckled. "Yes, she does," he said. "And she's right. So they eat whatever there is," he went on, "and at the end of the meal, Elijah the Prophet—"

"In disguise!"

"In disguise." He nodded. "So he says to this couple, 'Because of your kind hospitality, I will grant you three wishes. Whatever you wish for will be yours.'

"I wish I knew Elijah the Prophet," she said.

Her papa thought for a moment. "Maybe you do know him. Maybe one of your three wishes was to be right here listening to this story!" He tickled her, and she giggled.

"So the man says to Elijah, 'My wife and I are content with what we have, but to have a bigger house would be more place for my books.'

"Nu," her father said, looking down at Peninnah, "You know Elijah doesn't just give you things."

"He whistles!"

"That's right. Maybe he has a flute, or maybe he just uses his lips. In any case, he whistles. And just like that, the little cottage becomes a mansion."

"Papa?" she asked. "Does it have real big pillows like *Bubbe* and *Zayde*'s house in Harlem?"

He thought for a moment or two. "I believe they were even bigger."

"Papa?"

"Yes, little helicopter. What is it?"

"I don't know your papa."

He gave a small, sad smile. "That's because he no longer lives."

"What was he like?"

"You want to know now?" He looked at his beloved daughter's expectant little face and squeezed her shoulders. "Okay, okay, let me think. Your Zayde Hovchovich, my papa, he would always walk into a building with his right foot forward."

"Why, Papa?"

"Because people used to think that the right foot stands for goodness and success, honey. Nu, what does Elijah do next?"

It took her a breath or two to shift gears, but she enjoyed the story too much to dawdle. "He asks the wife! And she wants a necklace."

"And for the second wish, she wants some nice jewelry, that's right," he said. "And the husband asks for some nice clothes, too." When he caught her scowl, he asked, "You wouldn't want a necklace or clothes? What would you wish for?"

"I would wish for another doll. Or maybe a book."

"Well, maybe she had enough dolls and books already. Anyway, where was I? Oh yes. So Elijah gives a second whistle, and the woman is dressed like Queen Esther herself.

"And then for the third wish, they say some gold would be nice, to help others and serve nice food to guests for Shabbes. So Elijah the Prophet whistles a third time, and piles and piles of gold fill the room. Then Elijah disappears."

Peninnah fidgeted while her father watched her with obvious pleasure.

"Then Elijah gets busy with other things," he said at last, "and the years go by. One day, something reminds him of the old couple, and he wants to know how they are living, and if they are doing *mitzvot* with all those riches."

She frowned. "He doesn't like what he sees."

"No, tzugankele, you are right. "He doesn't like it at all. A big iron fence surrounds the mansion, to keep away people. Especially the poor. And the shutters are closed, too. As Elijah gets closer, the guards take a step toward him, and the dogs bark.

"Then the master of the house comes out and starts to holler, 'Get away from here, you beggar!' And you know what he does? He threatens to set the dogs on him!" The child nodded, her eyes wide.

"But Elijah says, 'So this is how you deal with strangers now? You, who have everything?'

"At that very moment, the man understands. He knows who this is, what he, the man himself, has done, and even what is going to happen." Samuel paused, extending the child's joyful anticipation of what was to come.

"He's a bad man!" she said.

Her father shrugged. "Nu, let's say he isn't a very good man. So Elijah gives a whistle, and all the gold disappears. And just as the wife comes running out in her fine clothes to tell her husband that the gold is gone, Elijah gives a second whistle, and all the—"

"The beautiful clothes and jewels! They disappear!"

"That's right. The husband and wife look down at themselves and once again they are dressed in rags. And then Elijah gives a third whistle, and the beautiful house becomes again just a simple old cottage. And only then does the couple understand how poor in spirit they have become, even with all the riches in the world."

Peninnah sank in closer to her father's broad chest and yawned. She was silent for so long that her father thought she had fallen asleep.

Then she asked, "Papa, are we rich?"

Looking down at her, her father smiled and rubbed her back.

"Only in spirit, *kindele*. In spirit, we have all the riches in the world."

THREE

Piano Lessons

As long as Peninnah could remember, the sheet music for Beethoven's "Moonlight Sonata" had sat on the black mahogany Marshall and Mendel upright piano in the living room. Before she knew what they meant, she was intimately familiar with the spidery lines on the ivory paper and the strange words and numbers that comprised the piece's official name: "Piano Sonata No. 14 in C-Sharp Minor, Sonata Quasi Una Fantasia, Opus 27, No. 2."

She had always known that her father was a distinguished chazzen and composer of Jewish music. She knew that with his resonant baritone, he taught other cantors complex liturgical melodies, and that his eldest daughter from his first family could play piano, read music and compose. So when her papa sat her on his lap on the couch and told her, pointing to those clusters of notes across the room, that one day she would learn to play his favorite piece of secular music, she had no doubt that she would.

"I especially like the bass chords," he said. "The low notes," he added in a bear-like growl, making her laugh. She was determined to play those best, to please him.

Peninnah was eight years old the winter that her parents decided she was ready to start piano lessons. Gold hoop earrings swinging to the rhythm of her footsteps, Mama walked her to the teacher's house, a small wooden building a few doors down from Bartlett Grammar School. Cottony clouds puffed from their mouths as they spoke.

All at once, Peninnah sneezed.

"Tzu gezunt, tzu laing yor tzu laing lebn," Mama said, as she always did when someone sneezed. To health, to long years, to long life. "Look, we're here, and soon you'll be plenty warm." When the child said nothing, she added, "It's so wonderful to be able to play the piano." She

squeezed her daughter's hand as they climbed the wooden steps to ring the doorbell. "I never had the chance."

"I know," Peninnah said with a brisk nod. When they reached the small front porch, she looked down at her plain black school shoes. "But I think it may be really hard."

Before her mother could answer, a middle-aged woman opened the door and smiled at her visitors.

"Good afternoon," she said, first to the child and then to the mother. "I'm Mrs. Spargo. Right on time, good. Do come in."

"I'm Peninnah. I am here to learn the 'Moonlight Sonata.'"

The teacher's smile grew wider, but she quickly suppressed it. "Beethoven," she said approvingly, stepping aside for them to pass into the house. "You have good taste."

Peninnah glanced at her mother, who was gently pushing her into the overheated hallway. "It's my papa's favorite."

"I see," said the teacher. "Then in time you will learn it."

The first thing Mrs. Spargo did after shepherding her guests into the music room was to bend down to feed the wood stove in the corner. She motioned to Peninnah to come forward and rubbed the child's cold hands over the heat while Mrs. Manchester took a seat.

"This will help," the teacher said. "No one should be expected to play a note with frozen fingers."

They began with scales in John W. Schaum's "Leading to Mastery of the Instrument," as well as simple songs. Up and down the notes, up and down the keys she played, falteringly those first few sessions with Mrs. Spargo, then over and over and better and better at home, until her little fingers ached. Through it all, her mother listened, to her early pieces with names like "Drifting Clouds," "A Rainy Day," "The Little Defenders" and "Graceful Stepper." Mama was so pleased with her daughter's progress that she started calling her Piannah, as a play on her name.

It soon became clear that music was not only in Peninnah's fingers, but also in her blood, her bones and her heart. Before long, she received her first real piece: Chopin's "Regentropfen, the Raindrop Prelude in D-Flat Major." It was challenging, she thought, to remember all those flats. But the child was grateful that the tempo was slow, and she focused on it measure by measure.

One afternoon, when she had finished the lesson to her teacher's satisfaction with a few minutes to spare, Mrs. Spargo turned to her.

"Would you like to hear me play it all the way through?" she asked. "That way you'll know what you're working toward."

The child flushed. "Oh, yes!"

The piece was beautiful, simple, and over in five or six minutes. Mama was already gathering her coat and scarf as Mrs. Spargo hit the closing notes.

"Could you—could you play something else?" she asked, avoiding her mother's eyes. Mama always had so much to do; Peninnah knew this time was stolen from her busy schedule. But it was as if she had gotten a nibble of something delicious and would do anything in her power to acquire a bit more.

Mrs. Spargo glanced at her mother, who nodded slowly.

"Just a little bit of something," she said. "This is by Ludwig von Beethoven. A wonderful classical composer, like Chopin. The man who wrote your father's 'Moonlight Sonata,' in fact.

From the opening notes, the girl's jaw dropped with wonder. Never had she imagined such a thing existed. Never had she heard anything so extraordinary. It was as though this were her first experience of music. She loved her father's chanting at Ahavath Chesed, their local shul, where he spent so many hours singing to God on behalf of the congregation. She always looked forward to the songs on the radio. But hearing this, she felt transported to another planet, an altered consciousness. The feeling was not only emotional. It was palpable. She felt as though she were floating.

When Mrs. Spargo stopped, Peninnah was speechless for several seconds. Then she asked, her voice just above a whisper, "Will I ever be able to play like that?"

The teacher smiled. "If you work at it, dear. If you work really hard, I believe you can."

Many months passed. One day, Peninnah rushed through the door of Mrs. Spargo's house and handed her a large, serious-looking book.

"I know now that I'm not ready for the 'Moonlight Sonata,'" she said shyly. "But I have something else I'd really like to learn to play."

The piano teacher looked curiously at Peninnah and then down at the cover.

"*Jewish Folk Songs*," she read. She thumbed through the pages. "Did you get this from your father?"

"Yes," she replied. "My father wrote a book of his own music for the synagogue, you see, and sometimes he goes to New York, to the Metro Music Company on Second Avenue, to give them more to sell. Last week, he came home with this book."

Mrs. Spargo smiled. "Well, is there a particular song you want to learn?"

The child tugged at the little slip of paper that had almost fallen between the pages.

"It's here," she said, flipping to the bookmark. "Page 29. It's the lullaby his mama sang to him when he was a baby. It's very old. A hundred years, at least." She glanced over at her mother, who at that moment was absorbed in looking for something in her pocketbook.

"My father's last name used to be Hovchovich, and he comes from a place in a country called Lithuania, a town called, um, Sapizishok. It's by a big river. That's where his mama sang him this song. In Sapizishok."

Now her mother was listening, and she didn't look happy. "Mrs. Spargo isn't interested in this," she said, her voice almost a whisper.

The piano teacher smiled. "I don't mind at all. It's impressive that she knows so much about her family, Mrs. Manchester. Now," she said, reaching for the book, "let me take a look at this piece. Hmm. Composed by Mikhl Gordon, in 1868," she read. Then, although her pronunciation didn't quite work, Mrs. Spargo gamely read the first line. '*Az ikh volt gehat dem keiser's oitzres. . . .*' What does it mean?"

In an instant, Peninnah was back in the living room at 28 Channing Street, on the afternoon Papa came home with the book. He sat down next to her at the dining room table and turned to this same page. With his finger following the notes, he began to hum the delicate melody. After a few bars, however, she noticed that his hand had stopped. She saw that his eyes had closed. And she knew at that moment that her papa was in his mind back to Lithuania, many years earlier, with his beloved mother Perel, singing to him. When he had finished the song, he slowly opened his eyes, and she watched him return, as if from a long distance.

Then his dark eyes twinkled. "Peninnah," he said, "bring this to Mrs. Spargo. Tell her she should teach you to play it on the piano."

Her reverie may have taken a moment, or ten minutes; she had no idea. With a full heart she told her teacher, "It's about loving your child, and not being as happy with anything else on Earth."

Within a few years, her father heard Peninnah master the lullaby he had loved as a child. He heard her practice his favorite "Moonlight Sonata" day in and day out, and he never tired of it. When she entered high school, she discovered the weekly convocations in the auditorium, where music students would take the stage to perform for their peers. The first time Peninnah appeared, she was excited, but confident. She sat at the piano, breathed a silent prayer, and began the famous repetitive triplets—which always reminded her just a little of the scales she had played all those years before. Except this was Beethoven. And this time, when she finished and curtsied to the audience, the students and teachers applauded wildly.

Before graduating high school, Peninnah performed several other pieces on that convocation stage, including some Grieg, and the brief "Warsaw Concerto," which had been so popular in Britain during the War. But nothing came close to the "Moonlight Sonata." Nothing else— except maybe that old lullaby—had the power to make her father, and her, so extraordinarily happy.

FOUR

The Book of Leaves

In the fall of 1945, the leaves in New London, Connecticut, seemed especially glorious. Maybe it was just that the War had ended, and people were still dazed, emerging, eyes bleary, from their emotional bunkers. Maybe it was due to some mysterious alignment of climate and chlorophyll. For whatever reason, during that September, residents enjoyed a dazzling array of colors: pomegranate crimson, pumpkin orange and hot lemonade. On windy days, the leaves sashayed like diminutive dancers on the swaying limbs of Norway, red and sugar maple, and the silver and pin oak. Chestnut and elm tree leaves carpeted the streets. When it rained, the pavement looked like nothing so much as sheet upon sheet of vivid watercolors.

From her bedroom, Peninnah could just catch a glimpse of the leaves swirl around Nathan Hale's statue in the park across the street. On mild weekend afternoons, returning home from a movie, she and her best friend Katherine tromped through crackling hills of leaves on the smooth, crisscrossing sidewalks around the tall, heroic figure.

One day that fall, Peninnah's fourth-grade teacher announced that the class was to collect the prettiest leaves they could find, dip them into melted wax, and make scrapbooks. At first she thought the students were going to simply find the leaves and do the rest at school. But as she listened to the woman flesh out the assignment, she felt dread begin to rumble in her stomach.

The idea of collecting the leaves and making a book from them was enchanting. But she couldn't do the wax part on her own. And Mama wasn't exactly what you would call an involved class mother. In fact, Papa's nickname for her was the *nein zoger*, the naysayer. So many times Peninnah had asked her for something, maybe a field trip, or a special treat. Unless the activity was clearly necessary for furthering her daughter's education, she would say, "No, you don't need to do that." Was a book of leaves going to get her into a good college? And God forbid it was something that didn't conform to Mama's idea of what a Jewish girl should do! She would never forget the time she begged to be allowed to wear a costume and go trick-or-treating with Katherine.

"Halloween is a Christian holiday!" Mama railed. She was right, of course. In the end, though, she did let her daughter dress up, adorning her in strands and strands of her own colorful beads and shawls, even giving her some makeup to dab on her lips and cheeks to complete her Gypsy costume. But it was Papa who walked with her at dusk, when all the stores were closed, to the very center of town with the exquisite library building of hewn stone, City Hall, and the County Courthouse on State Street, which led to the Thames River and the old train station, designed by a famous architect. It was Papa who let her take along soap from the bathroom and kept watch, laughing with pleasure, while she decorated a store window.

But Papa was not here now and this was something that was more in Mama's realm, anyway. What if she, Peninnah Pearl Manchester, were the only student who didn't fulfill the leaf assignment? The thought was too terrible to contemplate.

She knew Mama was always so busy. Everyone's mother cooked and cleaned. And of course hers accompanied Papa to shul, sitting upstairs in the women's balcony like a queen. But her mother was also a business-woman who bought houses, refurbished them and rented out the apart-ments inside. She was an exceptionally hands-on landlady, giving assis-tance and advice to her tenants—young Navy couples from the subma-rine base in nearby Groton—on everything from leaky faucets to infertil-ity. She didn't have time for things like class visits and art projects, even if she had approved of them.

Diligent as always, Peninnah was nonetheless the first in her class to begin the assignment, gathering the most beautiful leaves in the park. They put her in mind of colorful hands scattered throughout the city. Every once in a while, when she was alone in her room, she would dip her face into her overflowing shoebox of leaves just to breathe in the earthy scent. When it came to the next step, however, she waited until the last possible day. Finally, having trudged as slowly as she could through still more leaves, she arrived home from school the afternoon before the scrapbook was due, determined to ask for help.

She reached her large white Victorian house and stared up at the six stone steps rising from the sidewalk. To either side were large, jagged rocks that reminded her of inverted *dreidls*. She climbed the steps and reached the short, sloping walkway, then ascended eight wooden stairs leading to the porch. Next came the structure itself, with its double doors, paneled in oak, and ornate beveled windows. She loved the white lace curtains, made of silk, that graced the inside of the glass.

From the narrow front hall, Peninnah made her way to two more enormous doors—the height of the twelve-foot ceiling and wide enough for a small army to pass through—one of which was propped open. She saw her mother sitting in the dining room at the large table that dominated the room, opening bills, piling envelopes on one side of the rose-patterned tablecloth and important papers on the other. Some documents she slipped between the vibrant floral top cloth and a layer or two of the several cloths below. It was her singular, peculiar filing system. Peninnah imagined that sifting through those tablecloths one day would be like unearthing ancient treasures on an archaeological dig. Something like those dusty sites in the Promised Land she had heard about from Papa, containing multiple civilizations.

"Ma," she said, slipping into the closest chair. "I have an assignment for school I need help with."

Her mother glanced up from her piles of paper and began to sing in Yiddish, as she often did on setting eyes on her daughter.

Oy, mayn khane brayne,
Gotsaydank di bist shoyn mayne,
Kh'bin gliklekh on a shir,
Di geherst nokh mir.

She still feels really lucky that I am hers, Peninnah thought ruefully. That's because I haven't asked her yet.

"Sit, sit," her mother said, her gaze once more hovering over the mail. "What is it you need, kindele?"

"I have to make a scrapbook of leaves for school." She took a breath. Then, as casually as she could, she added, "I already have the leaves."

Mama looked up. "Nu? So what's the problem?"

"We need to dip them in melted wax. At home."

Her mother nodded slowly. Peninnah held her breath during what felt like an unnaturally long silence. She forced herself to exhale.

"Go get the leaves," Mama said at last. "I see what we can do."

Heart pounding, nearly unable to believe her luck, the child ran up the stairway to her second-floor bedroom. On the small landing, she paused, smiling at the reindeer head in the narrow Tiffany glass window before jumping up the last four steps. In less than a minute, she was in and then out of her room again, clutching the shoebox. When she returned downstairs, she didn't dare speak, so intent was she on not breaking her mother's good mood.

Mama was standing in the kitchen. She took one look at the box and said, "Now, come with me downstairs." In her hand, Peninnah noticed, were two white Shabbes candles. Her apron pockets looked strangely bulky.

Her mother led her through the room to the basement door and opened it. Mama reached up to flip the switch for the single bare bulb before descending the steep wooden stairs.

"Careful now," she murmured.

The first thing Peninnah caught sight of in the dim, overstuffed basement was the old coal furnace. In the adjoining room was the one-burner stove. Because of its high flame, Mama cooked steaks on it, with the meat folded between the hands of a steel mesh griller that she held with long handles. That was the only time she had ever seen her use the thing.

Now, Mama was reaching down beside the stove and pulling out a rusty, dented pot, too decrepit to use for cooking.

"I never saw that!" Peninnah exclaimed in wonder.

"And why should you, Perele?" she replied. "It's garbage. You know what I always say. *Varf gornit arois. Dos vet kumen tzu nitzt.* Don't throw anything out! It will come in handy!"

She dropped the thick white candle into the pot, lit the pilot light with a match from her apron pocket and lowered the flame. Then she placed the pot on the burner. The two watched in silence as the candles began to devolve into a soft, white opacity. In that still basement, it felt to Peninnah as though mother, daughter and melting candle were all that existed in the world.

When the wax had completely melted, Mama motioned to Peninnah, who handed her a single golden leaf. In one sure movement, as though she'd done it a thousand times, she swept it through the hot liquid, then held it over the pot for a moment to let the excess drip off. In an instant, the wax began to harden.

The child clapped her hands with pleasure. "Ma, look! It's beautiful! The color comes right through!"

Her mother gazed at the leaf for another moment, then handed the stem to her daughter. Next, from a second apron pocket, she pulled out a length of rope, which she fashioned into a clothesline. This she knotted between two pipes on opposite walls. From the other pocket, she removed a single wooden clothespin. She handed it to her daughter, who clipped up the first leaf to dry. They both gazed at the perfectly formed thing, at once so natural and so artificial.

"I wish I were an autumn leaf," the child said. "To be so beautiful, I mean."

"Nu, what kind of nonsense is this?"

"Oh you know what I mean. I wish I was pretty. I wish I had a better nose."

Before the final word was out of her mouth, Peninnah knew the answer she would receive. It was her mother's standard line when she disparaged her looks, and she didn't disappoint.

"*Vus retz du, narele maidel?*" Mama asked, hands on her hips. "*Du host azei fil chein!* What are you talking about, foolish girl? You have so much charm!"

Peninnah shrugged. As usual, she had no suitable answer for that statement.

The next morning, the child awoke earlier than usual, dressed quickly and took the stairs two at a time. She eased open the basement door, tiptoed down the cement steps, gingerly plucked each dry leaf off the line and piled them into the shoebox. Once back in her bedroom, she spread the leaves onto her rug. Using a mixture of flour and water that she had at the ready, she glued each leaf onto a piece of construction paper that her teacher had handed out. She slid a long piece of string through the pre-cut holes in the paper and tied the ends into a bow. On the cover, she penciled in her best handwriting, "Leaves by Peninnah Manchester." Satisfied with her work, she laid the book in the center of her bed, walked into the hallway, and, despite wearing a skirt and being almost a young lady, was so pleased that she slid down the bannister to breakfast.

When Peninnah left for school that morning, her mother said, "Be sure to wrap well your *farchailke! Gei gezunt un kum tzurik gezunt!* Go in good health!" She didn't call her over for a hug and a kiss. She didn't tell her that she loved her. As a matter of fact, she never had.

As far as Peninnah was concerned, Mama didn't have to. Seventy-five years later, she still has that book of leaves.

FIVE

The Farm

"Peninnah! *Vu bistu*? Where are you?"

She had known for several minutes that her father was home. He had a way of singing half to himself as he moved around the house. She had never asked him about it—for all she knew it was completely unconscious. But it seemed to her that even in his quiet moments, her father the chazzen couldn't stop himself from singing.

The child left her bedroom and appeared at the top of the stairs. "Yes, Papa?" she called down to him.

"Come take a ride with me in the machine to Uncasville. Mr. Brooks telephoned to ask me to come to his farm *tzu schechtn* ten chickens."

"To the Brooks farm?" From her seat at the table where she was opening mail, Mama's earrings shook with the intensity of her reaction. "Now, Chazzen? You haven't been home yet an hour! Rest a little while. Sit and have a glass tea and a *nosh* before you go. Lufkeh will wait for you. *Mehn ken nit tansn af tsvei chasenehs mit ayn tochis.* You can't dance at two weddings with one bottom."

"You know how my schedule is during the week," he said with a shrug. "What can I do? Yes, sometimes Brooks brings a couple of chickens here, but with ten of them, it's better I should drive to the farm. If I don't go, they won't have kosher chickens, simple as that. How could I do that to such good people? I'll have a glass tea at the farm. I just stopped home to change."

Mama tsked a couple of times. "They are good people, of course. I knew that already back when I met them in Europe. You have just had such a busy day already."

Papa opened his mouth to answer, but instead of words, he responded with a loud sneeze.

21

"*Tzu gezunt, tzu laing yor tzu laing lebn,*" she said. "A cold you got now!"

"We're not going far, Dvorele," he said with a laugh. "We'll be back soon."

"Nu, give Esther and Lufkeh my regards," she said, as her husband and daughter exited through the side door. "And drive slowly!"

Peninnah always jumped at the chance to travel with her father to the country in the four-door Packard Clipper, which he referred to as the "machine." The car wasn't new, but it was spacious. And she felt so grown-up, sitting beside him in the long front seat. She liked to think about the joke the nurses made to him in the hospital, where her father would go when he served as a mohel at a *bris* to circumcise an eight-day-old baby boy.

The nurses, who were well acquainted with the chazzen, would greet him and say, "With that Clipper, Reverend Manchester, you've got the best advertising in town!" Peninnah understood that a bris had something to do with clipping, although she was not sure exactly what.

Plus you never knew what would happen on a farm. Once, in his role of mohel instead of shochet, Papa was asked to circumcize a baby in the house. To her dismay, he wouldn't allow her in the mother's room while he performed the ceremony, however. He told her it wasn't proper for a young girl to watch.

Another time, wearing his chazzen hat, he officiated at a country wedding, and Peninnah went along. Later she confided to Katherine that the groom was the best-looking man she had ever seen, even in the movie magazines. She swooned over him for weeks, more than once fantasizing that she was the bride. At one point during the reception he had even asked her to dance, but she was too shy to accept.

The ride to Uncasville was almost due north, less than ten miles away. The traffic was light, and the weather balmy. They passed the Connecticut College for Women, after which they traversed a few miles of country roads, and then they reached the ripening fields, chicken coops and cow-filled paddocks that comprised a dozen or so family farms. Many of these, Papa had once explained, were owned by Russian Jews and subsidized by the German-Jewish philanthropist Maurice de Hirsch. De Hirsch believed that Jews should own land in places like America, Canada and Argentina, and work as chicken or dairy farmers. This was opposed to the Zionists, like Papa and Zayde, who thought it was best for Jews to settle in Palestine.

It wasn't long before they pulled up to their destination. Papa pointed out the children by the barn.

"Go see what they're doing," he said. Then he pinched her cheek. "Unless you want to join me in the chicken coop."

"Yuk!" she said, wrinkling her nose at the prospect. "It's too smelly!"

Peninnah knew the younger Brooks son, Frankie, and he introduced her to the other children, whose faces were streaked with dirt from playing in the grass. She wasn't dressed for rough play, but she offered to tell stories from her books. Before long, the boys and girls sat open-mouthed as she spun her tales.

Sometime later, Papa called that it was time to leave. When they were back in the car, he looked at her before turning on the ignition.

"Were they nice children, Gypsy?"

"Sure, Papa. Were they nice chickens?"

He laughed. "I hope so, because I would not want tzu shechtn a *shlechtn* chicken for them to eat."

She thought about her father's pun for a while, the idea of butchering a bad chicken. But surely a bad chicken deserved to die more than a good one? As she pondered, her eyes grew heavy. Papa began to sing in a soft voice the lullaby his mother had sung him in Lithuania that she was learning on the piano.

> *Az ikh volt gehat dem keiser's oitzres*
> *Mit zain ganze melikhe,*
> *Volt dos bai mir nit geven azoi nikhe,*
> *Vi du bist bai mir nikhe, mayn kind, mayn shain.*
> *Az ikh derzei dikh, dukht zikh mir,*
> *Di ganze velt iz mayn.*

Peninnah knew the song so well that she joined him for the chorus, and the rest they sang together.

> *Shlaf mayn kind, shlof mayn kind,*
> *Zolst lang leven un zain gezunt . . ..*

> If I could have had all the king's treasure
> And all of his lands,
> It would never bring me as much joy
> As you now bring me joy, my child, my light!
> When I see your countenance, then I feel
> The whole wide world is bright.

> Sleep, my child, sleep, my child,
> May life be long and fortune ever smile. . . .

They sang together the rest of the way home, then sat for a minute or two in the driveway until they finished the final verse. When they entered the house, they were both smiling.

Mama was making supper at the stove when they returned. "It's a shame you had to go, Chazzen," she said with a sigh, "but at least you made a dollar."

"Not today," he said, shaking his head. "They couldn't pay."

"They couldn't pay? After all, you charge only ten cents for each chicken!"

"Nu, what can I do?" He reached out for the glass of tea she set on the table before him. "If they have it next time, God willing, then they will pay me."

"And if not?"

He shrugged and picked up the sugar cube on the saucer. "And if not, the chickens will still have to be slaughtered in the kosher way. What can I do? That is the Law. I wouldn't want them to sin just because they don't have what to pay me tzu schechtn the chickens. I must do this *mitzvah* with or without payment."

Mama squared her shoulders and bit her lip. She certainly wasn't going to berate her husband, but she wasn't happy. This was not the first time a customer hadn't paid Papa, whether for a wedding, a bris or slaughtering chickens. He wouldn't even set a price to marry or circumcise. He would just tell them to pay what they wanted.

"Chazzen," she said, with a smile, "there is no one like you as a chazzen because you are the best in the world. There is no one who can shaycht as good a chicken, or sharpen as good a knife. But a good businessman, you are not."

Peninnah knew this wasn't the way her mother worked. She also knew that a man should be paid for the messy job of butchering chickens. Who knows? Maybe he said yes to these requests simply because he liked taking those car rides with her into the country. If it were up to her, she knew, she would do exactly the same.

SIX

Onstage

Twelve-year-old Joe Manchester burst into the living room like a fireball, his coat tails flying. "Ma! Pa! I've got big news!"

Peninnah, lounging with her legs stretched across one arm of the maroon armchair, didn't bother to raise her head from her book. As a rule she steered clear of her brother. Whether his mood was good or bad, there was rarely anything positive coming out of it for her.

"What is it, Yasef?" Mama asked, wiping her hands on her apron as she emerged from the kitchen.

"Dr. Bouvier! He's putting me in a Broadway show!"

His sister's ears pricked up, and her eyes widened. She was interested in anything to do with the stage. Her father was a performer, of course, albeit in the synagogue. And although she had never seen a professional play, Peninnah was an avid fan of radio drama. Fibber McGee and Molly's chaotic closet made her giggle with delight. She loved *Inner Sanctum*, *The Jack Benny Program*, and *Mr. Keen, Tracer of Lost Persons*. But there was nothing like *First Nighter*, with the screeching sirens on Broadway, and the descriptions of the audience entering the theater, the lights going down and the curtain coming up. She felt nearly the same about Alfred Lunt and Lynn Fontanne's radio drama program.

She cut short her reverie. "You mean your play?" she asked, despite herself.

Mama had told her that Joe had written a play, and that he had somehow managed to get it to the head of the English Department and Drama Society at Connecticut College for Women. Dr. Bouvier had actually called Mama and Papa to tell them that Joe had talent. That had been the big news of a month earlier.

"No, shut up," he said, his gaze stony. "I wasn't talking to you anyway."

Mama shook her head and shot the boy a pained look. "Don't talk like that, Yasef," she admonished, hands on her hips. "Nu, so tell us!"

Just then Papa entered the room. The boy strode over to him.

"Papa, guess what! Dr. Bouvier has given me a speaking part in a Broadway show!"

His father smiled. "*Kol ha kavod*, Yasef. I would prefer maybe you got a speaking part at shul, but I'm very proud of you."

"When is this play going to open?" Mama asked.

Joe beamed. "November sometime. I think the twenty-first."

"Mazel tov," she said. "Isn't that wonderful, Peninnah?"

From across the room, the young girl shrugged.

"The thing is," Joe said casually, jutting his chin in his sister's direction. "He wants her, too." Peninnah looked up in surprise. "Not in a speaking role, of course. She could never do that. Just to skip across the stage." He paused. "If she wants to."

Her family looked at her expectantly. Her first thought was: If Joe is involved, I'd rather be anywhere else. This is the boy who has treated me like a servant all my life, or worse. After my papa bought him a Shetland pony at his insistence, I took it for a slow, barebacked ride in front of the house. Joe suddenly slapped the pony's rump, and I had to hang onto its mane as it galloped away, praying with all my might not to fall off.

Then something else occurred to her. She would be on stage—in a Broadway play. Like the Lunts! How Katherine would envy her!

Not quite meeting her brother's eyes, she cocked her head. "Okay," she said, in as bored a voice as she could muster. "Sure. Why not?"

Peninnah was to attend two rehearsals, Joe told her grudgingly. She took extra pains dressing that first morning. What should she wear? Why didn't she own anything more sophisticated? New York City! Broadway! She couldn't believe her luck. It wasn't until they were in the car that she realized they weren't actually headed to the city.

"But how are we going to practice if we don't go to Manhattan?" she asked Joe.

He shook his head in disgust.

"First of all, the word is rehearse. Second, you don't think they'd put a kid like you on a Broadway stage, do you?"

"But you said—"

"What I said was we were going to be in a Broadway show. The show once played on Broadway. Now it's being produced at the College."

She was annoyed, but just a little. In truth, she had to admit that the idea of standing—not to mention skipping—on a Broadway stage had scared her. A lot.

The whole ride to the college, her brother didn't say two words to her. When Papa dropped them off, Joe even insisted that she walk a little behind him on campus. She didn't care. This was to be a special day; she felt sure of it. She just wasn't sure why.

When brother and sister entered through the tall doors to the Palmer Auditorium, Dr. Bouvier called out a friendly hello from the first row. Peninnah heard him as though in a dream. Looking around the elegant, professional theater, she lost any remaining traces of disappointment. All those velvet seats. The brass railings. The enormous stage. The superior acoustics, evident just from that one little word! The place even smelled special: to her unpracticed nose, the blend of cleaning products was intoxicating.

"You must be little Peninnah!" he said, with a faint French accent. "Love the pigtails. Nice touch. Let's get you on stage and take a look."

He showed her how to climb up, and just like that, for the first time in her life, she was on stage. The floor felt cavernous, much larger than she had imagined. When she raised her head, the ceiling was so far away it might as well have been the sky.

"Yes, you will do nicely," the professor said. "Now, let me see you skip a little."

She felt a little foolish, but dutifully she skipped across the stage.

"Yes, completely charming. Thanks, Joe! Our cast is now complete."

Joe frowned. Why did he even suggest me? Peninnah wondered. Maybe Dr. Bouvier had asked if he had a little sister. She couldn't imagine that she would have actually been on Joe's mind outside the house. Or even inside, for that matter.

"Now, you get up there with her, Joe," Dr. Bouvier instructed. "First, I want to see you run across the stage together. Then I want to see you skip." She loved the way he pronounced the word "skeep." Of course her parents came from Europe, too, but Dr. Bouvier's accent was different. More worldly, it seemed to her.

"Okay, sure. If you want." They were the first words she had heard her brother speak in an hour.

Joe clambered up and stood a foot or two down stage from her. On the man's signal, they ran from one side to the other. Then they skipped back across, from upstage right to downstage left.

Dr. Bouvier clapped his hands, not in applause, as she thought at first, but to get their attention.

"That'll work well. Now try the skipping again, this time holding hands."

Peninnah froze. She didn't know what to do. She couldn't recall a time when she and Joe had ever touched, except when she was five and had beat him up so badly—she didn't remember why—that he had called for Mama. She looked up at her brother's face. In an instant she saw that she didn't have to worry.

"We'll do it for the show," he called out. She wondered what the director would say to that, but he seemed to approve. It occurred to her on the way home that maybe he thought that a Jewish male and female couldn't touch unless absolutely necessary. Which, although they came from an Orthodox household, wasn't something that would have occurred to either of them to worry about. They were, after all, brother and sister.

On opening night, Mama and Papa were sitting up front, their faces shining with pride. Joe spoke his few lines clearly and forcefully. The two ran and then later skipped across the stage just as they had rehearsed, and in the glaring lights, Peninnah felt the pleasure hit her like a jolt of electricity. Sure enough, with the audience sitting before them, her brother held her hand. She found it cold and clammy, and when they arrived at the wings, she was sure he was as glad to drop the grip as she. She wondered for how long he would wash his hands after touching her. Probably not half as long as she would.

True to Joe's word, she didn't have any lines. She was glad of that. And true to his nature, he never touched her again. She was glad of that, too. Something else had touched her that evening, making an impression so deep that she knew she would never forget it.

In bed that night, she hugged herself in the darkness. "I was on stage," she whispered. "I belong on stage. The stage will be my home."

SEVEN

The Only Jews

Peninnah opened her eyes to the April morning sky beyond her window, glowing like an aura around the tops of the budding chestnut trees, filled with promise. For a moment, she felt the bliss of a day off. Then she remembered what day off it was. She pulled the pillow over her face and groaned.

For the past two weeks, she and Mama had been cleaning the house with more than their usual vigor, preparing it for *Pesach*. The child had already heard her mother making arrangements to dispose of any remaining *chametz* before the holiday, according to Jewish law. And now, the Seder was less than thirty-six hours away.

Mostly, she loved Pesach. Her father's adult children joined them for the ritual meal—at which, as the youngest, she had the honor of singing *Der Fir Kashas*. Why is this night different from every other night? She knew them by heart. Mama served her *kneidlach* the size of softballs, filled with an egg yolk that somehow always appeared smack dab in the center. These *matzoh* golfballs enjoyed pride of place in the chicken soup, which was eaten after the chicken entree in order, Mama said, to "wash it down." Another one of Peninnah's favorite dishes was potatoes with prunes. But her mother's matzoh cottage cheese *meikhl*, a sort of breakfast cheesecake for Pesach morning that the family called *gefilte matzoh*, was to her mind the highlight of the eight-day celebration.

What bothered Peninnah about this particular Pesach was that now that she was twelve and a young lady, it was exclusively her job to schlep Manischewitz kosher-for-Passover wine and a box of matzohs to each of the neighbors on the park, explaining to them as her mother had, with her tagging along every year of her childhood, the meaning of Passover. The Ten Plagues and the Sparing of the Firstborn. Moses and the Freeing of the Slaves. The Crossing of the Red Sea. And how Jews tell the story and eat the matzoh every year so that they can feel that God took them personally out of Egypt. She could feel her face grow warm with embarrassment at the thought of it.

But why, exactly, was it embarrassing? She was certainly proud to be Jewish, glad to observe Shabbes and the *yom tavim* with her family, to be the chazzen's daughter in the big Litvak shul with the enormous chandeliers. She was proud to see her friends in the women's balcony glare with envy each time she took her seat alongside her father on the *bimah* and watched his finger follow the Hebrew in the holy books. She didn't even mind that she was only ever allowed to eat ice cream at Katherine's parents' fancy, non-kosher restaurant, and not even that on Pesach. She was so proud of being Jewish that she once even wrote a letter to the editor of the *New London Day*, complaining about a comment written by a columnist—a fellow shul member—that matzoh tasted like cardboard. How indignant she had been at the scoundrel's treachery! Forever after, the man scowled at her when he saw her in synagogue.

Flying solo on the Pesach speaking tour was mainly embarrassing for the reason that her mother found it necessary in the first place. Mama was exquisitely conscious that the Manchesters were the only Jewish family in the immediate neighborhood of the park. (It would be years till another one moved in around the corner.) Their neighbors were New England WASPS, and Mama wanted above all else to be on good terms with them. Even now, Peninnah could hear one of Mama's favorite sayings: "It will come in handy," the phrase she reserved for used string, rags or safety pins. She realized that her mother may have had the vague notion that neighborhood friendship and support might come in handy, as well. There were still people in the world, after all, who believed the ugly lie that Jews baked the blood of Christian children into their matzoh.

When Peninnah opened her bedroom door, her heart leapt at the tiny, paper-wrapped gift her father had left on the hardwood floor, just outside her room. It was their ongoing private joke. Usually she heard the sound of the sliding package on the parquet, but this morning, she had been too annoyed at the day's upcoming task to notice. It was a dime, she knew. When he had learned years before that the girls at school called her Penny, he had asked, "Why so cheap? Someday you'll be a nickel or a dime!"

That morning, she dawdled over her eggs, but her mother watched her so closely that right after breakfast, she found herself knocking at the house next door, the one with the doctor and his wife and their four good-looking boys. Hopping on one foot and then the other while she waited on the front porch, she couldn't decide if she hoped the boys would be home or not.

To her surprise, the doctor himself answered the door. He was taller and even more distinguished-looking than she remembered. She took a step back.

"Hello, Peninnah," he said. "What can I do for you?"

You already know, she thought. Mama does it every year at this time. By now you probably know the story better than I do.

She flashed her sweetest smile. "My mama asked me to give you this." She handed him the paper bag from the A&P. "And if you don't mind, she wanted me to take a few minutes to talk to you about our holiday."

Like everyone else on her route, the doctor and his wife were gracious. After them came the mean-looking older couple on the street, and the people whose daughter would, years later, marry an officer friend of Fidel Castro and move to Cuba. There was the photographer who once took a beautiful photo of her father in his *tallis* and *yarmulke* that was reproduced in Papa's book. Efficient as always, she visited every house.

They were all nice people, her neighbors, but they were as different from her family as could be. They went to church on Sundays and mixed milk with meat and decorated enormous Christmas trees and didn't speak with accents and didn't know Yiddish and somehow had to be taught, year after year, about Passover. Sometimes she fantasized that they were wild beasts—polite and smiling and attractive beasts, to be sure—who needed to be placated with wine and matzoh to prevent them from turning on her and her family. It was far-fetched, of course, to think like that. Not true at all. If anything, their manners were better than those of her family. But still, although her mother never mentioned it, she knew that after what had recently happened in Europe, it wasn't totally crazy.

The next night at the Seder, surrounded by the people she loved best in the world, she sang *Der Fir Kashas:*

> *Ma nishtanah halailah hazeh mikol haleilot?*
> *Sheb'khol haleilot anu okhlin hametz umatzah; halailah hazeh, kuloh matzah.*
> *Sheb'khol haleilot anu okhlin sh'ar y'rakot; halailah hazeh, maror.*
> *Sheb'khol haleilot ein anu matbilin afilu pa'am ehat; halailah hazeh, shtei f'amim.*
> *Sheb'khol haleilot anu okhlin bein yoshvin uvein m'subin; halailah hazeh, kulanu m'subin.*

Why was this night different from every other night? Not just because they could only eat matzoh. Not just because they ate bitter herbs. Not just because they dipped twice in salt water, or because they reclined at the dinner table.

What was different was that this year, she reflected, she had become a representative of her people. It wasn't good; it wasn't bad. It just was.

EIGHT

What Joe Wants

"Hey, Peninnah! Get down here quick!"

For anyone else, her older brother's voice may have sounded melodious. In fact, he was considered a rather gifted singer. To Peninnah's ears, however, he thundered like a tank.

"Leave me alone, Joe!" she called down from her bedroom. "I'm reading!"

"Leave me alone, Joe!" he mimicked her in a high voice.

She squeezed her eyes shut in frustration. "What do you want?"

"What do you mean what do I want? What do you think I want? I want you to play Al Jolson for me." When she didn't respond, he added in a menacing tone, "Now!"

Her parents loved her. Of that she had no doubt. No doubt whatsoever. Papa had his six different pet names for her. Mama still sang to her when she entered a room. But her big brother was something else altogether.

Although her ability to focus on her reading had vanished, Peninnah didn't budge from her large brass bed. Instead, she gazed over at the familiar books on her nightstand, which had been there as long as she could remember. Aunt Naomi's maroon-covered *Jewish Fairy Tales and Legends*, a 1909 edition stamped with the seal of Papa's old synagogue in Utica. *Honi Ha Me'agel*, the tales of the ancient scholar, known as the Circle Maker. Even the titles of these books made her feel stronger.

Joe's voice had by now evolved into a roar. She knew he hadn't moved closer; he didn't need to. What he lacked in manners, she reflected, he more than made up for in lungpower.

"Peninnah!" he yelled. "I'm waiting!"

Her mother's figure appeared outside the bedroom door, which the child had left ajar a couple of inches. Now Mama pushed it fully open.

"*Kind mayne,*" Mama said, her tone gentle and calm. "You heard your brother. Go do what he wants."

Peninnah raised her eyes just enough to catch a glimpse of the familiar housecoat and flowered apron. Then she dipped her head again into the book, but for once, her eyes could not make out the words.

"Ma," she said, fighting to control her indignation, "I'm tired. I've been out all day. I just want to read." And then all at once—maybe it was the sight of her mother's placid expression that caused it, or maybe it was simply the final straw—she slapped a closed fist on the bed.

"You know what?" Peninnah glared at the open doorway. "I think I'm going to let him have it!" She started to rise, but her mother's grim expression stopped her.

"You have to learn to get along with your brother," Mama said softly. "Remember, a mountain and a mountain cannot come together, but a person and a person can."

Peninnah felt her eyes well up with tears. "He makes me so angry!"

"*Vos veintz du, nareshe meidel?* Why do you cry, foolish girl?" Her tears already subsiding, the child shrugged. "You know there's an old story about how important it is to hold in your anger," her mother began.

"I know that story, Ma. You've told me a hundred times."

"Well, then you're going to hear it a hundred and one." She paused as if daring her daughter to interrupt.

"There was a soldier who left his home and his beloved wife to go off to war and couldn't get home for twenty years. The pain at everything he'd lost was almost more than he could stand. But in letters, his wife promised to wait for him.

"After many years, the army let him go home. The trip was very hard; the war was still going on all around him. But he loved his wife, so he kept going. Then one day, he saw his house at last. He could hardly believe it, after twenty years! As he got closer, he even heard his wife's tender voice through the partially open door. And then, to his horror, he heard the low voice of a man!

"He was so angry that he pulled out his sword, planning to dig it into the heart of his wife's lover! He pushed open the door, ready to kill the *mamzer.* Luckily, she jumped between him and the young man in time. And it was a good thing she did, because the young man was. . . ."

"Their son. I know, Ma. But why can't Joe just wait? Why do I always have to jump at his every command?"

Her mother sighed. The ensuing silence lasted so long that the teen could stand it no longer.

"It just isn't fair!" she burst out. "Why is it that Joe always gets what he wants, when he wants it, no matter how much trouble it is to anybody else? Especially me? Why do boys always get their way?"

The first image in her mind at that moment was Joe's Bar Mitzvah, with all the family oohing and aahing over the sweets table, the three-tiered cake and her mother's delicious *aingemachts,* shredded white radish, honey and nuts, all cooked together. Still, even as she pictured the scene, she knew that there were other times when she too got plenty of attention. Her father bought her that pale blue taffeta gown with the pretty ruffle and the short, puffy sleeves. She had worn it when he walked her to the Mohican Hotel on State Street, the tallest building in town, and stayed down in the lobby while up in the penthouse ballroom, Mr. Harvey the gym teacher taught the young teens the foxtrot, jitterbug, tango, waltz and every other dance craze.

Mama frowned. Slowly, deliberately, she lowered herself onto the bed. For a full minute, she traced the lace coverlet. When she spoke, she looked fully into Peninnah's eyes.

"Do you respect me, *kindele?*" she asked.

Peninnah thought about the stories she'd heard as long as she could remember. How by 1923, her mother's father had already left their tiny *shtetl* of Dokshitz in White Russia, where pogroms and other, lesser terrors were an everyday fact of life, to settle in America. How due to quotas on Jewish immigration, Mama alone had had to stay put for three years in Cherbourg, France, until she could join the rest of her family members, who had been allowed through. She knew how in the States, her mother had quickly secured a job in a tie factory and put herself through night school to learn English. How four years later, she caught the eye of a widower twenty years her senior named Samuel Manchester. And then there was the part Peninnah knew from experience: how her mother went on to raise two children and care for Papa and create a thriving business as a landlady. No, she could never think of her mama as weak. When Ma agreed with Pa, or did what Pa asked, it just seemed natural. Like what you do when you're a loving couple.

"Of course I do. You're a successful businesswoman. You're the wisest person I know. You can do anything. It's just that. . . ."

"You know what happened that day at the bank."

Peninnah nodded. It was another one of her mother's favorite stories.

"You remember how the president of the New London Savings Bank, the president himself, how he held the door for me and said, 'Good morning, Mrs. Manchester.' He knows my name. Me! A woman! An immigrant! And him not even a Jew!"

She crossed the floor and perched on the edge of the bed. "Let me ask you something." She looked closely at her daughter. "This Al Jolson fella that your brother likes so much. You also like his music?"

This time, Peninnah nodded more vigorously. "You remember, Ma. He was wonderful. A cantor's kid, like us. You know Joe couldn't stop crying when he died. And Joe sounds just like him when he sings."

"So you like playing for Joe?"

"Yes, sure, I do. But you know that's not the point. I just—"

Her mother reached out her hands. She picked up one of her daughter's pigtails and ran her fingers over the smooth hair.

"Life is unfair in many ways, Peninnah. But many good things have come to you, yes? And many good things will come in the years ahead. You have a goldene keppele, as your papa says. You are clever. You are already accomplished, and as you grow up, you will only be more so."

The child was not convinced. "If I'm so clever, why do I need to be my brother's slave?"

Mama pursed her lips. "What can I tell you? When it comes to men and women, women give more than fifty percent to make *sholom*. That is the way it was when I was a child; that is the way of the world today. In the future, who can say? But you see me. You know I am independent; I am strong. I don't let it stop me. I go on and win. You will, too. Remember, when you have hardships in life, they make you stronger."

Peninnah nodded. A memory popped into her head: the time Joe threatened to throw her puppy off the roof if she refused to get rid of it. He was horrible to her; everyone knew it. But what was there to say?

"Make peace," Mama said. She rose from the bed and turned to leave. Over her shoulder she added, "Just remember, a mountain and a mountain cannot come together; but a person and a person—they can come together."

The young girl watched her mother's retreating back. She rose from the bed, placed a strip of paper in her book to hold her place, and laid the volume on the nightstand. Then she straightened her skirt. When she appeared at the foot of the stairs, her brother was standing at the piano, his arms folded. He was a nice-looking boy; she couldn't deny it. Looking at him now, it was hard to believe he could be so unkind.

Without a word, she approached the piano bench, passing on her way through the dining room the huge reproduction of Botticelli's famous painting of Judith. She had always loved that image, and she knew the story well. The pious Judith had managed to save her city from the Assyrians by seducing, and then beheading, their commander Holofernes. In the picture, she is standing, holding the wide sword with both hands, while in the background is the severed head. She had always wondered why that image held such a place of honor in the main room of the house, especially when it had been sitting in the attic when the family moved in. Now she thought perhaps she knew.

She sat down and began to play the music Joe had spread out for her. It was one of her favorites: "You Made Me Love You." When he started to sing, she had to admit that his voice was, indeed, just like Jolson's.

She did love that music. And when she played it, her large hands, with their long, nimble fingers, like those of her father, danced across the keys. Focused on the sheet music in front of her, she sat ramrod straight. And proud.

II

1952–1967: A Woman in the World

NINE

Shooting Star

Peninnah descended the front porch steps of the family house, crossed the park and climbed up toward the triangle of stately buildings that comprised WMI, Williams Memorial Institute, looking and feeling every inch the confident young lady she had long hoped to be. It didn't matter that she was to return home at noon for her mother's home-cooked lunch of meat, potatoes, and vegetables. She was finally entering high school. For fourteen years, she had been her mama's little girl. She had been the child who accompanied her papa on his excursions. She had been the adored granddaughter of her mother's parents, and the butt of her brother's foul temper. For fourteen years, she had been more a junior member of the Manchester family than an individual. She had been a child, cosseted and well loved, to be sure, but always subject to the whims and moods of her elders. Now, she was more.

It was a crisp morning in early September, that time of year when southeastern Connecticut sits on the fence, unable to commit either to embracing fall or to digging its heels deeper into a summer fading a little more with every passing day. She entered one of the turreted, Victorian-era buildings, its halls filling with chattering teenaged girls and smelling of equal parts shampoo and floor wax. With each step of her new shoes, she repeated under her breath, "I am a high school freshman." She could practically feel herself growing taller beneath the lofty ceilings, as if rising to meet them.

College-bound students in mid-1950s New London attended one of two public high schools: the males went to Bulkeley. The principal of the girls' school, WMI, was Gertrude Moon, an Englishwoman with a no-nonsense, patrician manner. After meeting her at the freshman welcoming convocation, Peninnah walked, a little starry-eyed, to her first Latin class. The teacher, Mrs. McAdams, was an older, dignified woman with pince-nez and a blue rinse in her permanent wave.

When Mrs. McAdams came to her name on the roll, she called out, "Pen-EYE-nah Manchester?"

Peninnah raised her hand, then said, rather sheepishly, "It's actually Pen-EE-nah, Mrs. McAdams."

One or two of the students giggled. The woman glared at them, then turned back to Peninnah.

"Well, that's how it is phonetically," she said, before returning to the roll. The following morning, the woman pronounced the name exactly the same way.

Before long, she didn't bother correcting her teacher's pronunciation. She almost got to like it, in fact. She considered it her Latin name. Anyway, if Mrs. McAdams thought that was how her name should be pronounced, who was she to say differently? She was happy to study Latin and anything else for hour upon hour, eager to please teachers who seemed miles above those in her other schools in terms of poise, knowledge and wisdom. She felt an almost physical hunger for what they had.

Looking at the posted after-school activities later that first week, Peninnah felt a little dizzy. There were so many new opportunities; she wanted to embrace them all. At last, having had a camera since she was a little girl, she decided to join the photography club. She loved the flash bulbs she had to change for every photo, the odor of the chemicals in the second-floor home darkroom that Joe had made in the kitchen once used by the Navy couples who had rented rooms during the War. As soon as he went to college, it became hers.

As if it were *bashert*, she soon became the school photographer, shooting pictures of the home economics class fashion show in Buell Hall and the couples at the coed dances. The nickel or dime that she charged the students for the photos she handed over to the club for expenses. And each time a picture of hers made it into the yearbook, she experienced the thrill of achievement, and of pride. I did that. That exists because of me.

Someone else shot a photo of Peninnah that represented her only foray into drama at WMI, and that was of her as the Mandarin of Wufu, in which she was costumed and moustachioed. Long after the play she thought of how happy her father was the night he and her mother attended. It was almost as though he were enjoying the work of a fellow performer. If only he could have heard her at morning convocation, when she played the piano for the assembly!

She didn't even mind gym class, getting dressed in those awkward one-piece blue suits with shorts, doing calisthenics and playing basketball. To her surprise and delight, she found that she excelled at baseball. Sometimes she had the sense that she wasn't so much growing as blossoming, like a flower that has finally reached its prime.

Mr. Johnson taught music and led the chorus at the school. A giant of a man, he wore a perpetual smile and was always ready with a witty comment. Adding to his mystique, he was a fireman in town. The students adored him.

After class one afternoon, he asked three of them to stay back, including Peninnah. She wasn't concerned; she knew she was doing well in the course. She only hoped she could get to her next class in time.

"Young ladies," he said, looking at each one in turn with a solemn expression that made Peninnah's heart jump a little. "I won't keep you but a minute. I have some news." They looked at each other and shrugged.

"I have the happy task of selecting three students to perform with the prestigious New England Conservatory of Music Youth Chorale." Her heart pounded. Could it be?

"And I wonder if you'd help me choose them." When he saw the mournful looks on their faces, he started to laugh. "No, I'm joking! You are my three best students! Congratulations!"

Their faces reddened, and then they too started to laugh.

"Mr. Johnson!" one of them said. "You are so mean!"

He grimaced. "I'm sorry, girls. I couldn't resist." Just then the bell rang for the next class, and the three stood up as if pulled by a single thread. "You will be going to Boston for three days. I'll give you all the details tomorrow. Congratulations!"

The girls ran into the hall to meet the crush of bodies. Before they disappeared to their respective classrooms, however, they stopped to briefly squeal and hug each other.

A few weeks later, they found themselves in a train bound for Boston, with reservations at the elegant Copley Plaza. For nearly two hours, trees and water whizzed by them as they passed from Connecticut through Rhode Island and the city of Providence to Massachusetts, but they hardly noticed. They were too excited to enjoy mere scenery, focusing instead on the other passengers, the clothing they had brought for the journey, and their fantasies about the Copley. When they arrived at last, they took a cab to the hotel, where they checked in as though they had done so all their lives. Following the porter to their room, the students could hardly keep from giggling.

"This is like a dream," Peninnah whispered. "I just hope we don't wake up too soon!"

The rehearsals went well, and the young women met other high school students from all over the area. And the concert was flawless. On Sunday morning, they were riding the elevator to breakfast, chatting about what they might do on their last day in the city.

"There are museums," one of them said doubtfully. "My mother said we should go to the Museum of Fine Arts."

"Maybe we could do some shopping," another one said.

An older man in a suit had been standing quietly behind them. Without a word of introduction, he suddenly asked, "Do you girls like baseball?"

They nodded and smiled nervously.

"Yes? Wonderful! I have box seats at Fenway Park to see the Boston Red Sox play tonight."

They looked at each other with delight. At last Peninnah said, "We would love to go, sir! How do we get there?"

It was the first professional baseball game of her life, and just like the hotel, and the concert, and being in the big city without her parents, it made her feel that the world was so much larger than she had ever imagined.

During her high school years, Peninnah felt as though she couldn't get enough of life, in classes or out. She joined the Zionist youth movement Young Judaea and the social organization B'nai Brith Girls (BBG). From a childhood with very few Jewish children, she was now basking in new acquaintances, with whom she learned Israeli dances and Hebrew songs. Despite her father's Zionistic beliefs, her home life was steeped in the Yiddish-speaking, Old Country tradition. But now Israel was a new country with a language and culture all its own, and she knew very little about it.

Some of these friends told her about the choir at Beth El, the Conservative synagogue. She had such a lovely voice, they said, she simply had to join. She wasn't so sure how her parents would take the news. After all, her family was Orthodox.

At Shabbes dinner a few nights later, Peninnah turned to her father.

"Pa, would you say Conservative Jews are bad Jews?"

Her father put down his fork and looked at her closely.

"Of course not, mayne katchkele. They are good, American Jews with a different philosophy when it comes to *halacha* and being more modern, that's all. Did someone tell you that?"

She shook her head. "No, nobody said a word."

"Then why you ask?" This was Mama, who was as interested in the question as Papa.

"Well, some of the girls at BBG are in the choir there on Friday nights. The conductor of the symphony plays the organ, and you know the chazzen. I thought I might sing in that choir—since I'm not allowed to sing in yours. It's later than your service, of course. After dinner, in fact."

Her father smiled. "I certainly do know the chazzen. Eliezer Bernstein. A fine man. So is Rabbi Kreitman. And Victor Norman plays the organ for the choir! My, my." He turned to Mama. "Let me give it some thought."

"How is she going to get there at night, a *meidelah* alone in the streets?" Mama asked. "It's not around the corner."

"If it's a good idea, I'll take her downtown myself," Papa said. "Let me think about it a little."

It was all she could ask for. She turned her focus to the boiled chicken on her plate.

Not many evenings later, Papa knocked on her door while she was studying, propped against pillows on her bed, her books and papers fanned out around her.

"I saw Chazzen Bernstein today," he said, lowering himself slowly into the chair.

"Oh great, Pa! Did you ask him about the choir?"

"No, ehre plansiche, I did not."

Her face fell. "But—?"

He interrupted her. "He asked me. He said, 'Why can't Peninnah join the choir? Our service doesn't start till 8:30, well after you've already *davened* and eaten.' I said, 'Nu, why not? She will be your number one soloist.'"

She jumped from the bed and flung her arms around her father. "Oh thank you, Pa!"

"Now, you're not going alone in the dark, you know. I'll walk you over there every week after Shabbes dinner and wait 'til you're finished."

"Oh that's wonderful!"

He rose from the chair. At the door, he turned back to her, already bending toward her book. "Just as long as you don't embarrass me and sing off-key!"

She looked at him and laughed. "I'm your daughter, Pa. I couldn't do that if I tried."

Only a couple of Peninnah's girlfriends lived right in her neighborhood; the rest were many blocks closer to the beach. The teens spent the long summer days during those high school years at Ocean Beach on the Long Island Sound, particularly Area 3, where the young singles hopping off the bus gathered on the half-mile strip of sugar sand from as far as Hartford, or even Springfield, Massachusetts, more than an hour's drive.

Occasionally one or another of the young men would give her some extra attention, ask her to take a walk over to the Clock Tower, or along the boardwalk, perhaps, but without meaning to, she found herself drawing inward, unable to socialize like some of her girlfriends did.

One particular steamy summer day, when the sand was too hot to walk on, she and her old friend Katherine were strolling down the boardwalk in their pink beach slippers, robes over their shoulders to shield them from the sun. Katherine, who dated the cadets from the military academy, pointed out the handsome young men with their arms around teens not much older than they. Each time she did so, Peninnah nodded silently.

"What is it with you, Penny?" she asked at last. "Don't you want to have a boyfriend?"

The young girl sighed. "It's not that I don't want to, exactly. I just—when I meet a boy, I feel myself sort of shut down. It's hard to explain." She didn't feel like reminding Katherine of the preadolescent crush she'd had on the handsome boy in dance class at the Mohican Hotel. She'd tried to cut in to dance with him, but he and his partner refused.

Katherine stopped and turned to her. "Well are you afraid, or just shy?"

"Who knows?" she said with a frown. "I mean, what's the difference?"

"But what's there to be afraid of? In all those movies and radio shows we like, don't people fall in love? Don't you want that, too?"

Penninah nodded. "Sure I do. But maybe all the young guys make me think of my brother. Or maybe I'm just quiet. Let's talk about something else."

In truth, she knew exactly why she was so hesitant. It seemed as though from the moment she could understand English, her mother had told her cautionary tales about the powders men put in women's drinks to take advantage of them.

"Watch," she would say, pronouncing the word, as always, the Old World way, with a "v" rather than a "w." Then she would add, "Don't let a strange man touch you. In the Old Country, a young man I knew once tried to kiss me, and I gave him such a push! And I never talked to him again!"

As they walked on, she thought of Irwin, the son of her father's friend, a kosher butcher in Springfield. Papa worked in that city sometimes as a cantor and floated the idea of a *shidduch* between the two young people. Irwin was a couple of years older than she and serving as a soldier in Korea. They exchanged letters. Among other gifts, he sent her a beautiful *hanbok*, the traditional Korean short, ribbon-tied jacket and long skirt, which she wore for Purim. She was happy to be friendly with a GI overseas, but try as she might, she couldn't summon up any romantic feelings for him.

When she was younger, her father would sometimes drive her to the Griswold Hotel, the magnificent mansion overlooking the Sound, just a few minutes from New London across the Thames River in Groton. They would sit on wooden lawn chairs watching the people go by, the dowagers on the front porch, like the set of the plantation Tara in "Gone with the Wind." There was a submarine base not far away, and officers striding to and fro, on, she presumed, important business. There were also guests who arrived by boat from Boston, and other romantic places. Living so close, Peninnah and her father would not have stayed at the hotel in any case, but they couldn't even walk into the lobby; not that he would have wanted to, in his position. In those days, it was not uncommon for resort hotels like the Griswold to post signs that read, "Christians Only."

Now, as if by magic, the hotel was no longer restricted. A Jewish businessman had purchased it, and that opened her summer social life like a key in a lock. That first day, she and her girlfriends walked into the hotel as if entering a palace, absorbing it all: the fancy carpeting and crystal chandeliers, the perfumed and coiffed socialites in their fancy resort wear, the important-looking uniformed staff. The Griswold was alive with activity, and she could have simply sat in the lobby to feel intoxicated from the assault on her senses.

On one of those forays, she locked eyes with a handsome bartender. He looked away in a moment, but that didn't faze her. She was, she told herself, just a child to a man of the world like that. Nevertheless, she stood stock still in the middle of the floor, feeling as though she had been hypnotized. For a full minute, she was aware of his face, of her heart pumping, and little else.

"Penny, come on," one of her girlfriends called out.

She came to her senses, but she made sure later on to get close enough to read his nametag. Marty. For the rest of the season they exchanged hellos now and again, although she was reasonably sure he didn't even know her name. By the time summer melted into fall, her one-sided passion had produced only one thing: she understood, at last, what all the fuss about boys was about. It was almost as though a switch had flipped in her heart.

As for Marty, she comforted herself by thinking what her mother would say, should she dare to bring a man like that to the house. "A *schlepper*, that one! He's nothing but a schlepper!" The putdown would, she knew, be sufficient to cancel all interest she ever had in the poor man. Not that it would ever come to anything with Marty.

It was a different story with the boys at the Coast Guard Academy in New London. The white-hatted sailors were looked down on in her household, but cadets were seen as a better class of military man: young college men. More respectable. Katherine could date any cadet she wanted; Peninnah was limited to the few Jewish ones. Thank heavens, she thought, she only wanted to date boys of her own faith.

One afternoon, when the sun was a ball of honey in the deep blue bowl of the sky, a Jewish boy from the academy asked her for a date in his Southern drawl, and she happily accepted. Her parents met him in the living room, and they were sufficiently impressed with his cadet credentials to wish them a good evening. They double-dated with Katherine and her own cadet. Peninnah wasn't overwhelmed with her date, who didn't seem to have anything in particular to recommend him. Still, she was pleased to go to the movies and out for ice cream. Despite her lack of experience, she was wise enough to know that sometimes people had hidden depths.

"Penny," Katherine said, a week later, when they were walking home from school through the park. "There's something I've gotta tell you."

Peninnah raised her eyebrows. Katherine usually blurted out her news. What could be so hard to say that it needed an introduction?

"You know the guy you were with when we went to the movies?" Peninnah nodded. As if there were so many! As if I could forget! "Well, the thing is, he's been calling me. He asked me out."

She kicked some leaves in a fruitless attempt to show she didn't care. There was nothing, really, to say. Her first response was a stab of disappointment. But then a single word popped into Peninnah's brain, uttered in her mother's voice. Schlepper! What she needed to date, she knew, was a *mensch*.

TEN

Higher Education

"Da-da-da-daah. . . ." She recognized the romantic melody, with its familiar mix of major and minor keys, as soon as she walked into the lobby of French House. It was "Autumn Leaves," which the residents of the French dormitory on the University of Connecticut campus, first and foremost Madame, whose phonograph was playing the song, knew from an Yves Montand movie years earlier. It was a sad song, which she loved, although it hardly fit her mood.

There had never been any question about Peninnah's going to college, just as her brother had done. Her mother reasoned that although her own poor education in Eastern Europe had not hampered her in life, this was due to her sheer force of personality, street smarts, and a head for business. Her daughter was different; she was a book learner. Mama was adamant that Peninnah go much, much further than she had in school.

"Education is the best thing," she told her. "And you are not going to work anywhere else instead of studying. When you are in college, you work at college by studying, not at a job."

Mama had it all figured out. Her daughter would go to nearby Connecticut College for Women and live at home. That was the most efficient plan of action.

"No," the teen retorted through gritted teeth. "After going to an all girls high school for four years, I am not attending an all-girls college—and live at home too!"

Before Mama could open her mouth to reply, Papa, who had been reading the paper in the other room, called out, "Dobke, you want she should get married someday, don't you?"

Her mother's answering silence closed the discussion for the moment. She rifled through her layers of tablecloth to uncover a bill to pay here, a list to add to there. Twenty minutes later, she said, as if the conversation had simply been put on pause till she was ready to speak again, "Then go to University of Connecticut. It's only what, Chazzen, maybe an hour from here?"

"Ma, I want to go to Columbia University. In New York."

"And what do you know from Columbia?" her mother asked.

She looked away. "Everybody knows Columbia. It's the best there is in the tri-state area."

"The best there is." Mama sighed. "Tell you what. You start at University of Connecticut. You don't like it, so you'll change and you'll go to Columbia."

If she were to really be strictly honest, Peninnah would have acknowledged that in fact, she felt a twinge of relief. It was a little scary, the thought of moving to New York City on her own. She agreed to apply to UConn, and she was accepted.

That summer after high school, Peninnah had a chance to work part-time as an arts and crafts counselor in a local day camp, about twenty minutes from home. This time, her father could neither walk her where she needed to go nor drive her over in the Packard. When she mentioned the problem to Mama, she received an immediate response.

"Nu, your papa taught you to drive. Now you need to have what to drive. We'll go and get you a car."

Not a week later, Peninnah drove a gray, four-door Chevrolet sedan out of the used car lot. She was to keep that car until after college graduation, when her mother sold it back.

Late summer came too soon for her parents, but Peninnah felt as though she'd been ready all her life. Although they had no idea how or what to buy or prepare for her, by checking in with some of her friends, she discovered everything that the university's welcoming material hadn't covered.

"You'll have what to eat there?" her mother asked the last day, while she and her father were packing his car.

Peninnah hesitated. "Well, um, Hillel is just half a mile away. So I can get kosher food there."

There was a heavy silence, while the woman who had fed her daughter kosher food all her life considered. "A long way in the snow it will be, no?"

Peninnah nodded. Some things, they both knew, were better left unsaid.

When the time came, Mama came to the door to wish her husband and daughter a safe trip. The two women knew they would see each other soon, and from long experience, Peninnah knew her mama was not one for long farewells. Mama did, however, stand outside waving, until all Peninnah could see from the rear windshield was a tiny blur of a human, extremely beloved form.

The University of Connecticut was founded as an agricultural college, and father and daughter were soon passing the farmland and buildings that constituted its enormous campus. This was as far from their small local women's college as she could imagine. They unloaded the car at French House, where she met Madame, the warm and gracious dorm mother. As she thanked her father and hugged him good-bye, she was already looking over his shoulder at the young women passing them in the hall.

From the first, Peninnah's college experience was a blur of playing bridge to the melody of "Autumn Leaves" in the dormitory lobby, French classes that helped her write better letters to her cousins in Paris, a lot of studying, and theater, theater, theater. Not only did she take as many classes in the subject as she could, but she also joined the drama club. She studied with professors Hinkel and Adelsberg, and when she auditioned for the production of "Father Knows Best," she cast as the servant.

She was to come onstage in her maid's uniform, white apron and all, carrying a tray with coffee. In rehearsals, she poured the coffee for "Father" and stepped back until he took a single sip and approved it, at which point she walked to the wings.

On opening night, she poured the coffee for the head of the house and waited. The lead role of Jim Anderson had gone to a good-looking Korean War veteran several years older than most of the other students. He took a sip of the coffee, and then, contrary to the stage direction, took a second sip. Then he said, "That's damned good coffee!" and held out his cup again. Unused to ad-libbing, she nonetheless took the hint, poured him more, and scurried offstage, hoping that her cheeks weren't flaming.

Backstage after the final curtain, the same student stopped her.

"Listen, I'm sorry," he said. "I have to explain. A buddy of mine was backstage doing the props. He put a little, um, Scotch whisky into the coffee pot."

She grinned. College was going to be quite a learning experience, she realized, both in and out of the classroom.

After the show, Peninnah walked into the dorm room that had been selected for the cast party. She picked up a soda and sat on the fringe of a circle of women.

"You know they only cast you as the lead once a year," one of the coeds was saying. "And freshmen are lucky for what they can get." Peninnah bowed her head. She didn't mind waiting for her big chance.

She loved everything connected with the school plays: the camaraderie of the cast, the costume fittings, staying out past curfew for late-night rehearsals, learning the lines, and the great, great thrill of appearing onstage. As soon as she was eligible, she was chosen to play the leads. She went on to play L.C. Moffat in "The Corn Is Green" and Helen Alving in

Ibsen's "Ghosts." But that first starring role, in her sophomore year, was that of Kate Keller in "All My Sons."

On opening night, her parents drove to the school. She spotted them in the hall on their way in; Papa in his serious black suit, Mama in a flowered silk top and one of her signature flowing skirts. How wonderfully familiar they looked, and yet how strangely out of place! They sat in the audience, beaming amid the professors, students and family members. In one particular scene, she was to sit on a porch swing, trimming the tails off string beans in a bowl. Remaining in character throughout, she suddenly had the strangest feeling. *I am my mother. These are the gestures my mother makes. This is the way my mother is.*

It wasn't a bad feeling, and it had, she knew, nothing whatsoever to do with her parents' presence in the audience. It struck her with an uncanny force, however. She had not often identified with her mother, feeling a much greater kinship with Papa. The two of them were the artists, the dreamers, the swans. Mama was the pragmatist who got things done, if necessary, by clipping their wings. Peninnah had always appreciated her mother's efficiency and effectiveness, even as she often silently rebelled against it. But never before had she identified with it. Never had she embraced it as part of who she was. The echo of that feeling remained with her long after the curtain came down.

At the end of the first semester of sophomore year, Papa picked her up for the winter break. They were in touch a little by telephone while she was away, but the hour's drive was her first chance in a long time to really talk with him.

"Nu, so tell me, Miss Manchester, how is university?" he asked, turning the car out of the campus onto the main road.

"So it's Miss Manchester now?" she teased. "What happened to calling me 'nove bransiche, ehre plansiche, pastechl, katchke, tzuganke, goldene kepele'?"

"Oh," he said with a wave of his hand, "you are too old and dignified and smart for such nonsense now. Now you are a university student. A Miss."

"I see." To her shock, she felt a tiny pang. "Well, this 'miss' joined Phi Sigma Sigma, one of the Jewish sororities on campus."

Papa pursed his lips. "There is more than one of these *pay samech samechs?*"

"Pa, those are Hebrew letters! This is Greek! And there is another Jewish sorority, yes. And two fraternities for the Jewish boys."

"And how did you choose this pay samech samech, in Greek?"

"That's a good question. Some of my friends were already in it, and they said the chef is great. And they're right; the food—she looked at him—which is kosher, of course—"

"Of course."

"The food is wonderful. But it's not the chef or the friends or the bridge games or even my wonderful roommate Audrey, who I will be living with forever, I hope, that took my breath away. Papa," now she turned fully toward him in the front seat, "they have a television set in the lobby! It's—it's wondrous!"

"Wondrous, you say." Her father rubbed his goatee. "Do you see a lot of this television?"

"Nope. No time. But I wish I could! It's amazing!"

He turned to her and winked. "So is this what you like about the university, my scholar? The television? The bridge games?"

"Oh Pa, you know me better than that. When I wake up in the mornings, I can't wait to get to class. I love everything about this place. It's just perfect."

He smiled. "Better than Columbia?" She nodded. "Then you might want to tell your mama. She will be glad."

They watched the hills roll by in companionable silence. Suddenly Papa said, "Your brother would like I think for you to play *shadchan* and find him a friend of yours."

She clucked her tongue. "Pa," she said, "He asked me to do that himself—or rather, he told me to. And I tried. I really did. But my friends don't want to see him again after they date him once." She paused. "He's not so nice to them."

He didn't look particularly surprised, just pained. "He doesn't hurt them, God forbid!"

"Not physically, no. But he's a bully. And he always has to be the center of attention. Face it, Pa. People don't really like him."

Papa nodded, and there was a small silence between them. But soon it was filled with the sound that Peninnah had missed most in those few months she was away: her father's tenor.

Mama had always told her children not to worry about money for college. As the businesswoman and primary breadwinner of the family, she had been saving tuition money for years. But Peninnah wanted some money of her own, along with the independence that came with earning it. The summer after her sophomore year, she and her friends got to know a few of the busboys at the Griswold. That gave her the idea to apply for a job at the only place she could imagine herself working: the hotel she had known since her childhood. The day she was hired as a waitress in the dining room, she almost hugged the woman who gave her the news.

She was sure she wore her uniform with every bit as much pride as the cadets at the academy wore theirs. Mr. Fisher, the maître d', was married to a Hawaiian woman, which meant that part of the staff show on entertainment nights was a hula. Happily, Mrs. Fisher was a good teacher; still, it was a far cry from Peninnah's years of foxtrot, jitterbug and tango lessons at the Mohican Hotel, or Israeli dancing at BBG.

She loved the job—from the elegant, round dining room to the happy guests, staff intrigue and good tips. Always a quick learner, she was soon balancing heavy trays on her shoulder, Catskills-style. She felt at home with the Jewish menu, with the many Jewish guests, more than a few of whom were big tippers, and with the friends she made, especially a young woman named Judith from the Boston area. The females bunked together in a firetrap of a house with room for several dozen young tenants. But it was an adventure, and it suited her just fine.

During one of her shifts, a soft-spoken elderly man who had come to breakfast with his wife asked what kind of juice she had.

"We have about twenty, sir," she answered sweetly, choosing not to point out that they were printed on the menu. "Would you like me to name them all, or would you rather just tell me what you prefer?"

The man looked at her a little sheepishly. "You wouldn't happen to have sauerkraut juice, would you?"

To her knowledge, it was the only time anyone had ever ordered it, but she had seen the cans in the pantry.

"Yes, sir," she said, "I'll get it for you right away."

She soon returned to the table and, like the good waitress she was, she opened the can to pour it on ice. To her dismay, the pungent sauerkraut juice sprayed all over her face and uniform. She would have to go and change, and then rinse it out as soon as she could. Sometimes, she reflected, she hated Jewish food.

"Oh, I'm so sorry!" she blurted.

"Not your fault," said the man kindly. "Sauerkraut juice will do that. Fermentation, you see. Don't worry, sweetheart. You've just earned yourself a big tip."

And to her delight, he was true to his word. Life was good.

On the last day of her first season at the hotel, the Fishers told her that the following summer she could be a captain. When she told her mother, she looked at her in confusion.

"You would be maybe on a boat?" she asked.

"No, Ma, in the dining room! Standing with the maître d' at the podium in front. He tells me where the people are going to sit, and I talk to them, make them comfortable, while I take them to their table. Then I give them menus and make sure the waiter knows when they're ready to order. And I don't even wear a uniform!"

"I thought you were proud of this uniform," her father said.

"Oh yeah, this year, when I just got the job, sure. But then I'll wear a black skirt and white blouse and heels. I'll be a professional!"

"You hear that, Chazzen?" her mother said. "Our daughter, the professional!"

Now it was the summer after junior year, and the Fishers had been true to their word. As much as she had learned on her first year at the job, her eyes were now opened to more of the goings-on at the hotel, some of which she would never dare tell her parents. Working around adults at a resort was certainly a different sort of education than she was getting in her college classes. After hours, she and others on the staff would creep into the back of the ballroom to watch the stage show. There was always a singer, a comedian, and two dancers from the staff. When the dancers came on, the Latin band lit up the room with cha cha, rumba and tango music. The staff had so much fun that they invariably got thrown out for being too noisy.

Meanwhile, her brother Joe decided he needed a motorboat. Her father dutifully bought one, and they found a place to dock it outside of town. Joe took it out on the water a few times, but he quickly tired of it, and as usually happened in such cases, its use and maintenance fell to Papa.

And Papa didn't mind at all. He loved going out on the boat, and in short order learned everything he needed to know about it. He learned how to use the motor, tilt it up and down, knew how to start it, put gas in it. Within weeks, he was taking the boat out on the Sound over to visit Peninnah at the Griswold.

She waited for him at the dock after lunch, when she had a couple of hours free. She loved to watch him emerge from the spray in his white shirt, his glasses dotted with water, his moustache and goatee moist. Was there anything her papa couldn't do? She sincerely doubted it.

He picked her up and they would drop anchor in the gray water, sometimes chatting, more often just lazing in the gentle rocking of the boat, baking in the late afternoon sun and watching the clouds in the azure sky. They both worked hard; they both needed the respite from the pleasant jumble of their lives. Neither felt the urge to move or, often, to talk.

One day, she noticed his fishing rod lying beside him.

"Caught anything today, Pa?"

He laughed. "Not yet. I will pick up my catch at the fish market on the way home."

"As usual?"

"As usual." He reached out to playfully swat her arm. "Now don't you tell your mama. She thinks I am a true fisherman."

She smiled. "Sure, Pa."

When they returned to the dock, there were two fashionable couples standing by a sparkling white yacht.

"Excuse me, Miss," one of the women called out to Peninnah. "You work at the dining room, am I right?"

"Yes," she said. "I'm your captain."

She looked at the others, hands on her hips. "I told you so!"

"We have a lot of fish here," said a man Peninnah took for her husband. "Do you think the chef would want some fish?"

"I think they have their own, sir," she said politely. "But thank you. I can ask."

"Well, maybe you would like some for your family? Sir?"

She looked at her papa. "Mama loves fresh fish," he murmured. To the strangers, he said, "You are very kind."

"That's settled then," the man said. "Come aboard, and we'll give you the bucket. It's got ice in it already. You can just take it home and enjoy."

She was astonished at the quantity of striped bass and bluefish the couples had amassed that day. All that fish looked surreal somehow, suspended on the sparkling ice.

"Can we pay you for this?" she asked. "Papa, you have your wallet on you?"

"Oh no, no!" the man said. "To tell you the truth, you're doing us a favor. What would we do with this? We're going out to dinner!"

"We should pay *you!*" the other woman said. "How much do you want us to pay you to take it?" They all laughed.

Afterward, it was just the two of them once more, enjoying the dip and rise of the small craft in the gentle waves against the wavering blue wash of the sky for another few minutes before she had to get back to work. She realized her father was gazing at her with a small smile that felt to her both pleased and wistful.

"What is it, Pa?" she asked.

"You are so grown up, my goldene kepele. You are an adult now."

She pursed her lips, a smile playing around her eyes. "I know. Isn't it wonderful?"

During the summer after graduation, she was still working as a captain at the Griswold. She hadn't forgotten the thrill of locking eyes with that bartender years before, and now her gaze was always on a particular dance instructor, who was, she told Katherine, "absolutely dreamy." The two would chat from time to time, but that was the extent of their relationship. He was strictly off-limits to the staff. It didn't matter to her much. She had already applied and been accepted to Columbia for graduate school, and she was beginning to feel sometimes that she was looking at the hotel through a rearview mirror.

On one of her shifts, Peninnah was instructed to show two distinguished-looking men to their table. As they chatted, she had a sense about one of them; he reminded her somehow of the old-world dignity of her father.

"What is your name, young lady?" the man asked her as she handed out the menus. She told him.

"Pleased to meet you," he said, extending his hand. "My name is Paul Kwartin."

Her eyes widened. She knew the last name well. Zavel Kwartin's recordings had played on the record player in her home countless times. He was one of the leading lights of what was known as the golden age of cantors, along with Pinchik, Sirota, Koussevitsky, and others. Her father had hung framed photos of some of them in his bedroom; he was so in awe of their talent. How strange to catch a glimpse of her father's world in the midst of the controlled chaos of resort life! She asked him if he was related.

The man's rather formal expression folded into a huge smile. "That's my uncle! Tell me, Miss Manchester, where do you live when you're not at the Griswold?"

"Well, I come from New London, but I will be going to Columbia for graduate school in the fall."

He pulled out his card from the breast pocket of his shirt.

"I am a cantor in Brooklyn, but I am giving a concert of Jewish music this fall on the east side of the city, at the 92nd Street Y, and I would be honored for you to come. It's an Italian Renaissance composer, Salomone Rossi. Remind me, and I will leave tickets for you at the box office."

She didn't know the name Salomone Rossi. She didn't know that the 92nd Street Y was a legendary Jewish cultural institution. She wasn't even sure where 92nd Street was. But she was determined to find out.

She graduated from UConn Phi Beta Kappa, the first year that the university welcomed the honor society, and was on her way to Columbia and the wide-open boulevards of New York City. She was delighted, but at the same time something was tugging at her heart that she couldn't quite identify.

When she was ready to leave for school that fall, Mama again saw her off at the door, as she had done four years before. This time, both mother and daughter felt the difference. New York was only another hour, hour and a half further than UConn, but it was also another world.

"Thank you for sending me to Columbia at last, Ma," Peninnah said, her voice choked with emotion.

Mama nodded. They stood facing each other in silence for many minutes, as if each could hold the other with her gaze.

At last Mama spoke.

"Just as I went away from my mama," she said quietly, "so too you have to leave your mama. *For gezunt un kum tzurik gezunt.* Travel in good health, and return in good health."

Her lovely lead actress, straight-A daughter nodded, her eyes wet.

"I know, Ma. I promise to make you proud."

Her mother nodded. "Of course, you will. You always do."

As Peninnah walked down the porch through the autumn leaves, a melody came back to her, as if from another lifetime. "Autumn Leaves." She whispered the words, this time in the original French.

ELEVEN

Tallulah Bankhead and Other Fallen Women

Peninnah stood in a circle of laughing, smartly dressed young men and women, a cold glass of fizzy soda in hand, when something suddenly occurred to her.

"Wait, wait!" she called out. "I've got a joke, too!"

Their smiles widened in anticipation, which gave her pause. What was she doing, telling a risqué joke at a party in a young man's apartment in New York City? She, a chazzen's daughter! But it was too late now; she had opened her mouth, and everyone was waiting.

"Okay," she began, "you know Tallulah Bankhead?"

"Not personally," a drunken young wit called out. "If I did, what would I be doing here with all of you?"

The others in the circle shushed him quickly and turned back to her. She swallowed. "Well, she was walking across—or slithering, really—across a hotel lobby when a man approached her. But Tallulah just kept walking.

"As she passed by, the man shouted out to her, 'Tallulah, don't you recognize me? I was your lover!'

"And the actress turned around and said in her sultry voice, 'Dahling, I'm so sorry. I didn't recognize you with your clothes on!'"

They all laughed, but the one who seemed to get the biggest kick out of it was Irving, the good-looking, slightly older man who had kicked off the joke-telling in the first place. Irving. She had caught his name when he was introduced to someone else, and it stuck with her. It was something about the way he looked at her, even when he was addressing the whole group. How he seemed to look for her approval when he said something funny. Was she imagining it? Maybe so, but there was something there, no matter how tiny the spark. She was sure of it.

The apartment belonged to a friend of Irving's named Mickey, who had invited her roommates to the party. When they asked her along earlier that day, she had demurred.

"Sorry, I'd like to," she said, "but I've got a blind date."

"Bring him along!" Sue uncapped a bottle of bright red nail polish and carefully dabbed the brush across her left thumbnail. The sharp odor wafted over to Peninnah on the other side of the room. "You know it's the more the merrier at these things."

She shook her head. "I don't know if he'd even want to."

"Hey, it's just around the corner. Stop in for half an hour. Say hello; see what's going on. And then do whatever you want."

The plan sounded plausible, and besides, you never knew what to expect with a blind date. Maybe the party would salvage the evening. At the thought, she shook her head in wonder. A year ago, she would have been thrilled at the prospect of a blind date in New York City. But after having lived with her sociable roommates for a while, she was less excited.

It's funny, the way things happen. One minute you're sitting in the plain old cafeteria of the plain old Columbia University dorm eating a plain old cheese sandwich waiting for your friend Sue, and the next you're moving into the fabulous apartment she's found for you both just five short blocks from school. It goes to show you've got to have faith.

From the day the two young women saw the enormous four-bedroom apartment at the vibrant corner of Broadway and 111th Street, they knew their graduate school experience was about to change forever. It was the fall of 1956. Elvis Presley, Fats Domino and Bill Haley and the Comets were on the radio. Everyone they met invited them to a party, sometimes to dance, sometimes just to talk, and before long they were throwing their own get-togethers. The whole thing would have been exotic enough for little Peninnah Manchester of New London, Connecticut. But when you added in the Indian samosas and dosas cooked by the roommate from Bombay, it was like being in somebody else's life. Best of all, that life included interesting young men. Dozens of them.

She had been interested in men in college and at the Griswold, including a heart-pounding, pulse-quickening crush on a grad student to the point where she learned his campus itinerary and would hide behind a tree and watch him pass, never daring to speak. Another was a good friend who would sit at the piano with her for hours, singing songs he had written. But this was different.

Take this Irving. He was thirty-three, she figured out from what he said about his wartime service. Clearly Jewish. In the course of their brief conversation she also learned that he was an international lawyer for the Revlon cosmetics company, and that he'd switched from Columbia to Brooklyn for law school because, he said, "Columbia made judges. I want to be a lawyer." She liked his looks—his blue eyes, light brown curls, good build, even his slightly bulbous nose—and that devilish sense of humor.

Even his joke she found adorable.

"There was a rabbit father and son," he began, his slightly watery eyes twinkling. "The father says, 'My son, I think it's time you learned about lady rabbits. I'm going to teach you everything you need to know.'"

"The little boy rabbit says"— here Irving raised his voice an octave or two—"'Yes, papa. What do I have to do?'

"So the father says, 'Son, I'm going to set up a line of lady rabbits. You start at one end, and I will start at the other. Then we'll meet in the middle. All you have to do is say *bonjour madame, merci madame* to each lady rabbit.'

"'Yes papa, I understand.'"

So the little boy rabbit went to one end of the line, the father started at the other end. And you could hear the father's voice, 'Bonjour madame, merci, madame, bonjour madame, merci madame.'"

"And from the other end, there was a high voice, saying, 'Bonjour madame, merci madame, *pardon* papa. Bonjour madame, merci madame, pardon papa. Bonjour madame, merci madame. . . .'"

Everybody laughed, and almost immediately someone else jumped in with another joke. From time to time, she and Irv would exchange a few sentences; they were standing just a few feet apart from one another. After a while, they broke off from the group to chat in relative private.

"So you liked my joke?" he asked casually.

"I guess I like just about anything French," she said with a smile, "even fries! My mother spent a few years in Cherbourg on her way to the States, and my father's brother actually made his way to Paris in 1914 and joined the French Army so he could learn the language. He and his wife still live in Paris. When I was in high school, their son Jacques was my pen pal."

"What, he never heard of language lessons?" She laughed. "So you like French? Then let me ask you something." He paused dramatically. "*Comment allez-vous?*"

"*C'est trés facile,*" she said. "*Je vais bien, merci. Et vous?*"

"*Trés bien maintenant*! Say," he added, almost as an afterthought. "You wouldn't happen to like baseball, would you?"

She had just opened her mouth to tell him about seeing the Boston Red Sox when her date apparently noticed her interest in Irving, or his in her. He tapped her on the shoulder and said, "What do you say? Ready to head out?"

What could she do? She thanked Mickey, and he asked for her number and address, saying that he would invite her and her friends to the next party. Then she scanned the room for Irving, hoping that he too would ask how to contact her. When she spotted him, she let out a sigh.

He was deep in conversation with his own date. She was very blonde and pretty, she thought, if maybe a bit cheap-looking.

The blind date might as well never have happened; she went to bed that night with Irving and only Irving on her mind. She thought of the first love letter her father wrote her mother right after they met, which was wrapped in string with the others in the credenza in her childhood home. It was dated February 25, 1930:

"Very respected Miss Dora Markman,

"I am thankful for the opportunity that was presented to me to make your acquaintance. . . . "I must tell you the truth . . . that you with your magic, found your way to my heart. . . . And the day should be blessed — or better said that the evening should be blessed when we met each other."

Her parents were two decades apart in age, and had lived entirely different lives when they met. And yet, she reflected, despite the differences between them, their great love and respect for each other was something she had long dreamed of for herself. Now, it almost seemed like it might be possible.

That was Saturday night. The telephone was so silent Sunday and Monday that she lifted the receiver several times to check that it was working. True, she hadn't given him her number, but he could have easily gotten it from Mickey. She paced the apartment. How could she have been so wrong?

By Tuesday afternoon, she had very nearly managed to put Irving out of her mind. She tried to console herself that there would be other boys. The city was full of them. But who was she kidding? Irving Schram was something special.

About five o'clock, the phone rang.

"Peninnah?" a male voice said. "It's Mickey, from the other night. I wonder if I could stop by tonight about eight for coffee?"

"Of course. That would be fine!"

"Oh, and if it's okay, I'll be bringing a friend."

She was barely listening. "Okay by me. See you later."

It wasn't till she opened the door at five minutes after eight that she realized who the friend was. Why was she so happy? She could have kissed that nose, right then and there. They were soon joined by her roommates, but Irving was all but laser-focused on Peninnah throughout the evening, and she on him.

It turned out that they had a lot in common. He too was close to his Eastern European immigrant parents; he lived with them just a block south of her, a few doors from their laundry/dry cleaning shop and their shul, Ramat Orah. Like her, he could speak and understand Yiddish. But he was a real New Yorker, born in Brooklyn, raised in the Bronx, now in Manhattan. She felt as though she could listen to his stories all night. It was like the cliché says: By the end of the evening, she felt she'd known him all her life.

"So where did a nice Jewish girl like you learn a joke like that?" he asked at one point.

"Probably at UConn. University of Connecticut. I was known as a great joke teller at my sorority. I hear a joke once, and I usually remember it. I actually have quite a repertoire."

"I wouldn't doubt it for a minute," he said. "I get the feeling you do everything well." She beamed.

When he asked if she was free Saturday night, she had to force herself not to answer too soon: Yes!

There was a hot new musical called "My Fair Lady" on Broadway that season, and everyone was learning the songs. The one that stuck in her head said it all. It had to do with being so happy, she could have never stopped dancing.

In fact, like Fred Astaire in "Royal Wedding," she could have easily danced on the ceiling.

They soon found themselves together every weekend, sometimes to stay in her apartment and discuss books and politics and their lives, sometimes to go to a movie or out to eat or to a party. They took trips to the intimate Frick Collection on the East Side, where they wandered among the Old Masters, and picnics under the trees in Central Park. Mostly, they talked. He seemed fascinated by her background. His parents were less educated, a good deal less formal than hers. She in turn wanted to hear anything he cared to tell.

"Really, I'm not that interesting," he said, lighting a cigarette and leaning back on the park bench they had stopped at, his arm casually draped over her shoulder. How she wished he didn't smoke! She was raised to hate smoking.

"I'd much rather talk about Willie Mays. Now there's a story! I could talk about him all day."

"I'd rather hear about you."

He held her closer. "Okay, I guess I could talk about Irv Schram for a change. Although I warn you: my stats don't come close to Willie's." He had been looking into her eyes; now his gaze settled on a squirrel some yards away. "We moved a lot when I was a kid, mainly because in those days you always got the first month's rent for free. I bet you didn't know that, did you?" She shook her head. He took another drag on his cigarette. "So—if you kept moving, you could save a bundle, and that came in handy, since business wasn't always great. We did that practically till I joined the service."

"And what was the Schram business, exactly?"

"Laundry. By the way, I should tell you, my family's name is Schrom. Mine is Schram." He winked. "More American, you know?"

She was so dazzled by his charm and wit that she had no idea if he was kidding. She decided not; after all, her father's surname had been Anglicized more than his.

"And you have two brothers?"

He frowned. "I did. Now I have one."

"Oh. I'm sorry."

"Hey, it was a war. We weren't the only ones. Not by a long shot." He paused and shook his head. "Excuse the pun."

"That must have been so hard for your folks."

"For all of us." He took another long drag on his cigarette and blew smoke rings. "You know how I got the news? Damnedest thing. Miltie and I were both in the Army in France. I had sent him a letter from my base to his, and it came back 'Deceased. Killed in action.' Damned Army. No sense of tact."

Her hand flew to her mouth in horror. "Oh that's terrible! I really feel for you and your family!"

She began to wonder if that was why he joked around so much, if that twinkle in his eyes were merely illuminating his darker feelings. The thought gave her a surprising urge to protect him. Protect him! The man who had not only served in the Army, but had told her he was a boxer — albeit in the lightweight division — in high school!

She had never met anyone so brainy, and yet so earthy at the same time. And he did everything with such authenticity, such decency. She was soon crazy about him. Her roommates adored Irving, too. He enlivened any group he joined. She loved that her two dearest friends and their husbands had become close with them both. They were soon part of a set of three couples that socialized regularly, and Peninnah had never been happier. This was all she wanted; there was no career beckoning to her, no special future plans. She wanted to love and be loved, and even though she may not have been at that point yet, she could see it on the horizon. For the first time in her life, she could see that she might have a marriage like that of her parents, and she blessed them silently for having shown her that such a possibility existed.

Seven weeks after they met, he came to pick her up as usual, only to announce that he'd forgotten his wallet. Could she come back to the house with him to get it?

"Sure. But if we're going to make that movie, we'd better hurry. I'll wait downstairs."

He said nothing until they reached the small lobby of the building minutes later.

"Just come upstairs for a minute, willya?" he asked. "I'm not so sure where I put it. You can help look."

Without a word, she followed him into the rickety elevator car. They soon reached his floor, then walked hand in hand to the apartment door.

Should she be nervous that a man was taking her to his apartment at night? She smiled at the thought. After all, this was Irv. By that point, she would trust him with her life.

The moment he opened the door, she knew why she was really there.

"Irving, that you? You forgot something, dahlink?"

He hadn't left his wallet; that much was clear. And he certainly hadn't meant to seduce her, either. Here were his parents, two warm, working-class immigrants from Ukraine, coming out of the kitchen to welcome her. They sat in the living room and shared a few pleasantries in Yiddish. She noticed that theirs was a Galitzianer accent; she had learned the more literate, Litvak dialect from her parents. She was thoroughly enjoying herself when Irv announced that it was time to go.

"Shame on you!" she said with a laugh, as soon as they reached the elevator. "I will never trust you again!"

He winked. "Pretty sly, huh? Bet you never fell for that old 'I left my wallet upstairs' routine before! I'm a master at the form!"

"Your parents are great; I really don't mind. It was fine. But you're just lucky I was wearing my good coat!"

"I checked you out to be sure you were presentable," he said, linking his arm through hers. "I figured you were on the line, but you'd pass."

"Thanks a lot!"

When she looked at him looking at her, she knew that in his eyes she was far, far past that line. And that made it more than fine. That made it positively sensational.

One drizzly Sunday evening, Peninnah was seated in the apartment on the living room couch, reading a book she'd just bought. Or trying to. In between pages, she and her roommate Sue were swapping jokes.

"Did you hear the one about the two Scottish girls in the meadow?" she suddenly asked, her head popping up from the book.

Sue shook her head. "No, I missed that one somehow."

"Well, these two girls were romping in the meadow when they spotted a young, kilted Scotsman sleeping under a tree. They crept up quietly and saw that he was sound asleep.

"One of the young girls says to her friend, 'You know, I always wondered what was under those kilts. I think I'll take a peek.' She tiptoed over to the sleeping man and lifted up his kilt. Then she let it fall back in place.

"They were about to go on their way when the girl turned to her friend and said, 'I feel bad that he doesn't know what I did. So she slipped off her blue hair ribbon and tied it around his—his private part.'"

Sue chuckled.

"Some time later," Peninnah continued, "the man woke up and felt something strange. He lifted his kilt and saw the blue ribbon.

"'I don't know where you've been, laddie,' he said to his thing, "but I'm sure glad you won first prize!'"

They were still laughing when the phone rang. Peninnah reached over and answered it on the first ring, hoping it was Irv. She wanted to tell him about the new book, and more importantly, she wanted to hear his voice.

But the call was from a woman, and it was for Sue, who was still seated on the other side of the couch. During the brief chat, Sue kept looking over at her. Peninnah felt a tiny fluttering in her stomach.

When her roommate hung up, she asked, "What?"

"It's nothing, really."

"What is it, Sue? Tell me, or I'll explode."

"Oh," she began, looking down at her hands, "my friend says she saw Irv with a flashy blonde last night, and she just wondered, did he have a sister in town? Nasty girl. Even if it were true, which it's not, Penny, it's none of her business. Anyway, weren't you with Irv last night?"

She didn't answer for several seconds. Then she said dully, "No. I was in New London."

Sue yawned and closed her book. "Oh that's right. Well, you know what? Maybe it *was* his sister! I'm sure there's a perfectly good explanation. Irv is a great guy. And he loves you. That's the important thing." She left the room, and Peninnah heard the refrigerator door open.

In a voice that was barely audible, she said to the empty room, "And Irv doesn't have a sister." Then she heard something at the window, and she raised her head to look. The rain had picked up. It was slapping furiously at the glass.

When Irv came to see her later that week, Peninnah was on edge after too many talks with her roommates and too many nights of poor sleep. But she knew what she had to do. She had tried to be as nice as possible when he called to make the date, because how do you break up over the telephone? But she was determined. She knew just who the "flashy blonde" was; he had been with her the night they met. But he had said—or maybe she had only imagined he'd said—that they had ended things. I will not be treated this way, she told herself, for the hundredth time that week. I am not garbage. I deserve better.

She was steely in her resolve till she opened the door, and there he was, leaning down for a kiss. How could she ruin their happiness? But what kind of happiness was it? Better to call it off now, before her heart was torn into a million pieces.

She had been told she was a terrific actress on stage, but it was infinitely more difficult to pretend her feelings in real life. That night they had the apartment to themselves. She was pouring him wine, listening without comment to his humorous description of an encounter with a fellow attorney. When his glass was full, she set the bottle on the table and sat down onto the couch, several feet away from him.

He stopped abruptly in the middle of a sentence. "Okay, what is it?"

"Huh? What is what?"

"Come on, Peninnah. You've barely said a word since I arrived. You are hardly making eye contact even now. And then there's this." He motioned to the expanse of couch between them. "This, this damned chasm here. This isn't like you. What's going on?"

She considered moving closer, but then she pictured the blonde sitting between them. She forced herself to raise her eyes to meet his.

"I heard a rumor. More than a rumor. I got a—a report."

He raised his eyebrows and said in mock horror, "A report?"

"It's not funny. Somebody saw you out with that—woman."

The laughter was gone from his face in an instant. He murmured, "You mean Gloria."

"I don't want to know her name. I don't care. That's your business, not mine. I just don't think we should see each other anymore, Irv. Not while you're seeing her."

He stood up so abruptly that he almost knocked his glass off the table. He didn't begin to pace as she expected; he didn't leave her side. It was as though he were rooted in place. For what felt like several minutes, he said nothing. Out of the corner of her eye she watched him, trying in vain to read his handsome features. Finally he sat down again, a little closer to her. When he reached for her hand, she pulled it away.

"Look, Peninnah," he said at last. "I love you. You are so bright, beautiful, amazing, so—fresh. That's what I thought the first time I saw you. Like a breath of fresh air." He reached down to take a long sip of wine. "I know her from Brooklyn. We're Brooklyn bums. What can I say? I've been seeing her a long time. I just can't—I just can't cut her off so easily."

"Do you intend to marry her?" she asked, her voice tense and quiet. "Has she met your parents?"

He chose, she noticed, to ignore the first question. "My folks don't like her. In fact, I even moved out of the apartment for a while because of that."

"Then what are we doing, Irv? Tell me, please, what we're doing. What are *you* doing?"

For the first time since they'd met, the brilliant, articulate lawyer was out of words. He leaned down, kissed her on the forehead, and reached for his coat. In silence, he walked to the door. Then he turned to face her.

"I really hope you'll change your mind."

She looked down at her clenched fists as if surprised to see them there. As though they belonged to someone else.

"And I really hope you'll change yours."

When he shut the door behind himself, she stood up and locked it. Then she sat back down on the couch, and her face dropped into her hands.

TWELVE

Leaving Home

When her old Griswold pal Judith told her that the drive along the Amalfi coast in southern Italy was breathtaking, Peninnah had assumed that she had been referring to the scenery. What she experienced was something altogether different, however: a terror so overwhelming that she didn't dare breathe.

It wasn't her traveling companion's fault, she reflected, dutifully gazing out at the dark peaks silhouetted against the sparkling sky, while her friend attempted to stay on the road. In fact, when Judith had called with an extra plane ticket to Europe so soon after Peninnah had broken off with Irv, she smiled for the first time in weeks.

"Wait, I don't get it," she had said. "Who was supposed to go with you?"

"Nobody, silly. I just didn't want to go alone. I figured I could always find someone. And you with your love of French were my first choice! Oh, and of course your scintillating personality."

When she weighed the prospect of a lonely summer without Irv or a European adventure with a friend, there was no question of turning down the offer.

"Take me, Judith!" she said, jumping up from her chair so fast she nearly toppled over in a heap. "I'm yours!"

Of course it wasn't quite as simple as that. Fresh out of college, Peninnah had very little money. She approached her father for permission and funding, although technically he was not the parent with the purse strings.

He leaned back in his chair and regarded his daughter seriously.

"Listen, Peninnah," he said, "better to go to Israel. You know I was there when you were a baby. You could go see my orange trees. . . . "

"But, Pa, I don't want to go to Israel!" She could hear the whining in her voice, and it infuriated her. Here she was, a college graduate at last, speaking to Papa like she was ten.

"I want to go to England and France and Italy," she said, struggling to steady her voice. "I want to see Buckingham Palace, the Louvre, and all the places and art that I've been studying for years in school." Did she sound convincing? She wasn't so sure.

"Pastechl," he said quietly. "Listen to your papa, please. I went to Israel three times in less than fifteen years. And you know why? You think I never heard of France or Italy? But Israel, Israel is like your mother. Sure, there are mothers who are more fashionably dressed, or better educated, or who speak English without an accent like your mother does. But your mama is your mama. Maybe there are countries with better museums, or older colleges, or more magnificent art and architecture. But you only have one Israel. You only have one mama."

Actually, she had a mother who agreed to give her the money, although, considering that Mama saw no reason for travel and sightseeing, no one quite understood why. Plans were made, flights were caught, and there the two friends were in Europe, with a schedule to stay eight weeks. With what seemed to Peninnah to be awe-inspiring confidence, Judith had bought the little Volkswagen Beetle, with the sunroof they called a *lokh in kop*, in Rotterdam, after a week spent touring Ireland and England. The plan was to drive through Paris to the Riviera, make a number of stops in various countries, and return the car in Scotland before flying back to the U.S.

The prospect of those car trips while enjoying the safety of her Manhattan apartment had been exciting. Having learned to drive on her father's Packard—manual transmission, mind you—at age sixteen, she was looking forward to getting behind the wheel. She thought of the ride to beautiful Ocean Beach, with the boardwalk, and its pure white sand, and the huge empty parking lot in the winter, where Pa taught her three-point turns and parallel parking. She was a pretty good driver, even if she had failed her test the first time. And that, she had always maintained, had been more due to the intimidating inspector than to her own expertise.

But now on the Amalfi Drive, she prayed silently that Judith would forget their deal: fifteen minutes of driving, fifteen minutes of enjoying the scenery, because it was frankly impossible to do both simultaneously. She had never seen a road so narrow and twisty. If they missed it by an inch, she knew it would be all over. It was madness, but by the time they had realized the danger, it was too late to turn back.

"Driver change, Penny!" Judith called out, as if reading her thoughts.

She felt her heart thump with fear. "Are you sure it's been fifteen minutes?"

"Just over twenty, in fact. You lucked out. I couldn't find a good place to stop. Quick, let's do it fast. This spot seems safe. Or at least safer."

Back behind the wheel, she prayed again, this time that no ongoing traffic would appear. It was hard enough with one car's width on the road. The prospect of two was devastating.

Some people might actually enjoy this kind of hair-raising risk, she reflected. But not me. I don't even cross the street by foot without looking left, right and left again.

And yet. The view was certainly out of this world. She only hoped she would stay in this world long enough to tell someone about it.

She thought: I haven't done this much praying since Yom Kippur.

They completed the drive in one piece, but it wasn't the only time Peninnah found herself praying during those two months abroad. There was that evening in Nice, which was overrun with tourists due to bullfights, when they desperately searched for a vacant *pension*, only to be tailed for miles through dark, vacant fields by a carload of rowdy young French soldiers. There were lesser mishaps, as well, when she stepped in a cow "pancake" in Lichtenstein, or when they pretended to make a date with two overly attentive policemen in order to be allowed to continue on their way—pale line on the men's ring fingers marking absent wedding bands notwithstanding.

She prayed even more, however, when she picked up her mail at the American Express offices throughout Europe. She leafed through the pale blue aerogrammes: a letter from Pa, one from Sue—ahh, another couple from Irv. Greedily she ripped open the flaps of the first one. They had patched things up before she left, but she was anxious for a proposal. Had he finally written what she was waiting to read?

She could hear his voice as she read the words. "I want nobody but for you to be my wife. But I need a commitment from you, too. When your trip is over, I will be waiting at the airport for your answer."

She lowered herself onto the closest chair. Judith must have seen her grow a little woozy, because she rushed over.

"Penny! What is it? I hope it's not bad news!"

Silently she handed her friend the letter. Judith, who had heard endlessly about Irving throughout the trip, stood scanning the page as harried travelers passed around her.

"Oh wow!" she said when she finished. "Oh my God! You're going to say yes, aren't you?" She dropped down on the seat beside her. "Well, aren't you?"

"I think so," said slowly. "I don't know. I told you he called to apologize and tell me how much he missed me before we left, right?" Her friend nodded. "Well, all I said was that I was doing the trip anyway, and that I didn't have time to see him before going. He really hurt me, Judith. I've just got to be sure that he's the one."

Judith placed her hand on Peninnah's shoulder. "You'll know what to do when you see him again."

When the young women arrived in New York, Irv was standing on the glassed-in balcony overlooking the runway. She saw him the moment she entered the terminal, and just as Judith had predicted, all the bitterness she had been feeling for months melted away like so much chicken *schmaltz* on her mother's hot stove. Judith struggled to keep up with her as she trotted to meet him at baggage claim. He was thinner and paler than he had been at the beginning of the summer; his allergies, or her absence, had clearly taken their toll. But it didn't matter; he was her Irv. They exchanged a friendly airport hug, and he reached for her luggage.

She said her good-byes to Judith, who was met by friends, and happily walked arm-in-arm with Irv to his car. On the drive to Manhattan, she couldn't stop herself from chattering.

"Oh Irv, the most wonderful part of the whole trip was Leontyne Price in 'Aida.' That was in an amphitheater in Verona; did I write you about that? During the overture, everyone held up these tiny lighted candles they gave out at the door, then they turned off the lights and just had thousands of twinkling flames and trillions of stars in the sky—it was spectacular. Then at every intermission, the people around us pulled out their baskets of food and wine and shared it all! Oh, and Maria Callas was in the audience! Can you believe it?"

Eyes on the road, he murmured, "Sounds great. I wish I'd been there." When she didn't reply, he added, "You know, when my mother told her good friend you were going to Europe for so long, you know what she said?" Peninnah shook her head, just once. "Mrs. Meyers said, 'That girl's crazy. He won't wait for her.' But I did."

At that, the conversation quickly faltered, and they sat in silence. Am I nervous? she wondered. No, not at all. Excited? Exhausted? Or just terribly, terribly excited and exhausted at the same time?

"Where are we going?" she asked after a time, unwilling to take her eyes from his familiar profile even to check their surroundings.

"I thought we would go to my parents," he said quietly. "They want to see you."

It was then that it hit her: He still didn't know. She had known back at the airport what her answer was to be, but he didn't. It was Irv who was nervous! As for herself, she had never been more calm about anything. The thought took her aback. She was so used to Irv's being in control that it never occurred to her that she held his future in her hand. She could hardly wait to deliver it to him, but she couldn't very well bring it up now. Not in a speeding car on the Triborough Bridge.

Soon they were in Manhattan, on West 110th Street, and he was escorting her up to his apartment. She thought of the first time he had tricked her into meeting his parents. How much had changed between them since then! How much she herself had changed!

Unlike that first visit, however, his parents were out of the house. He didn't seem to mind in the least.

"I'm sure it won't take long," he said. "They're always home around now."

"No problem." In fact, she was barely able to restrain her pleasure. "There's no place I need to be."

"Do you want something to drink, maybe? Or eat? There's gotta be something in the refrigerator."

She hadn't realized how thirsty she was until that moment. "Okay, yes. Thanks. Just some water is fine."

"I'm sure it's a treat to have good old American water out of the tap after that spritz from the bottle," he said with a grin. "You probably couldn't wait to get home!"

"Oh," she laughed, "it was terrible! Two months of hell!"

They were leaning up against the doorframe between the kitchen and the dining room, chatting and joking. The atmosphere was almost back to normal, she thought, when there was a sudden silence, filled only by the honking of police sirens on the street below. She closed her eyes. They were so close, she could breathe in his cologne, but other than that hug in the airport, they had barely touched.

He swallowed. "Peninnah?"

"Yes?" She held her breath.

He gazed into her eyes with what seemed to her a new tenderness.

"Will you marry me?"

When she spoke, her voice was trembling.

"Of course I will, Irv. Yes, yes, of course, of course!"

Their kisses, which she would always remember as delicious, lasted close to an hour. Just once did they break apart. That was when his allergies got the better of him, and he sneezed, apologizing profusely.

"Tzu gezunt, tzu laing yor, tzu laing lebn, my darling," she whispered.

The only other thought that came to mind during that hour was that once again, he had used a ruse to get her up to his apartment. And once again, she forgave him.

She and Irv gathered themselves together at last, returned to the car, and soon she was sitting alone in his big blue Buick, double-parked on Broadway while he "straightened something out" with the neighborhood florist. He emerged ten minutes later with a wrist corsage of red roses that he gently slipped over her shaking fingers.

Then they drove to New London, smiling all the way.

"Ma, Pa!" she called as they walked through the front door of her parents' house and set her luggage down in the hall. "I'm back! And I'm getting married!"

Mama jumped up from her seat at the table. For the first time in her daughter's experience, this strong, capable woman was at a loss for words.

After a moment or two, she said, "Sit down, children, and have something to eat! Then we'll talk," and hurried into the kitchen.

But Papa stood up slowly, with a warm smile that showed his dimple. First he embraced his daughter and welcomed her back from her trip. Then he shook Irv's hand, wished them both mazel tov, and brought out a bottle of wine and glasses to drink *l'chayim*. His exclamations of joy filled her head for hours.

So did her mother's instructions, which she delivered *sotto voce* when the two were alone in the kitchen toward the end of the evening.

"Two things you need to remember, my child: A mama will forgive and forget. But a mother-in-law will forgive, but never forget."

"What's the other?"

It was advice she knew as soon as she heard it that she would never keep.

"You should live ten blocks from your mama—and ten blocks from your mother-in-law."

The song that filled her head that night was from a Broadway musical of the past decade, *Kiss Me Kate*. She was in love.

Wedding plans are never easy. There were complications about the location and even the rabbi, because unfortunately, her father no longer had a license to perform wedding ceremonies in New York. For the venue, he suggested the Broadway Central Hotel on the Lower East Side, which had a lovely ballroom and chapel at which he had performed weddings when he was a cantor in Bayonne. Papa also recommended the rabbi, Benjamin Kreitman, a major talent and a dear friend who had been the rabbi at the New London shul where Peninnah had sung in the choir all those years before.

They were married on December 7, 1958, just three weeks before her twenty-fourth birthday, and the seventh night of Chanukah. Offsetting her simple gown with pearls sewn around the neckline was the elegant veil, complete with a two-inch crown her mother had absolutely insisted upon.

"Mama, I look like a princess in this!" she protested in the store. "It's ridiculous!"

Her mother frowned. "To your papa and me, you *are* a princess. And you want your husband to treat you like a queen from the very first day."

Cantor Eliezer Bernstein, who had been her choirmaster at Beth El, sang the traditional *shevah brachot*, the seven blessings—all except the last, which was a major cantorial piece and the showpiece of Orthodox Jewish weddings. That honor, along with walking up the aisle and singing a welcoming melody before the wedding party arrived, was reserved for her father, who at eighty was still able to bring the assembled guests to tears with the beauty of his resonant voice.

When she heard him singing, her bridesmaid Adrienne shook her head.

"Your father should really make records," she whispered. "He's amazing."

Peninnah nodded. "You know, when Papa would get ready to daven *Hineini* on the High Holidays, a local butcher, one of his biggest fans, would look up from the men's section at the women in the balcony and say, 'Ladies, please don't cry! You're going to flood us down here!'"

Her friend laughed. "He was definitely onto something. I'm about to dissolve myself."

The bride walked down the aisle holding a white Bible draped with white orchids and satin ribbons. Her first dance with her husband was "So in Love." Her life, it seemed, was a rose, blooming before her eyes.

During the reception, the bride and her father celebrated the holiday with the Chanukah duet he had composed years earlier, *Haneiros Halolu*. Instead of her playing the melody on the family piano, as she had done so many times before, Abraham Ellstein, a revered composer and conductor for Yiddish theater, accompanied them. He was also a member of the wedding orchestra, along with "the Benny Goodman of klezmer" himself, clarinetist Dave Tarras. A bass player completed the trio, which played under the *chuppah* as well as at the reception.

Later in the evening the band played *"Die Mezinke Oysgegebn,"* a tradition at the wedding of a youngest child. The guests placed four chairs in the middle of the floor for the four parents, then sang and danced around the chairs.

> Louder, louder, enlarge the circle
> God has brought me good fortune and happiness.
> Rejoice, children, all night long.
> My youngest daughter's getting married.

Someone took a photo of the two sets of smiling parents surrounded by singing and dancing young people. Both fathers, as different as they were, wore the identical gleeful expressions.

Her old friend Phil from New London had schlepped in a heavy reel-to-reel tape recorder in order to record the service. When they listened to the tape sometime afterward, they heard her father's chanting, the reading of the *ketubah*, the reciting of the vows, the rabbi's blessing, the breaking of the glass, and the accompanying applause and mazel tovs. There was a pause. Then they heard Phil's irritated voice say, "Oh shit, how do you turn this thing off?"

Peninnah and Irv stared at each other in horror for several seconds and then simultaneously burst into peals of laughter. Perhaps, they agreed, they wouldn't play the recording so soon for anyone else.

They laughed every time they thought of it for a long, long time.

THIRTEEN

Paris, by Way of Manhattan

At the very top of Manhattan Island, bounded by the Hudson River to the west and the Harlem River to the north and east, lies the neighborhood of Inwood. When the newly married Schrams moved there in late 1958, the residents were primarily Irish or Jewish, and the couple soon felt completely at home. The area's most beloved attraction, just four miles away in Fort Tryon Park, was the Cloisters. Assembled from four imported European cloisters in the 1930s, the exhibit of medieval art and architecture gave the impression of actually being on the continent. As fans of all things French, Peninnah and Irv appreciated the proximity to a piece of the Old World.

The young Mrs. Schram took to married life the way she did most other things—wholeheartedly, with energy and enthusiasm. Over the course of her twenty-three years, she had adopted the credo that if a thing was worth doing it was worth doing well, and that strategy extended now to everything from cleaning the house to following her mother's chicken soup recipe to learning about her new husband on a deeper level than she'd ever known anyone, even her childhood friend Katherine. She reveled both in her independence as a married woman and on her growing dependence on the man she loved. As each day passed, Peninnah was more and more sure of her choice. Sometimes she would stop herself in the course of a day, in the market down the street or in the living room of her apartment, and wonder once again how she had been so blessed to marry the most wonderful man on the planet.

The couple celebrated their first anniversary with their parents and some of their siblings in their 215th Street apartment. Not long afterward, Irv came home from work to tell Peninnah that Revlon was talking to him about a transfer to its Swiss office.

"You're kidding!" she said. "Living in Switzerland? We could go to Paris whenever we wanted! Oh Irv, how fantastic. What an adventure!"

He held up a hand. "Now, no counting chickens before they're hatched, please. We're still in the discussion stage." But they hugged each other with joy nonetheless.

A mutual friend introduced them to another couple also planning to move to Switzerland. They shared a few dinners, got along well, and foresaw for themselves a comfortable and enjoyable sojourn in that country. Ever the conscientious student of life, Peninnah began reading about the country and its history. As for language, her French was good, and she figured her Yiddish would help her understand the German. For weeks, her delight at the prospect of this new move colored everything she did.

She had been ladling out soup at the stove one evening when he told her there was a change of plans; the Switzerland job was no longer available. When she swung around to face him, he couldn't tell whether her face was red from the heat of cooking or the disappointment.

"Oh no," she moaned. "Damn! That would have been so wonderful!" She dropped down into a kitchen chair. "Oh Irv, I know nothing was for certain. But I am so damned aggravated!"

"Well maybe this will cheer you up," he said, in a voice as casual as he could muster. "We're being sent to Paris instead."

The expression on her face, he told friends later, was worth everything. She looked surprised, dazed and over the moon at the same time. He didn't even mind when she playfully punched him in the arm for teasing her.

That evening, over a celebratory bottle of French wine, she told him again about the family on both parents' sides that she had in Paris.

"Judith and I met them when we were over there," she said. "They're wonderful."

"Jacques was your childhood pen pal," he replied. "I remember your telling me." To her happy nod he added, "And you thought I didn't listen to you."

"Never did I say that! If anything, you listen too closely. I'm afraid sometimes that anything I say may be used against me in a court of law!"

"What can I say? I've been trained well."

Peninnah leaned across the table to plant a kiss on his lips. "Tonight of all nights, Irving Schram, I dearly love the lawyer in you. And everything else besides."

The plan was for her to remain with his parents at the 110th Street apartment while he got himself situated in Paris. After a few weeks, he promised, he would return home to help her pack up the Inwood apartment. He would then return to Paris, and she would join him as soon as possible. She could barely contain her eagerness to go. Sometimes just strolling around her neighborhood, she would suddenly start to smile broadly, and it was all she could do to restrain herself from dancing down the street. Paris! I'm going to live in Paris!

On 110th Street, his mother had fixed up his old room for her, and the novelty of being there somewhat dampened the longing she felt for him, along with the anticipation of her new life. At night sometimes she would lie awake hour after hour, thinking that she was looking up at the same ceiling that he must have stared at for years, and wondering at the odds of being sent to the one place on earth she wanted to be above all others. For her father, she knew, that place was Israel; he still dreamed of moving there permanently. He still had the orange grove there he had bought in the early thirties, expecting to visit for several months while his wife and children remained in the States. For her mother, paradise was America, with its freedoms and opportunities for advancement. Whereas for Peninnah, the French capitol had long ago put a spell on her that she could not explain.

Somehow the purgatorial waiting period passed. Irv returned to New York to prepare for a lengthy stay in Paris. The New York apartment was vacated. The suitcases were packed, and what they wouldn't be taking they put into storage. Irv returned to Paris, and Peninnah waited for him to tell her to confirm her flight. Finally, the relatives and friends were kissed and hugged. When she walked toward the plane the evening of November 16, 1960, she felt as though she were already up in the air. Only at the last minute, as she stood at the entranceway, did she turn one last time to wave good-bye to her family, and to her past. Something altogether new was going to happen to her. She could feel it. The little Jewish girl from New London was more than ready for a taste of sophistication.

On entering the airport in Paris, she received a message explaining that Irv was stuck in a meeting, and she would have to make her way to the Hotel Raphael on her own. She was exhausted, and she had been looking forward to being swept up in his capable energy, but in truth, she didn't mind in the least. The hotel, which had been built at the end of the War, was situated in the 16th Arrondissement, the middle of Paris, just steps from the Eiffel Tower and the business district beyond. She had studied the map for the tenth time on the plane, and in any case, she would be taking a taxi. The ride north to the city took less than half an hour, and her gaze never wavered from the window. To Peninnah, Paris looked both extremely exotic and strangely familiar at the same time.

When the cab pulled up in front of the sculpted stone facade, she was perplexed. Yes, it was beautiful and elegant, but small, and she could see no sign indicating that it was a hotel. But the driver insisted, first in broken English and then in French, that they were at the right place. She paid him and entered the lobby, which she noticed was decorated with all manner of antiques. After she checked in, the bellhop led her to an enormous elevator with a velvet bench, and when she reached her room, she was sure it was larger than her entire apartment back home.

She had just toured the enormous bathroom, furnished with two of everything, including bidets, when the telephone on the bedside table rang.

"Hello?" she almost whispered.

Not very French of you," Irv said. "What kind of way is that to answer a phone in Paris? You say, *oui*? Or *allô*?"

"Oh, Irv! This place is incredible!" She proceeded to describe the velvet-flecked wallpaper and the king-sized Louis XIV bed.

"Well it better be incredible, for what the company is paying. It's a five-star hotel, after all."

"What I don't understand is why there's hardly any sign from the street. Does anybody know about it?"

"Only the likes of Ingrid Bergman and Anna Magnani. It's the kind of thing that you either know about or you don't. And you, *ma chérie*, are in the know."

"So when are you coming to share the king-sized bed with me?"

"That will have to wait a little, I'm afraid. But I'll be back around seven, and we'll get something to eat."

"Okay." She heaved a mock sigh. "I'll unpack and keep myself busy somehow. *Au revoir, mon beau mari!*"

"*Au revoir, mon petit chou. Et à bientôt.*"

Peninnah was exhausted by now, but she couldn't bring herself to lie down. Then she remembered the going-away gift a friend had given her, a brand-new invention, the pocket-sized Sony transistor radio, with its own leather case. All at once struck with a wave of homesickness, she turned it on. She almost jumped when she located a station. Why, the announcer spoke in French! She chuckled. Of course, she chided herself immediately. If it hadn't struck her before that she was in a different country, she knew it now. She couldn't understand all of what was said, but fortunately the program turned to music soon after. That she was born understanding.

She must have slept at last, because she awoke to Irv's gentle kiss on her cheek. He lay down beside her, and they held each other for many minutes.

"Tired, huh?" he asked after a time.

She wrinkled her nose. "Twelve hours in a plane will do that to you, I guess. You would have thought I actually flapped my wings all that time. But Irv, now that you're here, the picture's complete. I feel like I'm living a fairy tale. I couldn't be happier."

Over the next few weeks she explored the neighborhood, mainly shopping while Irv was at work. They visited with the Sorkines, her mother's Russian cousins, and treated her father's brother Benjamin, his wife Rose and son Jacques to room service hot chocolate, *café aux lait* and pastries when they visited them in the hotel. These relatives were French Communists, and she felt more than a little embarrassed at the decadent lifestyle she and Irv were enjoying. But to her delight, everyone was gracious as could be.

Over supper one evening, Irv asked about her day.

"Well, I'm really getting to know Paris by walking everywhere," she began. Parc Monceau is already one of my favorite places. All that old architecture. I'm thinking of signing up at the Alliance Francaise to improve my speaking, though. Maybe three times a week? What do you say?"

"Great idea! Then you can deal with all the tradespeople and the landlord for us."

She poked his arm. "I have a feeling your French will always be better than mine. And your accent? *Très magnifique!*"

He held her gaze. "And you don't mind not working, right?"

"Are you kidding? *C'est très très magnifique!*"

After three weeks at the hotel, they found a charming, seven-room apartment on Avenue McMahon, on one of the streets radiating from the Arc de Triomphe. It seemed that from that moment on, their social life exploded. Apart from relatives, they became friendly with a retired American executive from Revlon and his wife, Burt and Ethel Reibel. In his post-retirement role as senior consultant, Burt mentored Irv, while Ethel showered Peninnah with VIP tickets to fashion shows and took her to fancy cafes. What's more, it sometimes seemed to them that every friend they'd ever had came to visit, including her dear college friend and fellow actress Lenore and her husband, with whom they traveled for a ten-day trip through the Loire Valley wine country.

On one of their winery tours, Lenore took Peninnah aside.

"My dear," she said quietly, "this life is all very well, but we both know you are a performer at heart."

"We both are," Peninnah replied. "You know either you or I starred in every play there was in school. People complained we had a monopoly."

"That's what I was thinking exactly," she said. "When you get back to New York, I think you and I should start a little theater company. Bring shows to synagogues, men's clubs, sisterhoods, that sort of thing. What do you say?"

She didn't hesitate for a moment. "I say that if I were anywhere, and I mean *anywhere* other than Paris, I'd go back and start this theater company immediately!"

The Cole Porter hit "I Love Paris" said it best: she was completely in love with Paris, and Irv felt exactly the same. She caught him at times just sitting and reading a French dictionary, or looking out the window while he drank his morning coffee. There was an expression about doing things with French eyes, and that is what he had. The place fit him like a bespoke suit. For her, being with family was every bit as important as the place. And Uncle Benjamin's family meant the most to her. They heard them mix Yiddish with French and watched them greet each other with a kiss on both cheeks so often that she and Irv started doing the same.

After they'd been in the city for several months, Irv returned from work one day with a dinner invitation from Monsieur Justine, who owned the Revlon boutique on the fashionable Champs-Elysees. It was a rare honor for Americans to be invited to French people's homes. Dressing for dinner that evening, Peninnah was delighted at the prospect of an evening full of chic and sophisticated people.

"Irv," she said, standing at the mirror smoothing down the neckline of her little black dress.

He was standing behind her to one side, tying and untying his tie.

"Hmm? Damned thing. You'd think after all these years I could get it right the first time."

"Honey, listen." She turned toward him. "Seriously, your French is so much better than mine; and people tend to speak so fast here. I don't want to look or feel like an idiot. Will you be sure to sit next to me at dinner?"

He released the wayward tie and placed his hands on her shoulders.

"I would be honored, Madame Schram. Hey, that almost rhymes!"

She laughed. He had a way of erasing her fears that never failed to amaze her.

"It would rhyme if you hadn't changed your last name from Schrom!" she said.

Before dinner, Peninnah was sipping a cold drink and admiring her host's collection of paintings by the Jewish expressionist Chaim Soutine when she summoned up the nerve to ask him, in French, how he had come to amass such superb art from a single painter.

"Soutine was a starving artist when I first knew him here in Paris," he explained. "Whenever he was hungry, he'd sell a painting for food. I scooped them up. I was lucky to have had a good eye! Do you know, Madame Schram, that he once kept a bloody animal carcass in his studio for ten days, just to paint it?" When she wrinkled her nose, he laughed. "The neighbors were livid!"

They chatted a bit more until they were summoned to supper. She was feeling pretty good until she saw in the center of the magnificently appointed banquet table an enormous silver platter that held a bed of glazed tomato slices and deviled eggs, on which lay two enormous lobsters, their antennae tied together with blue ribbon, arranged to face each other as if deep in conversation. Just about the least kosher food in existence, she thought. How can I insult these lovely people that Irv depends on for his livelihood by not eating the entree? And then: What am I doing here, where I so obviously don't belong?

It got worse. When they were invited to sit, Madame Schram was placed across, and at the other end of the table, from Monsieur. She felt the panic rise in her throat.

"What am I going to do?" she mouthed to Irv.

He mouthed back, "Allergy?" She realized that he didn't seem to notice that she was referring not only to the food, but also to sitting on her own.

Out of nowhere a smiling servant appeared at her side, holding a large fork.

"*Madame?*"

"*Une tomate, et des oeufs, s'il vous plaît,*" she stammered. The tomato and the eggs filled her just fine, and, to her infinite relief, it turned out that the lobster was not the main course after all. During conversation, she said, "*Repetez s'il vous plaît*" and "*lentement,*" or "slowly," more times than she had before or since. Then, gradually loosening up, she found that she enjoyed the five or more hours of eating, five or more bottles of wine for maybe twice that number of people, and French conversation more and more, until the guests began to rise from the table at midnight.

In the cab back to the hotel, she kissed Irv's cheek and leaned her head on his shoulder.

"That was amazing," she whispered. "An absolutely amazing experience from start to finish."

"Don't forget the two amazing lobsters." He reached for her hand. "You know, I'm really proud of you, Peninnah."

She raised her head and looked at him. "You are? Really? Why?"

"Because you handled yourself so well, even though you were caught off-guard. I got the feeling tonight that whatever life throws at you, you'll be okay."

She lowered her head once more. "Thank you, darling. That means a lot."

In the course of their stay, they grew close to the Reibels. When the couple announced that they were returning home to New York, Irv and Peninnah decided to host a small good-bye party. A few days before the date, Burt Reibel called her.

"Peninnah, do you mind if my cousins come too? They're visiting from the States."

"Of course," she said. "We know all about visitors! And besides, I always think the more the merrier. It would be our pleasure."

Peninnah had packed just ten records to bring with them to Paris, and she had bought some more during her shopping expeditions. In the midst of an Aznavour hit she had put on the turntable before the party began, the doorbell rang and in walked the Reibels, accompanied by an older couple, their cousins the Jagendorfs.

While he was exploring the apartment, Peninnah asked Moritz Jagendorf if he would like a drink.

"Tell me," he said instead of replying, "do you know Ruth Rubin personally?" Peninnah looked down at the album covers by the phonograph. On the top was a record by Rubin, the singer and scholar who specialized in Yiddish folksongs.

"No," she replied. "We love her music, though. Especially when she does the Yiddish songs *a capella*."

"Tell you what," he said. "When you get back to New York, I'll introduce you to her. Yes, that's it! I'm going to invite you to dinner to meet Ruth Rubin and her husband."

"Wow, that would be wonderful! How do you know her?"

"I'm a folklorist; she's an ethnomusicologist. We travel in the same circles. I'll be sure to get your number from my cousin. Ruth will adore you!"

She had no idea how he knew that after three minutes of conversation, but she certainly wasn't going to argue. Ruth Rubin! That would be *formidable*! Absolutely fantastic.

Some time later, a wealthy French advertising executive invited them to attend their daughter's wedding at the magnificent Grand Synagogue of Paris. Opened to the public in 1875, it was designed in the classical style, with Byzantine ornamentation. At the elaborate entranceway, Peninnah saw the verse from Genesis, "This is none other than the House of God, the very gateway to Heaven." As she moved further into the sanctuary, she pointed out to Irv more Biblical quotations, as well as the names of the prophets.

To their amusement, they realized that the ushers were dressed as Napoleonic guards. They were surprised to see that the bride and groom sat in high-backed thrones on the bimah, with the rabbi facing them, away from the congregation. The reception afterward took place in the garden of the father-of-the-bride's enormous country villa, complete with uniformed, white-gloved staff. If it hadn't been for the ketubah, the breaking of the glass underfoot and the mazel tovs all around, Peninnah reflected afterward, she would have thought she was taking part in a play rather than a Jewish wedding, especially when they arrived at the villa. On their arrival, they were ushered inside in order to descend from the house to the magnificent gardens, at which point one of the ushers announced them to the assembled crowd: "Monsieur et Madame Schram!"

On second thought, she still felt that none of this could be real, beginning with her life in this great city.

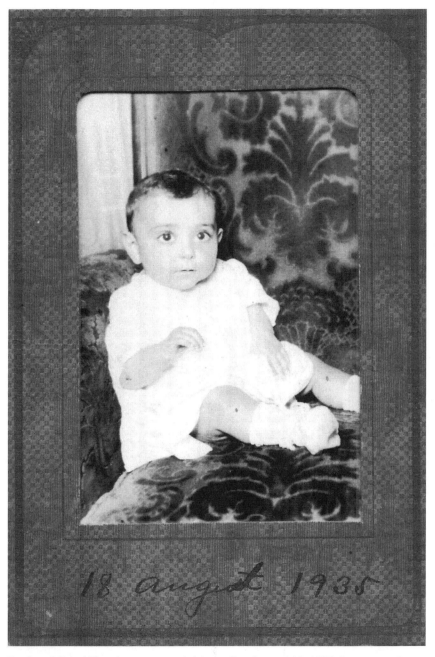

Peninnah Pearl Manchester, age eight months, August 18, 1935. *Image courtesy of Peninnah Schram*

Cantor (Chazzen) Samuel E. Manchester, from his self-published book *Kol Rinah U'tfilah*, 1942. Victor Castaldi, photographer. *Image courtesy of Peninnah Schram*

Manchester family, 1945. (From left) Dora Manchester, Samuel Manchester, Peninnah (on lap), Joe, Rivke Markman (grandmother).
Image courtesy of Peninnah Schram

High school graduation day with best friend Katherine Peterson, 1952. *Image courtesy of Peninnah Schram*

Official high school graduation photo, 1952. *Image courtesy of Peninnah Schram*

Wedding to Irving Schram, Dec. 7, 1958. *Image courtesy of Peninnah Schram*

The Schrams, New Year's Eve, 1967. *Image courtesy of Peninnah Schram*

Creative movement with Stern College students and children at 92nd Street Y, mid-1970s. *Image courtesy of Peninnah Schram*

Storytelling at 92nd Street Y, mid-1970s. *Image courtesy of Peninnah Schram*

ADULT EDUCATION A SELL-OUT

Pictured above is Isaac Bashevis Singer as he appeared in 1963 at the home of Peninnah Schram-Thaler.

Isaac Bashevis Singer was at the home of Peninnah Schram-Thaler in 1963 to oversee the first dramatized version of any of his stories. "Gimpel The Fool" was performed by "Theatre A La Carte, Inc." a professional touring company based in New York City. Gimpel The Fool was performed in the tri-state area for temples and various groups.

From left to right, Cantor Paul Kwartin (who appeared in Wings Of Song on radio), Isaac Singer, Marc P. Smith, playwright, Dr. Ernest Simon, Professor of French at Ramapo College, and seated, Peninnah Schram-Thaler. The picture was taken in 1963.

Isaac Singer will appear at the Yorktown Jewish Center on April 29th as part of the joint Jewish Adult Education Program. The tickets were completely sold out an hour after they went on sale.

Images courtesy of Peninnah Schram. The Center Reporter: The Publication of the Yorktown Jewish Center. March 1979, Vol. XIV, No. 4.

Dov Noy with Peninnah Schram at 92nd Street Y, 1988. *Image courtesy of Peninnah Schram*

Elie Wiesel with Peninnah Schram at 92nd Street Y, 1990s. *Image courtesy of Peninnah Schram*

Gerard Edery and Peninnah Schram, publicity photo, mid-1990s. *Image courtesy of Peninnah Schram*

Publicity photo, 2000. Clarence L. Thorne, photographer. *Image courtesy of Peninnah Schram*

Peninnah Schram's grandchild Ilan's Bar Mitzvah, 2012. (From left) Mordechai Schram (son), Sonia Gordon-Walinsky (daughter-in-law), Tzahi (grandchild), Dorielle Zafrany (grandchild), Ilan Zafrany (grandchild), Peninnah Schram, Rebecca Zafrany (daughter), Emile Zafrany (son-in-law), Aaron Zafrany (grandchild). *Image courtesy of Peninnah Schram*

FOURTEEN

Coming Home

After her father's yearning to emigrate and his quietly heated conversations with Mama on the subject, after his orange groves in Gan Yavne, not far from Ashdod, after his impassioned "Next year in Jerusalem!" at every Seder, and the framed portraits of the great Zionists Theodore Herzl and Chaim Weitzman over the piano for as long as she could remember, Peninnah was finally taking the advice he had given her to heart: "Go better to Israel!"

He had said it years earlier, of course, when she announced that she was going to Europe for two months. Then she and Irv moved to Paris, where her in-laws visited them on the trip back from the Jewish State, still basking in the glow of the new country. From the descriptions of the quality of light to the smells of growing things to the desert and the jaw-dropping antiquity, the country was calling to her more every day.

"Well, if we're ever going to do it," Irv said over dinner soon after his parents left, "we might as well go when we're already more than halfway there." So it was that they decided to take a cruise to the home of their ancestors, a land both ancient and less than fifteen years old.

It was the fall of 1961. They booked passage on the ZIM Line, a stunning, pure white ship called, appropriately, the Herzl, the founder of the Zionist movement. The train ride from Paris to the port at Marseille took eight hours, during which she read about the ship, its exotic Mediterranean styling, its movie theater—a luxury to be sure—its synagogue, dining room and, perhaps most important, air-conditioning. They had purchased first-class tickets and were looking forward to being spoiled from port to port, bow to stern.

But when they finally reached the dock, they learned to their dismay that their ship was undergoing maintenance in Italy.

Irv went to investigate their options, while Peninnah sat with the bags, watching her fellow passengers jostle each other. After a time, she fell into conversation with a pleasant-looking couple. Anita Engle was a writer and collector of ancient glass, and her husband Nelson Berkoff was a professor at Hebrew University in Jerusalem. She also met their son, who looked to be in his late teens. The family had lived in Israel for years, and was returning home from a trip to England.

When Irv returned, Peninnah made the introductions. Then he explained the situation. She couldn't help noticing that a fine sheen of sweat had broken out on his normally cool-as-a-cucumber brow.

"Okay," he said, reaching for her hand. "We have two options. We can get on another train and pick up the ship in Genoa, or we can go there on a Greek tanker."

She shuddered. "I hate the thought of getting on another train. How long is it by sea?"

"About two hundred miles. It's an overnight trip."

"What do you think?"

He smiled. "I think we've been looking forward to a boat; let's get on a boat!"

"I agree. And a tanker! That's something to tell our grandchildren!" The Berkoffs came to the same conclusion and went off to make their own arrangements, promising to catch up with them later.

The good news was that due to their connections, they were eligible to book a first-class suite. The bad news was that there was only one such cabin, and the captain's guests were entitled to it. Instead, they learned that they and another couple were to share a rather unappealing berth with two bunk beds, and a shared bathroom.

They reached the cabin, and Peninnah glowered at the bunk beds. "There is no way I'm getting up there," she said, pointing to the top mattress. "I'd rather swim."

He brought his hand to his eyes as though blocking the sun to survey the upper bunk from a long distance.

"I think I can make it," he said. "Don't worry about me all the way up there. I'm sure I'll be able to breathe."

When he pointed out the shared bathroom down the hall, she shook her head. "What a sad way to start off a holiday," she said. "This ship is just awful."

"To be fair, it's not meant to be a luxury liner, just a working tanker. And it's only for one night. C'mon, it'll be fun. Where's your spirit of adventure?"

She knew he was as aggravated as she, and for his sake, she tried to work on her attitude. But the dinner was inedible; even the coffee was awful. All she could manage to get down was some bread and butter.

He leaned over during the meal to whisper in her ear.

"You know Willie Mays got only one hit in his first twenty-five at bats with the Giants, and he still went on to win Rookie of the Year?"

Despite her terrible mood, she was helpless in the face of Irv's good humor. With a laugh, she asked, "Wait, what is the moral here? That the best is yet to come?"

He rewarded her with a dazzling smile.

They passed an uncomfortable night, but when they walked on deck in the morning, they were greeted with a happy distraction from the terrible food. There before them was the sparkling Mediterranean Sea and the sleek and elegant *Herzl*, waiting for them at the dock.

The ship was as different from the tanker as two seagoing vessels could be. But despite the art gallery and dancing and gourmet kosher food—including her first perfectly cooked medium-well steak—and the casual-dress Rosh Hashanah services in an actual synagogue, she felt sick from the gentle rocking of the ship. She was nearly as miserable as she had been on the tanker, albeit for entirely different reasons.

And then, early on the fifth morning, they stood on deck surrounded by more than five hundred other passengers watching the outlines of Haifa and the golden dome of the Ba'hai Temple emerge like beacons from the fog. As if on cue, the crowd burst into the new state's national anthem, *Hatikvah*. The Hope. They sang in Hebrew, but for Peninnah the meaning was clear:

> As long as in the heart within,
> The Jewish soul yearns,
> And toward the eastern edges, onward,
> And eye gazes toward Zion.
> Our hope is not yet lost,
> The hope that is two thousand years old,
> To be a free nation in our land,
> In Zion, Jerusalem.

She joined in with the others as the sun rose, astonished to feel the tears rolling down her cheeks. It had never occurred to her when planning this trip, and certainly not while suffering through the travel, that coming home to the land of her people would be so moving. Yes, Judaism was a major part of who she was: kashrut, shul, all the beliefs and rituals. But Israel was something else again, she realized. Israel was all of that and more, writ large and proud for the world to see. It was less than twenty years since the war that had killed millions of her people had ended. Israel was survival.

The emotion was so strong that she turned to Irv and hugged him for all she was worth. Whether or not he understood why she had done so, he was glad to hug her back.

As soon as they checked into the hotel, they phoned her Haifa cousins, Tanya and Seva Sherell. The couple had been expecting their call and immediately extended an invitation for supper. When Peninnah, who still hadn't regained her land legs, protested that they had only just arrived, Tanya said she would not take no for an answer. And so they soon found themselves in a taxi meandering across the city.

"How is Seva related to your mother again?" Irv asked. She was looking out the window when he asked the question. Neither could take their eyes from the feast of green and gold and the activity of Jewish settlers that surrounded them.

"They're second or third cousins. I don't know if even they know which."

It was easy to see by the warm welcome that this couple didn't have many relatives alive after the war. The apartment was simple and clean, with a few artifacts and pieces of furniture from those years, which they had spent in Shanghai. While the Schrams snacked on cake and fruit, they asked and answered questions about their families.

After quite a while they moved on to the dinner table, and Peninnah realized that she was famished.

"So how are your parents?" Seva asked her. "Everyone okay?"

"Everything is wonderful, thanks." They were still talking when Seva's wife brought out the main course, chops as white as snow. Such exotic food, Peninnah thought.

"How interesting that looks!" she exclaimed. "What kind of meat is it?"

Her hostess smiled with pride. "Only the best for our honored guests! It's pork!" Then she saw Peninnah's face. It was approximately the shade of the chop. "Oh, Peninnah!" she said. "I'm so sorry! I will bring you fish right away!"

"I really appreciate that,"

In the cab on the way back to the hotel, after the dinner, the conversation, the hugs and promises to see each other again soon, Irv patted her arm.

"You know, Seva told me that pig farms are very popular here, and that pork is a special, special dish for guests." He paused, then added dryly, "At least for guests who don't keep kosher."

She put her face in her hands. "I understood about the lobsters in Paris, sure. But my first meal in Israel! Pork!"

"At least you didn't have to eat it. How was your fish, by the way?"

"Wonderful. How was your pork?"

"I feel bad saying it was good, considering that your face was the same color as the chop when she introduced it to you. But it was *geshmak*."

She laughed at the Yiddish word for "delicious."

Over the next ten days, they reveled in the food, the jasmine-scented air, the tours of the Dead Sea, Masada and the winding streets of the ancient, multi-leveled city of Haifa. They rode to Jerusalem and davened at the Kotel, the remnant of the Second Temple, destroyed nearly two thousand years earlier.

They also visited her dear friend Paula, the one who had gone to Israel for a year, met her Jewish-Iranian husband Benjamin and decided to stay. Peninnah had received special instructions from Paula's mother—relayed at the restaurant in B. Altman's department store in Manhattan—to meet her new son-in-law, and to send her a full report as soon as possible.

At last it was time to go, and once more they boarded the ZIM line. As hard as it was to leave Israel, they were convinced that they would return before long. On the way back, the ship made a few stops in Europe. The Schrams took the train back to Paris from Venice.

Fall flowed into winter flowed into the following year. When Irv wasn't working, they were busy entertaining and visiting their many friends and relatives. Their closest relationship, however, was with Benjamin and Rose. They were sitting in the couple's home one evening when Irv made the announcement they had both dreaded.

"Uncle Benjamin, Aunt Rose, we've got to tell you something. We're going back to New York."

The older people's faces fell in unison. "But why?" Rose asked. "You children don't like it here anymore?"

"It's not that," Peninnah said quietly. "It's just that we want to start a family."

"So there's no problem!" He clapped Irv on the back. "Many people have families here in Paris!"

"It's not that simple," Irv said with a frown. "We don't want to be ex-pats. We want to raise our children American. We love this country, but we love the U.S. more. Besides, our parents aren't so young anymore. We really ought to be closer to them. Our children should be closer to them."

Her uncle tsked a time or two. "So is Revlon going to transfer you back?"

"That's the plan. They don't have any more work for me here in Paris."

"There are other jobs here, Irving. You're a young man, much in demand."

Rose reached for her husband's hand. "Benjamin, they have to go. Don't make them feel worse than they already do."

Peninnah saw the tears in her uncle's eyes and hung her head. They sat in silence for a full minute. Then she leaned over and hugged each of them in turn.

"We're sorry, Uncle Benjamin," she said at last. "We really are. But we have to do this for our family. The one we have and the one to come, God willing."

After two years abroad, they traveled back to the States on the new SS France. For Peninnah, the trip was another shipboard nightmare. Despite the modern stabilization system to calm the rocking ship and another movie theater to distract her, she was light-headed and nauseous for nearly the entire cruise. As if I weren't miserable enough already, she thought.

When they arrived in New York Harbor, they took a taxi straight to Manhattan to stay with Irv's parents. It wasn't long before they found the perfect apartment: two bedrooms in an attractive building on quiet, stately West End Avenue, a little over a mile south and just one block west of his parents' home. As the weeks and months passed, they found themselves missing Benjamin and Rose and the Tuileries and the Eiffel Tower and the Louvre and the Champs d'Elysees and the corner bakery a little less all the time. There was only one thing missing in their lives that would complete their household. So they set about trying to create it.

FIFTEEN

Peklach of Joy

It was a fine spring morning in 1962, the air so clear and sweet that New Yorkers could almost forget the wet, bitter winter just passed, in which pure snow had turned to gray slush and suede boots to sodden sludge. The Schrams had been back from Paris just a few weeks and were still settling into their new apartment. Peninnah was rinsing the breakfast dishes, thinking about where she was and what she was doing that same day, that same time, the year before. Glad as she was to be back in the city, she nonetheless looked back on those two years away with a nostalgia bordering on homesickness. Irv had just left for work, and she was looking forward to her second cup of coffee with the *Times*.

Once again, Peninnah was perfectly content with the life of a housewife. Washing the dishes, doing the laundry, sweeping, cooking—these tasks took on an almost sacred meaning when she did them for herself and Irv in their own apartment. It wasn't as though she had ever had any great professional ambitions. As far as she was concerned, all they needed now was a child. And they were trying. She blushed when she thought of how much they were trying.

When she heard the telephone, she had no idea how long it had been ringing, so deep had she been in her reverie.

"Is this Peninnah Schram?" The voice was vaguely familiar, but she couldn't place it.

"Yes? Who is this, please?"

"This is Moritz Jagendorf. Burt Reibel's cousin?"

She smiled, remembering the man's surprise at her record collection in the Paris apartment.

"Yes of course! Moritz! How nice to hear from you! How is Sophie? How are the Reibels?"

"Everybody's fine, thank you. Listen, you remember our conversation the first time we met, about Ruth Rubin?"

"Of course! I had one of her records of Jewish love songs, and we talked about it. I couldn't get over it when you said you knew her."

"Well, at the time I said I'd arrange for you to meet, and I didn't forget. My wife and I want to invite you for dinner to meet Ruth and Harry." He paused. "And to eat, of course, and drink some of the wonderful wines I've made."

She sighed. "Moritz, it would be so great to meet Ruth Rubin that you wouldn't even have to wine me and dine us."

"Well, that's tempting, my dear, but Irv might not feel the same way. We'll expect you next Saturday night. Say about seven-thirty?"

The ethnomusicologist, singer, and poet Ruth Rubin was thirty years older than Peninnah and born in Montreal, but apart from that, they had a lot in common. Their parents were both Jewish immigrants from Europe, and they both grew up speaking Yiddish and felt a deep connection to Yiddish culture. What was more, both women also spoke French and loved to sing.

Ruth Rubin was petite, with a short, gray bob and an animated, affectionate personality. The two couples took to each other immediately. That dinner party was followed by several more, as well as, over the years, Rubin's intimate salons at her seven-room apartment at Broadway and 107th Street and, later, long, luxurious tête-à-têtes over tea with just the two of them in her Gramercy Park home. Peninnah also attended Rubin's concerts at YIVO, the Jewish Museum, the Workmen's Circle and Town Hall, and she arranged for Rubin to perform for a Jewish education conference at Rutgers University. At every performance, her friend contextualized the song she was about to sing, rooting it in a number of sources. Then she sang a cappela, except when she performed or recorded with her good friend Pete Seeger, who played banjo and guitar.

"Pete and I did some live television together a few years back," she told Peninnah one afternoon. "I remember one song in particular we did. You know the riddle song 'Tumbalalaika,' don't you? What can grow without rain, what can burn for many years, what can cry without tears?

"Sure I do," she said. Together they hummed the refrain. "Sometimes I think I should have been a singer. I would love to perform the old Yiddish songs, like you."

Ruth Rubin thought for a moment. "Tell you what, Peninnah. I'm going to teach you a *cante fable* that combines story and song. Then you can do both at the same time!"

This is the story she taught her:

There once was a wealthy textile merchant. Although he himself was not a learned man, he wanted his daughter to marry a scholar. So he went to the yeshiva and told the rabbi he was looking for a son-in-law who would go into business with him, but also spend his days in study.

The rabbi knew just the student, a poor young man named Hayim who composed *niggunim* that were unforgettable. Every Shabbes the yeshiva students clamored for him to teach them more of the tunes.

The merchant met the young student, and they both agreed to the marriage.

"Here are a hundred rubles," the merchant said, reaching into his pocket. "Go into town and purchase satin cloth for the wedding coats."

Hayim walked to town the next day, but on his way he overheard a shepherd playing a magnificent nigun on his flute. The shepherd agreed to teach it to him—for fifty rubles. The young man gladly handed over the money. Later that day he heard another melody on another shepherd's flute. Again he paid fifty rubles for it. He marveled at the wonderful sound the two melodies made when sung together. He couldn't wait to get back home to teach the new nigunim to his fellow students!

At the thought of home, he remembered the prospective father-in-law who had sent him to town to buy cloth. Without money, he had no business in town, so he returned from whence he'd come.

When Hayim presented the nigun to the merchant instead of the cloth, the older man knew this was not the groom for his daughter. But why should Hayim mind? He could find a bride any time. What was more important was that he had a new nigun for Shabbes!

Three decades later, near the end of her dear friend and mentor's life, Peninnah regularly visited Rubin, by then frail with dementia, in a nursing home in Westchester. One day she sat with Rubin in her room long into the afternoon, much later than she had planned. She had so much to do, but she couldn't bring herself to let go. As the sun began to descend behind the branches of a nearby park and the shadows lengthened on the wall, they looked out the window and held hands in a companionable silence. She wasn't sure her friend even knew who she was.

Then she had an idea.

"Do you remember the story 'The Nigun?'" she asked.

The old woman shook her head.

"Well," she said, with a gentle squeeze of the woman's hand, "you gave it to me once, and now I'll have the pleasure of returning it to you." As Peninnah proceeded to tell the story, interweaving the two melodies, her friend's eyes began to shine, just a little, and she started to hum along. In the midst of her sorrow for her friend, Peninnah was comforted to know that the magnificent Ruth Rubin was listening, with all her heart.

She had been back from Paris about two months when she met her college friend Lenore at a neighborhood diner for coffee.

"So good to see you!" she said, unbuttoning her coat and hanging it on the rack by the booth. "And you said you have some news?"

Lenore leaned forward and grabbed Peninnah's hands.

"Do I have news! I've got the money for my share of the scenery and costumes, and I talked to some Equity actors who might agree to work under assumed names for a fraction of their regular fee."

It was the theater company they had discussed briefly in Paris. They had decided to call their enterprise Theatre à la Carte, because the plan was to produce one-act plays that could be mixed and matched depending on the needs of their Jewish audiences. They planned to use portable backdrops of painted cloth stretched between two metal poles, which they could roll up and easily transport in a station wagon They even found a venue in case the client didn't have a performance space handy: a barracks-cum-theater at Idlewild Airport in Queens. They had lined up a playwright to dramatize short stories, and a director they knew from UConn. The two friends were delighted that Lenore's brainchild was coming to fruition.

Not long afterward, in the early fall, Peninnah noticed that she was feeling a little off. Not ill, exactly, but not quite herself, either. She made an appointment to see her doctor, and when Irv came home from work that evening, she was sitting at the kitchen table, waiting for him.

"Are you hungry?" she asked, after he had kissed her and they exchanged a few words about their respective days.

"Sure," he said. Then he turned to look at the empty stove. "But I don't see anything cooking."

She winked. "That's because we're not in the restaurant yet."

"Oh! Are we celebrating something, or does the great theater impresario just not feel like cooking tonight?"

"A little of both," she replied with a glint in her eye. "At least I'm not quite up to cooking for three."

There was a long pause, and then Irv's face grew very red. In seconds he was at the other end of the table hugging her.

"I'm so happy, my love," she said.

"Oh, me too," he replied. "Oh Penny, me too. Now the parents can get off our case."

She laughed. "You know that's not true. They never even asked. We were the ones who were worried. They were the most patient Jewish non-grandparents who ever lived!"

He held her at arm's length. "You know who's not going to be thrilled at our news." She looked at him questioningly. "Lenore. What are you going to do about your theater? Who works pregnant, especially onstage?"

"Irv, it'll be fine. Of course I won't act, but I can do everything else. I'll just be extra careful. You'll see."

"Well, Little Irvele will never forgive you if you're not."

"Little Irvele?" She had been reaching for her pocketbook; now she wheeled around in mock disapproval. "What about little Peninnele?"

"Her too." He grinned. "It really doesn't matter which. I'm just so damned delighted."

When she told Lenore, her old friend hugged her.

"I'm really sorry, kiddo," Peninnah said. "By the time we get rolling, I'm going to be huge. You know as well as I do I can't be on stage in that condition."

"Sorry?" Her friend laughed. "I should be thanking you! This means I get more roles, and you do more grunt work. Tell me, how could that be a bad thing?"

Now, the new theater company needed material. Peninnah contacted the rabbi she had known since her teenage years, Benjamin Kreitman. Ever since Rabbi Kreitman married her and Irv, their relationship was one of adult to adult, and she valued that connection.

When she called him to ask for a story suggestion, Rabbi Kreitman did not hesitate.

"Look at DeMaupassant," he said. "His stories are wonderful, and there is one I think will be perfect. It's got Jewish characters and a nice little twist in the end. It's called 'The Venus of Braniza.'"

"Oh I read him in French class in college!" she replied. "'The Necklace' is unforgettable.

"Yes," he said. "This is sort of like that. A real surprise at the end."

When the two friends looked at the story, they were overjoyed. It was, indeed, perfect. A Talmudic scholar is blessed with the most beautiful and virtuous wife in the city. One day, she asks him when the Messiah will come, and he explains that it can only happen when all the Jews were either entirely good or completely depraved.

"How likely is it that every Jews will be good?" she asks.

"I wouldn't count on it," is his curt reply.

The story ends with the scholar's learning that his wife is unfaithful to him with an Army captain. When he confronts her, she answered calmly, "But husband, I was just doing my part to help bring about the Messiah!"

Their playwright set about dramatizing it. Next they came across a Chekhov farce that made them giggle every time they thought about it. "The Marriage Proposal" centered on three characters: a father, his hypochondriac neighbor, and his daughter, to whom the neighbor wants to propose. She wants to marry him, but the pair can't stop arguing. Maybe it wasn't exactly Jewish, but it certainly could have been. It was just the sort of thing they were looking for. And all in one act.

They still needed at least one more play. It was then that Rabbi Kreitman called with an idea.

"Peninnah," he said, "it just occurred to me. I don't know why I didn't think of this before. You see, I'm kind of related to Isaac Bashevis Singer."

"What?" The great Jewish author was not yet quite at the height of his prominence, but he was already well known for his fiction. An adaptation of one of his stories would be a coup for the company.

"Well, not closely related, but my cousin married his sister. And I was thinking, why don't you ask him for a story? He lives right in your neighborhood."

She could feel the excitement rising in her chest.

"Oh that would be too much! Yes, yes, Rabbi!"

He gave her the great man's telephone number, and as soon as the call was over, she dialed the number with shaking fingers.

"Ah, Mrs. Schram!" he said when she introduced herself and explained her mission. "Yes, I would be glad to meet you. Say, can you meet me this week at the Tip Toe Inn?"

The diner was just two blocks from her apartment building, on Broadway at 86th Street. They set the time and the date. When she hung up the phone, she could not call Lenore fast enough. She had an appointment with Isaac Bashevis Singer!

The day of the meeting, she chose her outfit with special care. How does one know what to wear to meet a prominent man of letters? As she reached for the hairbrush, she stopped and held out her hand. Why, it was still shaking! She laughed at herself for being so star struck, but there it was.

Peninnah arrived at the restaurant a few minutes early. The air smelled of coffee and the familiar scents of Jewish food, and every table buzzed with animated conversation. In the midst of it all sat Isaac Bashevis Singer, sipping a cup of tea at a corner table. She strode over and extended her hand.

"Mr. Singer," she said. "I'm—"

"You are Mrs. Schram, I hope," he replied, with a courtly little bow. She nodded. The waitress was already hovering. "Nu? Sit, I'll order for us. Something I especially like, and so delicious." He proceeded to do so.

When the waitress had gone, she said, "Please. Call me Peninnah."

He nodded. "Peninnah."

When it arrived, the apple pancake, what she knew as a *kuchen*, was like nothing she had ever smelled or tasted. Bursting with cinnamon and sweetness, it was served on its own pedestal, like the delicacy it was.

"Peninnah," he said, between bites. "Excuse me, but I can't help noticing that you are expecting a child. Don't you think maybe you should stay home instead of working so hard?"

"But I love theater," she said hastily, as if he were planning to stop her. "And besides, I'll be backstage."

"A modern woman. I see." He sipped his coffee. "So what can I do for you?"

"We wondered, that is, my partner Lenore and I, if you would have a short story that we could make into an adult play? It would mean so much to us to have a dramatization of an I. B. Singer story to present to Jewish audiences in synagogues."

"Why not?" he replied, without a moment's hesitation. "Take whatever story you want. However, I suggest 'Gimpel the Fool.' Very interesting story. Perhaps a little shocking, too."

"That's so kind of you!" Then a cloud passed over her sunny smile. She looked out over the noisy restaurant and back to his face. "But we don't have any money, you see. We barely have a budget for sets and costumes. And the actors are working below scale."

He waved off the thought. "Enjoy it. When you're ready, you'll talk to my literary agent. She handles all of my business affairs. Just be sure to invite me to a performance."

Half an hour later, she walked out of the restaurant feeling that she'd won first prize—in life.

When they read the story, she and Lenore laughed with delight. The plot, about a good-natured baker who was the butt of the townspeople's jokes, was equal parts amusing and philosophical. It was just saucy enough—with illegitimate births and inappropriate urination—to give it the adult edge they were looking for. There was also so much dialogue in it that it was practically dramatized already. Within a month or two, Singer approved the script. They signed a contract for the rights to the dramatized version of "Gimpel" for two years, the first time anyone had presented his work on the stage. During rehearsals, Peninnah decided to have a luncheon at her apartment for everyone connected to the production. Of course, she invited Singer, who was well known to be a vegetarian.

She didn't think much of it till she started to plan her menu. What did you serve a vegetarian? In 1963, few people knew. She had never met one, as far as she could recall, and all she could think of was a plain salad that filled the entire table. Some people called themselves vegetarians who ate fish and eggs. What would Mr. Singer eat? What was she to do?

She decided to boil vegetables. Carrots. String beans. Cauliflower. She made a green salad, of course. Then she prepared tuna fish and egg salad, which would at least feed the other guests. And she put out some bread. Everyone eats bread, right?

The room smelled to her a little like moist earth, but when they sat down to eat, she was relieved to see that her guests were happy.

"Peninnah," one of the cast members called out during a brief lull in the conversation. "When are you due?"

"Any minute!" she said with a laugh. "Oh, that reminds me. Did I tell you what the theater manager said?"

They all looked blank.

"Last week, Irv was helping me sweep the stage. And the theater manager looked at my husband and said," here she put on a strong New York accent, "'Mista, take your wife home, willya please? She's gonna pop any minute!'" The guests roared with laughter.

The talk continued, ebbing far less than it flowed, and Peninnah was delighted. At one point in the festivities, she turned to the guest of honor.

"Mr. Singer," she began, "I made this meal because I read that you've been a vegetarian for a long time. Could you tell us what made you decide to do that?"

The table turned quiet. The author patted his lips with his napkin, folded it and lay it neatly beside his plate. "I'll tell you the truth, Peninnah. I like chicken. But I like chickens better."

It was, everyone agreed, a perfect answer.

Theatre à la Carte soon presented, among other things, an original musical of Hans Christian Andersen's "The Nightingale" called "The Emperor's Nightingale," written by Elsa Rael, with a score by Philip Fleishman. It was produced at a makeshift theater they set up in a hotel ballroom on West 73rd Street. But their first booking was at a synagogue in New Jersey, an hour or so south of Manhattan.

The president of the men's club had chosen "Gimpel" and the Chekhov, and Peninnah sat back and watched the actors with awe. Everything, it seemed to her, was as professional as if they had been on Broadway. Someday, maybe. Why not? Anything was possible. She was smiling so hard she hoped no one around her was distracted from the performance.

Afterward, when they were packing up, she approached the president for their check. It was only a couple of hundred dollars split among them all, but it was a start.

"Excuse me," she said. Was it possible the man was avoiding her eyes? "Are you the one who pays us?"

"Yes, but no. I'm not paying you," he replied bluntly.

She felt her hands ball into fists at her sides. "But why? We gave you the shows you asked for, and they were terrific!"

"We never asked for a dirty play." His crossed his arms, as if daring her to disagree.

"A dirty play?" She shook her head in disbelief. "What are you talking about?"

"A baker who—pees in the challah dough? Tell me, is that nice for a Jewish audience, Mrs. Schram?"

"Sir," she said, with as much poise as she could muster. "Have you read the Singer story? Better yet, have you read Sholem Aleichem? These are earthy writers writing about earthy characters. These characters were peasants; this was shtetl life. We were true to the text!"

He frowned and hemmed and hawed, but he finally did hand her the fee. She couldn't help noticing that he didn't say thank you. But she did. And Theatre à la Carte walked out of that shul with its head held high.

In the middle of the night of June 7, 1963, Peninnah went into labor. Not wanting to wake Irv too early, she sat in the rocker in the living room, timing her contractions. She rocked for hours, singing softly, although whether to calm the child or herself, she couldn't say. There was so much she wanted for this new member of the family. Some expectant parents, she knew, promise their babies they will give them all the love and material pleasures they never knew themselves. But not Peninnah. That night, she prayed that the baby would be healthy. She prayed that she could be as affectionate and supportive as her father and as good a role model as her mother. If she could do that, she reflected, her child would turn out fine.

At seven in the morning, she went into the bedroom to wake Irv. They called the doctor, who told them to check into Doctor's Hospital on East End Avenue later in the morning. To her extreme annoyance, the birth itself was less than a blur; without knowing she had a choice, she was given a heavy sedative and was asleep for hours.

When she awoke at last and was handed her baby girl, she marveled. I cannot believe the beauty of this child, she thought. Her next thought was: I never diapered a baby! I only babysat sleeping children! What do I do?

Then the nurse came in to take back the newborn to the nursery, and Peninnah missed her as though missing a part of herself. Which in fact she was.

Later, when she was able to walk to the pay phone in the hall, she called her parents.

Mama picked up so quickly that Peninnah imagined she had been standing with her hand on the black receiver.

"Peninnah?"

"Yes, Ma. It's me."

"*Mayn hartz hut mir gezogt. . . .*" My heart told me that it would be you.

"I had a *meidelah*," she cried out. "We're naming her Rebecca, Ma, for your mother. Will you be able to come to New York to see us in the hospital?

Her mother clicked her tongue. "And what are we going to do for you in the hospital? When you come home, we'll come and help you." Then Mama gave her a blessing, and one for her new grandchild.

She hung up with a smile. My mother. The strong role model. With a pedigree like that, she reflected, Rebecca will have no choice but to rule the world.

Peninnah's dream of Broadway, or more realistically off-Broadway, grew more persistent with every production. With Rebecca safely cared for during the day by family, she and Lenore decided to try to raise the funding. This time, they needed serious angel investors, and they needed a theater to show them what their money would buy. Summoning all her *chutzpah,* she made a cold call to Irving Maidman, who owned a string of off-Broadway theaters. He invited her to meet him at his office on West 42nd Street to hear her out. When she arrived, she explained that as a young company, they had no money. She wondered could they possibly use a theater for one night to perform some of their material in order to find investors for an off-Broadway run? After what felt to her like a long and tortuous meeting, Maidman agreed to let them use a ninety-nine-seat house for one evening for free; as long as they covered the fee for the security guard.

The space was pretty seedy, but, she told herself, it was only for one night. She and Lenore sent invitations to everyone they knew. To her relief, the audience loved what they saw. Among them was Singer, who had not seen his story dramatized before then and was very pleased. Now, it was time to figure out costs.

"Mr. Singer," Peninnah said in the lobby after the show. "What would we need to pay you to put this on?"

"I don't handle the money," he said, putting up his hands. "Talk to my literary agent. I'll agree to anything you figure out with her."

The following morning she called the woman, who proceeded to tell her what the royalties would be per performance.

"Is there any chance you would let me use it for one percent of gross?" Peninnah asked. "That's about all we can afford."

She could practically feel the phone line grow cold.

"That's impossible, Mrs. Schram. Mr. Singer is a big name, you know."

"I know, and I'm grateful. But we're young. We're just getting started in this business. That extra half percent might just be the straw that breaks the camel's back. I really think he would be okay with that. Could you maybe discuss this with Mr. Singer?"

"That's not Mr. Singer's problem, I'm afraid. And frankly, I don't think he'll be 'okay with that.' Good luck to you."

And that was the end of the professional theater dream, which was beautiful as long as it lasted. It would have been wonderful had it come true, but she really didn't mind. Life was sweet. Peninnah already had more blessings than she had ever imagined.

One of those blessings arrived after midnight on December 11, 1965, when her second child arrived in the world. This time, she received just a spinal anesthetic, so to her joy, she was able to fully experience the birth.

When the obstetrician had asked her what she would call the baby if it were a boy, she responded promptly, "We've decided on Mordechai Benjamin."

"And if it's a girl?"

She frowned. "Actually, we haven't chosen a girl's name yet."

The Schrams' luck held. The baby was a boy, and nine days later, as soon as her parents could come to New York for the bris, the ritual took place. Unable to perform the ceremony due to his advanced age, her father instead filled the role of the *sandek*, the honored guest who holds the infant during the circumcision.

Looking around at her guests before she took Mordechai to the bedroom to nurse him after the ceremony, she breathed a sigh of relief. Her family was complete, and so, she suspected, was her life.

SIXTEEN

Peklach of Sorrow

When Peninnah appeared in the living room one chilly February evening, Irv looked up from his paper and let out a low wolf whistle. She laughed and struck a pose. Then she reached for the heavy sweater she'd laid neatly on the arm of the sofa that afternoon. She had bought it specifically to match the dress she was wearing. Maybe she was going a little overboard for a simple dinner party with Irv's fellow executives and their wives, but she had only met one or two of them before. It was important to her to make a good impression, at least with the other women.

Then her gaze fell on the pack of cigarettes on the coffee table, and her mood shifted like the changing of the tide.

"Oh, Irv," she said, pointing to the table. "C'mon, honey. You know what my mother would say, don't you?"

Irv lowered the *Times* to his lap, picked up the unopened pack and, sliding it into his jacket pocket, looked at his wife in mock confusion.

"Hmm, what your mother would say? Let me think: That you should spit three times when startled? Or maybe, 'One hand washes the other?'"

His wife started to smile, despite herself. "You sure know her well."

"After eight years of marriage, I know every one of her expressions, believe me." In a strong Yiddish accent he said, 'If everybody threw their *peklach* of sorrows in the ocean, you would take out your own.' Wait, I know. Much more appropriate for a dinner party on a cold night. '*Dos geit nit in lebn. Beser shtei in der heim.* It's not a matter of life and death. Stay home, better.'"

Peninnah sighed and shook her head. They'd talked about cigarettes before, heaven knows, but because she insisted that he only smoke at the office, she had usually been reminded of the habit solely by the aura of tobacco around him, not the actual offense itself. But now the evidence was right in front of her. Her handsome husband was planning to smoke that evening.

"Are you done?" she asked. He hung his head in mock apology. "What I meant to say was, she would tell the sailors in her rental apartments during the war—twenty years before the Surgeon General's Report came out, by the way—that cigarettes were poison, and they should throw them away. And with those terrible allergies of yours! I just don't understand it."

Irv dropped the paper on the coffee table and rose to his feet.

"Well, thank God I'm not allergic to cigarettes," he said, moving forward to help her on with the sweater. "And besides, I don't have any other vices to speak of. Unless you count my cigars and pipe. And of course there are all the women in my life who *do* let me smoke in front of them."

She hit him playfully with her purse. "Speaking of mothers," she said, more to change the subject than anything else, "I already said good-bye to yours along with the kids. Did you?" He nodded. "Good. Really, Irv, we'd better get going. You said it's about an hour's drive to Perth Amboy, right? Oh, what did you say your boss's wife's name was, again?"

He put a forefinger to his chin in mock contemplation. "Umm, is it Peninnah? No, that can't be right. I'll think of it."

The house in Perth Amboy was well heated, which she appreciated after the freezing weather that had trailed them from the city. The noise level was a little louder than she normally liked, however, so she soon joined a small circle of young wives in a corner, which was a respite from the general *kibitzing*. Children and husbands. She could talk about them all night. Clearly she had been worrying about this party for nothing.

Sometime in the middle of the evening, Peninnah loaded a plate with hors d'oeuvres, filled a glass with wine and set off in search of Irv. Strange, she thought. He didn't seem to be in any of the party rooms. She knocked and tugged on the door to the guest bathroom down the hall; it opened to darkness.

"You looking for Irv?" a passing man in a plaid blazer asked her. "I just saw him go out the front."

"Thanks. Thanks very much."

I won't say anything about the smoking, she promised herself, tugging open the front door. He's always had so much tension in his life, between the War, his brother's death, his job. And then his father dying so recently. What do I know? Maybe smoking helps him cope. Besides, he's a big boy. I shouldn't be telling him how to live his life. What can I say? I just love him so much.

The cold stung her like a blast of needles as she made her way over to him.

"Irv!" She reached for his icy hand. "Darling, it's freezing out here! What are you doing?"

"I—I don't feel so good."

She had realized it before he'd opened his mouth, though she didn't know how. She could barely make out his features in the near-darkness, but the slightest misfire of neurons, the most ephemeral misalignment of molecules that comprised her handsome husband's body and soul—she had always sensed them, sometimes even before he noticed them himself. That is what love is, she thought. You learn your beloved. You memorize him like you memorize a sonnet in school.

At what point did she run back to the house, call for the men closest to the door to come help, watch in disbelief as they half-walked and half-carried him back inside? She was vaguely aware of following them into a little den where they lay him on the couch.

She heard herself say, "I love you, darling, I love you," over and over like a prayer. Then some other people rushed in, pushing past her to grab him. What was happening? Where were they taking him?

"To the bathroom," an older man called over his shoulder. "Looks like he's about to lose his lunch." Why had he said that? Had she asked the question aloud? Minutes passed. They brought him back to the den, but they wouldn't let her near him.

The women kept plying her with drinks she couldn't have gotten down if she'd wanted to. The room was still noisy, or maybe no one made a sound. She had no idea. Was the tumult inside or outside her head? Did someone say he was calling an ambulance?

Why am I so cold? I have never been so cold. Look, I'm shivering. How do they know to put a blanket around me? And another blanket. Where are they finding so many blankets? Did they take them off the children's beds? Off their own beds? Why aren't the blankets helping? Why doesn't someone turn up the turn up the turn up the heat. . . . Someone keeps repeating, "Keep breathing. Just keep breathing, Irv." I think it might be me.

It seemed to her that the ambulance took forever to arrive. When it appeared at last, she was unable to catch so much as a glimpse of him carried out on the stretcher, to speak to him, to tell him that she would follow in another car, that she would always love him.

The same couple that drove them to the party took her, trailing the ambulance, to the hospital. Did they talk on the ride over? When they walked inside the big sliding doors, the husband spoke to the people at the desk, while the wife took her to the waiting room. After twenty minutes? Two hours? Three? After some period of time, she spotted two orderlies through the windowed door to the hall. The older one was shaking his head. She read his lips: Heart attack.

I am no longer a wife, she thought, with a strange calm. I am a widow. Wi-dow. She may have tried out the word on her tongue. The unfamiliar syllables kept time with the rhythm of her heart. But there must be a mistake. A widow is not thirty-two years old.

When a frowning young nurse tried to give her a sedative, she mindlessly slapped away the woman's hand.

"Where is the doctor? I need to see the doctor!" Was she screaming? Was she speaking at all? Why wouldn't anyone meet her gaze?

At some point, a gray-haired man in a rumpled lab coat entered the room. Her companions stood up as if he were the Pope, so she stood, too, although her strength was already failing her.

"I'm sorry," the doctor said, taking them all in in a single sweep. Whose pain was greatest here? He didn't stop to ask. "We did all we could. I'm very sorry."

Two a.m. She must have left the hospital and climbed back into the car on her own two legs, although she had no knowledge of doing so. Were there more forms to fill out? More chances to write her signature, linking her first name, the name given to her by her parents, with her last, the name that had bound them together less than a decade before? If Irv is dead, and I am one with Irv—her mind met a locked steel door, and stopped cold.

The woman sat with her now in the back seat.

"Did you call everyone you needed to, honey?" she murmured, draping a shawl around Peninnah's shoulders and reaching for her hand.

"My mother-in-law is with the children," she said dully. "I called his brother Sonny from the hospital. He's meeting me in the lobby of our apartment house." And then she felt a squeeze of panic in her chest, like a sudden jolt of electricity. "My father-in-law just died last summer. They've already lost one child in the War. Now it's the youngest. Oh my God."

"Do you want one of us to come in with you?"

She shook her head. "No, I can do this." And then she imagined telling the children in the morning. *No. I can't do this.*

She did it. Before entering her apartment, she and Sonny woke her neighbor Dr. Fox from down the hall, who took along his medical bag in case her mother-in-law needed a sedative. Then she and Sonny woke her to give her the terrible news and held her when her legs began to wobble. She sat with Irv's family in the living room 'til it was time to wake up Rebecca and Mordechai. A little later in the morning, she called her parents. Then she began to organize the funeral, which by Jewish Law had to be done as soon as possible, and the subsequent *shiva*, a week during which mourners wear a ripped garment or piece of black cloth, perch on low stools or hard, straight-backed chairs, cover their mirrors and clutch at the comfort offered by visitors.

At some point during that first day, she lay down for a short nap. Picked at some food. Washed a few dishes. Bathed her young children. She put one foot in front of the other, all day. Still every once in a while her mind said, No! I can't do this.

She buried Irv on Sunday. Her parents came into the city by train, and her father chanted the traditional prayer *El Maalei Rahamim.*

O God, full of compassion, Who dwells on high, grant true rest upon the wings of the Divine Presence, in the exalted spheres of the holy and pure, who shine as the resplendence of the firmament. . . .

Through it all, she had one thought in her head, and it wasn't Irv. She would break down if she thought of Irv now, and she mustn't do that, she told herself. Instead she thought of Jackie Kennedy at her young husband's funeral. She remembered the black dress, the veil, the dignified demeanor, the chin held high, even in grief. And she held that image with her throughout the ordeal, including when she followed the casket up the aisle of the funeral home and following the hearse in the limo.

There was a point during shiva when, after sitting on her own in a corner of the living room for several minutes, she looked up to see her mother at her side, holding a plate laden with food.

"*Ess, ess, mayn kind,*" she told Peninnah. "You must eat, my darling. *Shtark zech.* Strengthen yourself." It was her perennial advice for mourners. Dutifully Peninnah reached for a dinner roll. At the moment, it was all she could keep down.

At some point during shiva, her mother-in-law knocked on the door of her bedroom, where she had been sitting on the edge of the bed, staring into space.

"I got a letter from your father, honey," she said, holding up an envelope with familiar writing on it. "I want to read it to you. It's a story."

Peninnah nodded. As a man of God, her father well knew the Jewish practice of giving comfort through stories, and he had always known the right ones to tell. She closed her eyes.

In the second book of Samuel, her father had written in his elegant Yiddish, there is a story in which King David's much-loved son falls ill. The great king refuses to eat or sleep. Dressed in sackcloth and ashes, he sits on the ground all day and night, weeping, reciting psalms, and praying for his restored health.

Many days pass, and then the young man dies. The servants murmur among themselves. Who should be the one to tell the king? What will happen to him now, if just the boy's illness took such a toll on him?

Being a wise ruler, David understands why the servants dare not approach.

"My son, he has died?" he asks them.

A trusted adviser comes forward, bows and says, "Yes, sire."

And then, to the servants' surprise, the king rises from the floor and commands the servants to dress him in his royal robes and bring him food and drink.

One or two retreat immediately, but the adviser remains behind.

"Sire, if you please, will you help me understand?" he asks. "Why is it that now that your child has died, you are ready to rejoin the world, but not when he still lived?"

The king nods. "I see this is hard for you to understand," he says, "but consider. When my son was ill, I had reason to beg God to intercede. But now the worst is over. My son is gone from me, and in the fullness of time I will join him. Now there is nothing more from God for me to seek. I simply must go on and live what life is left to me."

The two women were silent for a full minute. Peninnah saw that the older woman's eyes were brimming with tears, but she was smiling nonetheless.

"My dear," she said, "your father is a wise man."

Before she could respond, little Mordechai began to cry. Peninnah took one last look at her mother-in-law and went to him.

"His diaper is full," she said. The older woman nodded.

Lifting her son in her arms, Peninnah suddenly started to laugh. Her voice was strained, little more than a whisper, but she was laughing all the same. Her mother-in-law looked up in surprise.

"I guess I must go on and live what life is left to me," she said. "Even if it starts with one full diaper. L'chaim! To life!"

Her voice sounded so convincing that she almost believed it herself.

III

1967–Present: A Woman of Valor

SEVENTEEN

Those Who Can . . .

The morning sun poured like peach schnapps into Peninnah's bedroom, illuminating her features before waking her far earlier than she'd wanted. In fact, she hadn't even realized she'd fallen asleep. She held her eyelids closed as long as she could, at first counting sheep, then just counting. But it was no use. She might as well get out of bed. Put one foot in front of the other. Make coffee. Check on the children. The housekeeper will be here soon.

Even in grief, the Earth spins on its axis; the sun rises and sets beyond the Manhattan skyscrapers; the snow carpets the sidewalks and melts and falls and melts again; the city sprays its cacophony of taxi horns, truck engines and jive-talking hotdog vendors; the rooms in the apartment emit their layers of dust; the clothing attracts spills and sweat; the children grow, demanding equal parts food, affection, security and freedom; the paper is delivered; the coffee takes forever to boil and minutes to cool. Even in grief, the strong, insistent forces of life roil beneath the surface.

That is the way of Jewish death. The *Kaddish* prayer, intoned on a regular basis the first year after a loved one's death, is itself enveloped in life:

> May His great name be exalted and sanctified, in the world that He created according to His will. May He establish His kingdom during your lifetime and during your days and during the lifetimes of all the House of Israel, speedily and very soon! And say, Amen.

Among the people who paid their respects to Peninnah and her family that first week after Irv's death was Alan Schwartz, her old friend from Ocean Beach and UConn, where they had appeared together in plays. About five years older than she, with a thin face, dark hair, and a sweater and pipe that had seen better days, he had nothing of the buttoned-down visage of his father, the Hartford chief of police. She had always enjoyed Alan's humor and breadth of knowledge. More recently, he had invited her to give a talk in his role as chair of the Speech and Theatre Department at Iona College in nearby New Rochelle.

"You were in Paris two years," he had said on the phone when he was trying to convince her to come. "I'm sure you have something to say about French theatre."

"Well, I did go to the Comedie Française a few times."

"There you are, then. You'll be great."

She had approached the lectern and gazed out at the class, wondering how she had gotten there. She ran her hands over the playbills she had brought from the Comedie Française and the Olympia Theatre, took a deep breath, and began. The students seemed to enjoy her talk, and that was that. What had she said? Did she say *"Bonjour"* when she walked in, or *"Au revoir"* when she finished? Did she say everything she had prepared? She had no idea. On her way out of the building, she had already forgotten the whole thing.

Now Irv was dead, and they sat across from one another in the cozy living room of her once-happy apartment, which seemed to have grown bigger and emptier overnight. The children were out for a brief respite in nearby Riverside Park with her mother-in-law.

"Are you sure you wouldn't like some more coffee?" Peninnah was already halfway out of her chair.

Her old friend gently waved her back down. "Relax," he said calmly. "You've been waiting on me since I got here, and I've come to help you."

"Help me!" She let out a hollow laugh. "You help me just by being here. Giving me someone to talk to who isn't connected with—" She glanced at the table, where the tray of cookies and fresh fruit she'd put out was sitting untouched. "You're sure you're not hungry?"

He shook his head and leaned forward in his chair. "Look, I'm going to be frank with you. We've known each other a long time, right? You trust me?"

She raised her dark brows. "Of course. Why?"

"You're at loose ends, and I've got a proposition for you." He swallowed. "A faculty position opened up in my department for the fall, and I think you'd be perfect for it."

"Me? A professor?"

"Why not? You were an A student in college. You majored in Speech and Theatre and English, and you're Phi Beta Kappa! You're at least as qualified as some of the faculty I've inherited over the years."

Even as she stared at her friend in disbelief, her mind raced with the possibilities. She thought of her childhood games of playing school with Katherine, and of how her best friend's parents would ask her, just a year older, to teach their daughter to be as good a student as she was. Then she thought of how her assimilated uncle had asked her to teach his daughter about being Jewish. To have the chance to make a living doing something she cared about—it was a miracle. Still, she had her doubts.

"Look, Alan, I appreciate this, I really do. But all I have is a year teaching seventh grade at a yeshiva in Crown Heights! I've never taught a college course. Why would your boss ever agree to it? I've never even taken an education class!"

"Well as a matter of fact, the dean has already signed off on the offer. He heard your lecture, remember? When I suggested you to him, he said he thought you'd be a great fit." He stared at her, his mouth set in a thin line, mirroring hers.

Once again, her mind was miles away, and her eyes took on a faraway look. She was reliving a scene that had occurred a few days before with her mother. They were companionably feeding the children when Dora had suddenly shaken her head.

"Look at these *sheina punnums!*" she said. "Just over three years Rebecca is already, and Mordechai a year. Nu? Come live here in New London, and I will support you so you don't have to work. You can all day take care of your children. And I can help you. If you don't want to live in this house, maybe, I'll prepare an apartment for you and the children next door. A beautiful four-room apartment on the first floor."

Peninnah had almost dropped the spoon. The baby looked up in surprise, his mouth still open. "Ma, what are you saying? I'm not moving back to New London! Our lives are in New York!"

Her mother drew herself up a little straighter in her chair.

"It's such a terrible place to grow up?" She frowned. "New London is a good town for children. You have the park across the street, the beach in the summer, clean air. You think it's so much better in the dirty city?"

"It's not that, Ma," she said, stirring the dish of mashed banana before tipping the spoon toward Mordechai's waiting mouth. "It's that I have a home already. And I can work again!"

"Work, you call that theater? How much did it pay you, tell me that!"

"We had quite a reputation, though." Here she allowed herself a small smile. "And you know what you always told me, Ma. 'A good name is worth more than all the riches in the world.'"

Mama clicked her tongue. "And who will look after the *kinder*?"

"Irv's mother."

She was picturing the expression of disbelief on her mother's face when Alan reached out and placed a hand on her arm. She jumped in surprise.

"Hey, I'm sorry," he said. "I thought you'd be pleased. In fact, I thought you'd be over the moon. But I should have known it was too soon. Anyway, you've got your theater business with Lenore from UConn, right?"

She shook her head. "Actually I sold her my share. And look, don't apologize, Alan. This is fantastic. It's a gift. It's just that I haven't given a thought to what I'm going to do. My head is so buried in the past and present I haven't taken a minute to look into the future. I guess I know what I don't want—but not what I want. Until this minute."

"Wait, are you saying you might give it a try?" He looked uncertain. "You know you can always sign the contract now while it's offered to you and change your mind later. Lord knows we'll have plenty of applicants to choose from if you decide against it."

Now her face lit up, and for a moment she nearly felt like herself again.

"Of course, I'll try it! Just tell me what I need to do, Pastor Manders." She paused, then added in a haughty voice, "I find it seems to explain and confirm a lot of the things I had been thinking myself. That's the strange thing."

His eyes narrowed in confusion for an instant. Then he winked and replied, "Good God! Do you seriously believe that most people—?"

They stood up and hugged. No further words needed to pass between them. The exchange was from the first act of Ibsen's "Ghosts," the play in which they had co-starred in college. He, she was saying, was a man she could count on. A man who knew who she was and what she could do.

On Alan's recommendation, she enrolled in a few courses at Teachers College and completed her master's degree at Columbia. It was the summer of 1967, regrettably tagged the Summer of Love, when it seemed as though everywhere she looked on campus and everything she saw in the media was draped in sexual innuendo. College students kissed on the steps of the grand old Lowe Library. Hippies danced half-naked on television. She was grateful that she had something to distract her from these reminders of what she had lost.

The first thing that struck her when she walked into Iona College that fall was the cross with a figure of Jesus over the classroom doors. She should have expected it, she chided herself, given that it was founded by a Christian Brothers Order. Some time later, a student asked to lead the class in prayer. "Bless us, oh Mother of Speech," he began. Despite herself, she smiled. It was the most unique blessing she heard there. She wondered what her father would have made of it.

The fact that the students at Iona were exclusively male meant that she didn't encounter hand-holding or kissing in the halls, which further helped take her mind off thoughts of what she'd lost. Still she was shaky that first semester, despite the support Alan gave her through a steady stream of advice and handouts, and a four-day-a-week schedule that got her away from the house and its memories.

Apart from being with Rebecca and Mordechai, all she wanted out of life at that point was to teach the students who came into her classroom to speak their truth in a public forum. She took to the job as if she'd been born to it, as if she'd created it herself. Perhaps she saw the young Irv among those teenagers, although he'd been ten years older than these students when they'd first met. Or maybe she even saw herself, at an earlier, more hopeful time, when her dreams were still fresh. In any case, she set about teaching the way she would have liked to have been taught, through humor, kindness, stories, and above all, listening.

One of her students was an unusually gentle, soft-spoken young man, a star student from the first day, a little rough around the edges in appearance, perhaps, but that was perfectly in keeping with his chosen profession of folksinger. When he arranged to meet her in her office for a required private conference, she suggested that he bring his guitar to work on voice projection. He did, and the hour passed quickly as they compared the sound of the instrument to that of his voice and, when they were through, talked a little about songwriting.

Such a sweet soul, she thought, when he left that day. Not long after he graduated, she would see him again when he was featured at an outdoor concert at Lincoln Center.

"Are you going to say hi when he comes out, mom?" ten-year-old Rebecca asked, her large dark eyes on the stage.

"Oh, he won't remember me, silly," she said, shaking her head and holding a little tighter onto Mordechai's hand. "He's a star now. He's interested in young people. What does he want with his old professor from Iona College?"

Twenty minutes later, the performer took the stage to thunderous applause and whistling from the mostly blue-jeaned, mostly longhaired crowd. He reached for one of the waiting guitars, slung the broad strap over his shoulder and strummed a few chords, looking around at the expectant faces. All at once his gaze settled on Peninnah's, and his eyes lit up.

Without a moment's hesitation, he called out, "Oh, Professor Schram!"

Peninnah waved shyly, but Rebecca bounced on her toes and hugged her mother's long coat. "He really knows you!" she cried out. "Wow! Don McLean knows my mom!"

It was the spring of 1968. She had to admit that she and the children had settled into a sort of routine, although "unsettled" often felt like a more appropriate word. One day after work, she was sitting at her kitchen table opening mail when she came upon a cream-colored envelope. Opening it, she realized it was an invitation to a wedding reception for a man she and Irving had known mostly in Europe, Jim Goodfriend. They hadn't been close, but were fond of him and had gotten together a few times back in New York.

There were few things she wanted to do less in those days than attend a wedding. It wasn't purely that she was feeling so alone. She hadn't been to a party since the night of Irv's death, and this event, at the Grand Concourse Plaza in the Bronx, promised to be a lot more than simply dipping her toe into the waters of social life. She sat down to send her regrets, holding the pen inches above the reply card. She certainly wasn't going to tell them that she was alone and didn't know anybody besides the groom and couldn't bear to attend. She would have to make up an excuse.

Then her father's voice came to her, almost as though he were whispering into her ear: It is a mitzvah to celebrate with a bride and groom.

"Okay," she said aloud, to the four walls. "I'll go and fulfill the mitzvah. I'll say mazel tov, I'll have a nice dinner, and I'll come right home." She filled out the reply card, marked the date on her calendar, and didn't give it another thought.

Six weeks later, she walked into the reception hall in the Bronx wearing a cocktail dress she had unearthed from her closet, feeling conspicuously out of place in the midst of so much elegance, with the blazing chandeliers and the well-heeled crowd. Still, she told herself, she had decided to come and was determined to make the best of it. As soon as she was able, she delivered her mazel tovs to the bride and groom. That task complete, she figured that since she had come all this way, she might as well have some sustenance. She picked up a drink from a passing server. She hadn't taken three steps toward her table when she heard, "Peninnah? Hello!"

It was one of her former professors at Teacher's College, Peggy Clarke, whose husband worked with the groom and was his best man.

"Who do you know here?" Peggy asked, after giving her a hug.

They chatted for a few minutes. Suddenly Dr. Clarke said, "Come with me. I want to introduce you to someone special."

Taking her arm, she led Peninnah over to the table of a distinguished-looking older man.

"Dr. Tauber," she said, "this is Peninnah Schram, a brilliant former student of mine. Peninnah, this is Dr. Abraham Tauber, the chair of the Speech and Drama Department at Yeshiva University. Actually more than the chair; he founded the whole program."

There are moments that happen during the course of a life that, when you look back at them later, should have been accompanied by a clap of thunder, or a display of fireworks, or at the very least the clanging of a gong. When Peninnah talked for a few moments with Dr. Tauber and his lively, attractive wife Rhea, however, she knew only one thing: she hoped to be friends for life with the lovely Mrs. Tauber. What she couldn't know, couldn't possibly have imagined, was what was to happen next.

From humble beginnings in the Lower East Side of New York City in 1886, Yeshiva University had grown into a prestigious, multi-faceted institution of Jewish and secular learning that boasted an acclaimed teaching hospital and had conferred honorary doctorates on the likes of Lyndon Johnson, Robert Kennedy and then-future Israeli prime minister Yitzhak Rabin. So when Dr. Tauber called Peninnah soon after the wedding and asked her to interview for a position at YU's men's college uptown, she was floored. She met with Dean Isaac Bacon, who was disappointed to hear that she wanted to stay on at Iona for another year. It wasn't just that she felt the need of more teaching experience under her belt. She wasn't quite ready to take another job teaching only young men.

But Abraham Tauber didn't forget her. In the spring of 1969, he called again. Hearing his warm, resonant voice, she immediately sat up straighter in her chair.

"How are you, Peninnah?" he asked.

"Baruch HaShem," she replied, summoning every bit of her acting training to control her feelings. As casually as she could, she asked, "How are you?"

"Baruch haShem. Look, something has come up. There's an opening in the Speech and Drama Department at Stern College." She knew of Stern. It was the sister school to Yeshiva University, downtown. "It's a good place to work. In fact, my daughter June is in the same department. I would like very much for the dean to interview you for an open position."

She could hardly believe her luck. If she got the job, she could get to work by subway—Stern was in Manhattan, at Lexington Avenue and 35th Street. No more car or train rides to New Rochelle. And she would be teaching young women! She soon interviewed with Dr. David Mirsky, who hired her on the spot. Not only would she make more money, but she would only be working three days a week. Iona had been good for her, but it had never quite felt like home. Maybe it was because her students were all male, or that it was a Catholic college. Maybe it was the ride out of the city to New Rochelle. Whatever it was, now, for the first time since Irv's death, she had found someplace she felt like she might actually belong.

EIGHTEEN
Kaddish

While her father sat dozing on the couch, Peninnah, sitting beside him, felt her eyelids droop as well. Her fingers rested just inches from his on the cushion. They had the same hands, she noticed for the thousandth time. Expressive. Strong.

She could smell Mama's fragrant chicken soup simmering on the stove. *Dos goldene yoich iz geyad ha melech!*" her mother had called out as usual, tasting it as she seasoned. "This golden chicken soup is fit for a King!" They all three knew that that king always was and always would be Papa. Mama had waited for her to come in from the city after work before she would stray more than a few feet from his side to shower or lie down. No nurse was good enough for Papa. He was ninety-two. His kidneys were failing, and he was dying.

Sitting beside him, Peninnah felt herself drift into a lucid dream, knowing that she was asleep, but unwilling to awaken. It was no longer 1970, and she was no longer a widow in her mid-thirties. She was a child again, and it was summertime. Her father, in his prime and in control, had invited the half dozen or so men and single young boy from the shul choir to rehearse the liturgy for the upcoming High Holy Days. Despite the heat, she helped serve the requisite glasses of hot tea. She dutifully handed out the parts Pa had handwritten in each singer's notebook. Then she left the dining room as instructed, and sat here in the living room, holding her breath so as not to miss a note. Every time there was a voice even the slightest bit off-key, her normally sweet-tempered father would strike the table and shout, "Ach, Ach, Ach," stopping the rehearsal until the offending choir member got it right. At that moment it all felt so real she could have sworn she was there.

She felt Papa's hand knot into a weak fist. In an instant she was fully awake.

"What is it, Pa?" she asked, gazing at his pale face. "Do you need something?"

"*Nayn*," he said softly, his eyes still closed. As if lost in prayer, he chanted his old string of pet names for her. "Nove bransiche, ehre plansiche, pastechl, katchke, tzuganke, goldene kepele. You are so good to your papa."

"Of course, I am! You are my papa! You are Chazzen Samuel E. Manchester!"

"Hovchovitch." Pause. "Shuster." A longer pause. "Manchester."

She smiled and leaned closer, now holding his large hand in both of hers.

"Yes, I remember. You told me that you bought a passport with the same of Shuster in order to escape the Russian Army. And you changed Hovchovitch to Manchester in the U.S. because, why? It sounded more sophisticated? Or less Jewish?" He nodded weakly.

She reached over to the side table and held up a large get-well card with a gold Star of David on the front and at least a dozen different signatures in blue-and-black ink inside.

"Look, Pa, you got a nice card from the people at Ahavath Chesed. Did you see this?"

His eyes opened to half-mast. "I was a long time chazzen at Ahavath Chesed," he murmured.

She heard the soft ping of raindrops on the window. Looking out at the slice of sky between the curtains, she was surprised to see how quickly it had turned from the gleaming purple of an amethyst to the dark purple of a bruise.

"I know, Pa," she replied. "Nearly twenty years. You remember I learned my alef-beis there, in Talmud Torah classes. Do you remember the Chanukah parties, all those latkes the Ladies Auxiliary fried? And Mr. Gordon with his Chanukah *gelt* for the kids? We got a penny for each year we were alive."

"Federal."

"That's right. In those days, the shul was on Federal Street. With all those bulbs in the chandelier. And the lions of Judah on either side of the Ten Commandments above the ark. And the balcony for the women, who wept so much when you davened—it was so heartfelt and beautiful— that the butcher told the women not to flood the shul with tears!

"I love the story of how you got that job," she continued. His eyelids fluttered, and she pressed on in a soft voice. "How you went to a cantor's association conference in New York in 1930, I think, when you were still working in Bayonne. That's where you heard about a chazzen's *shtele* at the *Litvak* shul in New London. Everybody said, 'Oh, that job is impossible to get! They're so critical of the chazzen's voice.' But you said, 'I'm going to get it.' And the rest is history, right, Pa?"

Lying back against the pillow Mama had strategically placed behind him, he gave her hand a small squeeze.

"You know where I heard that story?" she asked. "Not from you! Remember Cantor Nulman, the Dean of YU's Cantorial School? He was at that conference, and he told me the story when I met him years later at a YU commencement." Silence. Keep going, she told herself. He was always a good listener.

"Did I ever tell you how much I loved sitting next to you on the *bimah* as a little girl, Pa? My friends sitting upstairs with their mothers were so envious! When you started the *Musaf* on the High Holidays from the rear of the shul, first standing with your back to the open door, in your *kittel* with that high, tasseled yarmulke and the huge tallis, with that silver *atarah* that I would polish for you. And then walking slowly up the aisle, chanting the *Hineni*—I can still hear your voice, davening with your whole heart in your beautiful second tenor, pleading with God on behalf of the congregation! You were the perfect *sh'liach tzibur*!"

Were those tears seeping out beneath his shut eyelids?

"You know what I remember?" she asked, her voice now almost a whisper. "I remember watching you at your desk, writing those musical scores, using that pitch pipe." She could just make out the edges of a smile around his lips. "And I remember hearing how when you went to Israel for a couple of months, they had to hire three shochets to replace you. I remember so much, Pa."

Maybe she should change her tone? Maybe it hurt him to think about what he could no longer do? A random image came to her. The Shetland pony Joe had insisted Papa buy him during the War. How her father had built a stall in one section of the garage for the animal. He took such good care of that pony, shoveling out the manure and putting it into the Victory garden, buying the feed and walking him over to the school grounds to eat grass. Topsy; that was his name. No, this was not a story for today.

"You know my favorite childhood memories, Pa? When we went out to the boardwalk on Ocean Beach, you in your white linen suit, white straw hat, white shoes that I would shine for you with that smelly polish. You were so dignified! You'd always buy me a vanilla ice cream cone, remember? And the orchestra played on the big platform they put up in the middle of the boardwalk, and Katherine and I danced and danced." When she smiled, it was wholly genuine despite her sadness, so entranced was she in the memory.

"Sometimes, you would give someone you knew a ride home instead of taking a bus. And the person would say, 'Chazzen, I'm sorry to take you out of your way,' and you would always answer, 'The car goes anyway.' And you would take whoever it was directly to their house." Was she talking for him, or for herself? Did it matter? They both needed happy pictures in their heads. "And then there were those days you would say, 'Come Peninnah, I'm going to drive up to the arboretum at the college. You want to ask Katherine to come along?" She could almost smell the pines and see the huge grassy area, the pond with the lily pads. All so beautiful. "And you would set up a folding chair by the trees, take out a bag of fruit and your Yiddish newspapers, and you were in heaven. So were we. Katherine and I played around the lily pads, or sat in these clearings—they felt almost like rooms—inside the walls of trees. It was absolutely delicious."

Hearing his soft snore, she dropped his hand gently into his lap, stood up, and let him sleep.

When she got the call that Papa was in the hospital, that it was very near the end, she drove as fast as she could from her job in the city, almost hoping that a state trooper would pull her over and lead her, siren wailing, lights flashing, the rest of the way. But it didn't happen, and she was late. Terribly late. She arrived at the room breathless, to find her mother, Joe, and Pa's children from his first marriage sitting in various seats and positions around the room as if flung from above, their faces grim. Papa had already given everybody his blessing; now he was unresponsive. She said nothing, just bent over to kiss his hand.

A man she had been dating for a while accompanied her to the funeral. Only years later did it occur to her that she would have liked, been thrilled, in fact, to deliver the eulogy. She knew just what she would have said:

"My father was my first and best mentor, but he never formally taught me to tell a story, to teach, to be a mensch. The greatest gift he gave me was not in a lesson, but through his example. Was it also the genes? Maybe so. But more probably it was all those days we spent together in shul, all those afternoons at the arboretum, or the boardwalk, or the resort, or visiting the farms. I learned by absorbing my father's essence, his very being. I carry my father with me wherever I go."

He had always said that the sea air was healthy. As he walked down the boardwalk at Ocean Beach, dressed in white, the summer sunlight glinted off the lenses of his eyeglasses. Gulls cawed overhead. The summer scents of salt and sweat and suntan lotion mingled in the air.

She pictured him there, and she wept for them both. She wept for them all.

NINETEEN

The Storyteller

Standing at the foot of the wooden steps with her eyes closed, Peninnah reveled in the hum of conversation, punctuated by gentle laughter and the distant roar of a train coursing through the outskirts of town. Five hundred people sat, or stood around in small groups, or searched for the best seats in the huge tent that cool fall afternoon at the National Story-telling Festival in tiny Jonesborough, Tennessee. A fellow storyteller serving as emcee took the stage, and the crowd began to settle. She spoke for a few minutes, but Peninnah had no idea what was said. The ensuing applause when her name was announced was like the crack of waves in a tumultuous ocean. By the time she stood smiling before the audience in her flowing black skirt and hand-woven silk jacket, even the train had fallen silent. And in that moment, it seemed to her that every face smiled back.

It was the first Friday in October, 1985. Before this weekend, she had rarely performed for such diverse crowds. The age range alone was a typical storyteller's nightmare: how to engage the demographic from ninety days to an equal number of years? More to the point, she saw before her a sea of types: the softly chatting librarians in wire-rimmed glasses and comfortable sweaters; the mountain men in long beards, blue jeans and flannel shirts; the other storytellers, some of whom appeared to be former hippies in their thirties; and the Southern tourists, sporting festival tee shirts and brightly colored windbreakers, gulping thermoses of coffee while struggling with varying degrees of success to shush their squirming offspring.

"*Shalom aleichem!*" she called out to the crowd. "That's the Jewish greeting that means 'Peace be unto you.' Now, you would answer '*Aleichem shalom!*' Unto you be peace." She repeated her line, pointed to the crowd, and they returned the greeting. The energy felt so exhilarating that she knew all at once that she would be all right.

"Well done! I am so glad to see you all," she began. "Now you may not believe it, but I don't come from the South." A smattering of encouraging chuckles. "I come from New London, Connecticut. My parents were born in tiny towns, or shtetlach, in Eastern Europe, and my father was a cantor and a rabbi, a Jewish ritual butcher and a circumciser. So I grew up steeped in what we call *Yiddishkayt*, that is, Jewish culture. In some ways it's very different from the cultures I'm guessing most of you grew up in, but in most ways it was exactly the same, just maybe with different window dressing.

"In fact it's sort of like the folktales you'll be hearing this weekend. The stories are the same all over the world—we share what are called tale types and motifs. Only the details are different."

She proceeded to tell them a cante fable that Ruth Rubin had taught her in Gramercy Park years before. Again and again she sang the wordless melodies, before and within the story, leading the audience in the simple tunes. And by the end of her set, five hundred disparate people, of all ages and backgrounds and walks of life, were singing together as one.

She couldn't say who was more moved, she or they. But she did know how she had gotten there.

The Jewish Braille Institute of America was located at East 30th Street, not far from Stern College. One day in 1969, Peninnah was recording in one of the Institute's studios as part of the cast of "The Tenth Man," by Paddy Chayefsky. It wasn't something she normally did; her friend Maram had asked her to take a part. After the session, Richard Borgersen, who headed the Institute's recording studio, walked over to compliment her on her work and asked her to stop by his office before leaving the building.

"Take a seat, please, Mrs. Schram," he said, pulling out the chair across from his desk. "Want some coffee?"

She was surprised at his attention, but also intrigued. "No, but thank you."

"I wanted to ask if you'd like to do something more for us," he said, steepling his fingers.

She nodded. "If I can, I'd be happy to. You have a wonderful organization."

"And you, my dear, have a wonderful voice. I was thinking, would you like to volunteer to record books for us? On your own schedule, of course."

Her heart leapt. "That would be terrific!"

"I'm thinking of a few different titles. You must like I.B. Singer?"

"I know him personally, as a matter of fact. I'm a huge fan."

"As am I. I'm thinking of *Zlateh the Goat*, his first children's book. Chanukah stories. We'll get you set up."

"I'm looking forward to it."

"Just one thing. When you read for the blind, you can speed up a little. Because they're so used to listening, they catch on to things they hear much quicker than sighted people do."

Her eyes widened. "Wow, that's fascinating. And it makes good sense. Thanks for the tip!"

Weeks passed, and she began volunteering for the Institute. Walking out onto 30th Street after a recording session one day, she loosened her scarf. It was the tail end of an afternoon in late fall, but the cool air felt soothing after the heated studio and the concentration required for the work. With half her attention on the traffic and her fellow pedestrians, she found herself replaying in her mind the book she had just read.

The title story was about a family that had fallen on hard times. The father Reuven was a furrier, but one particular winter was so mild that he had no customers. He decided that they must sell the family's beloved, aged goat Zlateh to the butcher in order to have the money to celebrate Chanukah. Aaron, his twelve-year-old son, had the unhappy task of taking Zlateh to the butcher. Unexpectedly, on the way to the butcher, the weather changed, and the two were stuck in a blizzard that lasted three days. They stayed warm by snuggling together in a haystack. The hay fed Zlateh, and so she was able in turn to feed Aaron fresh milk, which kept him alive until the snow cleared. When they returned home at last, both boy and goat were welcomed with tears of delight. First and foremost, they were safe. Beyond that, the cold weather meant there was plenty of work for a furrier, thus no need to sell the goat. Not that they would have anyway, after she had saved Reuven's life.

The values of family responsibility, respect and equality in the story warmed Peninnah's heart, as did Singer's love for animals, which she remembered well from the vegetarian luncheon she had held in his honor years before. Making her way through the rush hour crowds to the bus stop, her thoughts flowed like sand through an hourglass. First she smiled at how Richard had given her the circular finger motion to speed up her rate of speech in the recording studio. She would have to remember to forget some of her training in interpretive reading! Then she thought about having told "Zlateh" to Rebecca and Mordechai the previous evening, how they had enjoyed it, but told her they preferred the story in the same book with the demon and his wife. . . . A few blocks later, just as she approached 34th Street, something else occurred to her: recording these stories for blind children was so deeply moving, such meaningful work. A mitzvah, to be sure. She knew how important it was for all children to absorb Jewish values through stories, just as she had done throughout her childhood. (Although she hadn't always loved her mother's use of her stories as a prod toward good behavior!) If her chil-

dren enjoyed storytelling so much, why not do something like this for all
Jewish children? But where? How?

Unlike when she'd first arrived in New York, Peninnah now knew the
92nd Street Y to be one of the premier cultural centers in the city, with
classes, lectures, performances and other activities for all ages. The
Young Men's—eventually Young Women's—Hebrew Association had
been serving the Jewish community since 1874, finally securing its current location on Lexington Avenue between East 91st and 92nd Streets in
1930. Over the years, she had attended dozens of events at the Y, including Paul Kwartin's concert during her first months of grad school.

She had a much closer connection, as well. She and Lenore had produced two musicals there in 1964 and '65 as the Jewish Heritage Theatre:
"King Solomon and Ashmedai" and, for Chanukah, "Mattathias of Mod-
in," the first Jewish theatrical content at that Y. She thought of how they
had located the playwright, the composer, the director and cast. In other
words, she felt at home there. So why not bring stories to children under
the auspices of the Y? Why not bring a proposal for a program? Well,
why not?

She was so astonished at the beautiful simplicity of the idea that she
stopped still in the middle of the street. A taxi driver honked impatiently;
a messenger bicyclist swerved. As if coming out of a dream, she blinked
her eyes, looked around and walked on to her destination, and, she suspected, her destiny.

Nathan Kolodney was the director of education at the Y. It was, in fact,
his father who as program director had engaged Peninnah and Lenore
for the Jewish Heritage Theatre. Sitting across from the young man in his
office the following week as he scanned her one-page resume, she settled
back into her chair, crossed her legs, and took a long swallow from the
glass of water he had handed her. She couldn't say for certain that she'd
get the job of facilitating a weekly storytelling class for children, but she
knew it was a great idea. If he didn't want it, she was sure someone else
would.

He looked up at the paper, placed it on his desk and said, "So, Mrs.
Schram, why don't you tell me what you want to do and why."

She took a deep breath. "Here it is, Mr. Kolodney. I want to tell stories
to young children. I want to do interactive arts with them like drawing
and dramatics that reinforce the values in the stories. Now you might
ask, why use stories to teach values? And I would say that questions,
especially 'heart' questions—'Who are my people? By what values did
they live? What is the legacy I should leave for world?'—stories answer
these questions in ways that are long-lasting and memorable. We connect
through narrative to Jewish identity and are motivated to live according
to Jewish values and actions. It happened to me as a child; my parents

were always telling me stories. And I can make it happen for other children. I know I can."

He didn't respond, so she kept talking, leaning forward in her chair as she grew more enthusiastic. Somewhere down the hall a telephone was ringing; people were walking back and forth, chatting and laughing. But Nathan Kolodney's eyes never left her face.

"I believe that shared stories become guides for desirable conduct and values," she was saying. "That when they're passed down from generation to generation, these communal stories educate and help develop group identity in a creative and inspiring way. And people remember stories, and so they remember what they learn."

With a broad smile on his face, Kolodney closed his eyes and shook his head.

She frowned. "Is something wrong?"

"No, not at all! It's just so funny. Nobody talks to me about children's storytelling the whole time I have this job, and then this month, two people come to me with a similar proposal." He shuffled through some papers till he found what he was looking for. "Laura Simms. Do you know the name?"

"No. Who is she?"

"She calls herself a professional storyteller. Whatever that is. A young woman, but I gather she's been doing this kind of thing for a while. I'd like you to work together to come up with something. Meanwhile, I'll find somebody to underwrite it."

She almost clapped her hands with joy. "That's wonderful! I never knew there was such a thing as a professional storyteller! I'd love to meet her."

From the beginning, Peninnah and Laura Simms found they were of like minds. Together they designed a program they called "Fire, Water, Stone and Air." Every Tuesday afternoon, together or individually, they told world folktales—Jewish as well as African, German and everything else—using a blend of creative dramatics, music, movement and art. For a year, the two wildly creative women played off each other well.

One afternoon, Peninnah stood before the children and drew out an enormous pomegranate from the folds of her skirt. "Beautiful, isn't it? Does anyone know what this is?" She held out the wine-colored globe to both sides of the room, then set it down on the stool to her right. "This is a pomegranate. It grows in the Land of Israel, and it's very symbolic for Jews and others. For example, you know the Ten Commandments, yes?" A dozen heads nodded. "Well, in fact, Jews are supposed to follow 613 commandments. And some people say there are 613 kernels in this small fruit. Anybody care to count them?" She pretended to reach for it and laughed. "Just kidding. I'd rather you sit back and enjoy."

She launched into her retelling of a folktale that, wherever it was told throughout time and around the world, was about an apple. Instead,

Peninnah made it a pomegranate, which, along with the fact that it grew in Israel, she considered more magical. She titled her story, "The Magic Pomegranate."

Three brothers went their separate ways in search of an unusual item to show the others. When they reunited ten years later, the eldest had found a magic telescope, the second a magic carpet, and the youngest a magic pomegranate from a tree that replenished its single fruit as soon as it fell off.

With his telescope, the eldest spotted a princess who had fallen ill in a distant kingdom, and the middle brother sped them all to her side on his magic carpet. When the youngest fed the princess seeds from the pomegranate, she was cured. Whom did the princess choose to marry in appreciation?

She married the youngest, because, as she said, his mitzvah was the greatest. Because he could never recover the lost seeds, he gave of something of his own.

When Peninnah had finished, there was a satisfying pause, as the young minds drank in the story, as well as the lesson. Then Laura took the floor and began another story. Peninnah enjoyed every aspect of her colleague's voice, gestures and language.

Then it was Peninnah's turn again, and she told an African tale about a classic figure, Anansi the spider man. Afterward, she and Simms led their charges from the children's library through the glass doors to a spacious room, its floor covered in butcher's paper and crayons. The boys and girls were well used to interpreting the stories they heard through art. Rebecca and Mordechai were among them, happily diving into the colors. They scuffled to be seated with children they'd met on previous occasions.

The program was a success. After the last child was out the door, Laura called her over.

"Peninnah. Can we talk a minute?"

She had been humming a nigun to herself while cleaning up a few odds and ends. At the sound of Laura's voice, she turned toward her partner.

"Sure. Of course."

Laura led her to a chair and sat down beside her.

"Listen, I was thinking. That story you just told? You know it's in my repertoire."

Peninnah had no idea where this was going. "Oh? I didn't know."

"Yeah, I've told it forever, and I do it really well. And you told that pomegranate story really well. So I was thinking, why don't you just stick to the Jewish stories—and I'll take the rest of the world. That okay with you?"

Peninnah sat stone still, as if paralyzed. The only part of her that moved was her mouth, which said, to her surprise, "Okay."

"Good. That's settled then.

While Laura turned to leave, Peninnah still couldn't move. Tears welled in her eyes, threatening to spill onto her flaming cheeks. She felt as though she'd been slapped. The cyclone of emotions that boiled up in her was like nothing she'd ever felt. Who was this young woman to tell her what stories she could tell or not tell? How dare she? And why had she, Peninnah, agreed so quickly? It was the shock. The shock at having been treated so shabbily. But now what? She had already agreed. What could she do?

For the rest of the program at the Y, Peninnah told only Jewish stories. When she started teaching storytelling at Stern in 1974, she brought her students to the Y every Wednesday to teach youngsters Jewish values the same way, as an alternative to traditional Hebrew School. The program, which she called "Kernels of Pomegranate," introduced a different Jewish value every week. It was the College's first collaboration with the Y, and the administration in both organizations was delighted, as was she. But every time she walked into that building, she felt the full force of Laura Simms' words, and she felt her heart squeeze in her chest.

About a year after she started recording at the Jewish Braille Institute, Peninnah ran into Richard Borgersen on her way from the studio to the water cooler.

"Peninnah!" he said. "My favorite Jewish storyteller! Got a minute?"

She laughed. "For you? I'll give you two. What can I do for you?"

"What would you say to recording LPs and cassettes of these stories? I'm talking about producing commercial recordings, of course."

She had just bent down to take a drink; now she very nearly did a vaudeville comic's spit take.

"Are you kidding! Oh Richard, I would love that! When do we start?"

"Okay, well, first I need to book studio time for this. Meanwhile, why don't you come up with a name for our little record company, since you're so creative?"

"You know, I have a friend who's an artist who can do the cover design." He raised his palms as if it say, *B'shert*. It's fate. "You know, Richard, I'm feeling a little like Judy Garland here."

"Huh?"

"Well, it's sort of like, 'My father's got a barn, let's put on a show!'"

She heard him laughing all the way down the hall.

She decided to name the company POM Records, short for the pomegranate that had so much symbolic meaning for her. When Richard remarked on the name, she told him, "You know, in the Talmud, one of my favorite quotes comes from *Shir HaShirim Rabbah*, in which children sitting in a row studying Torah are compared to the kernels of a pomegranate. It always makes me think of children listening to stories."

He shook his head in wonder. "What can I say? Sounds perfect, Peninnah. I love it!"

They secured the rights to record the ten stories from Molly Cone's book *Who Knows Ten? Children's Tales of the Ten Commandments* for the first two records, entitled "A Storyteller's Journey" I and II. For the third, she recorded three stories from the folklorist Howard Schwartz's book *Elijah's Violin*. While her friend Jacqueline Kahane designed the covers for the first two, they used the illustration on Schwartz's book for the third. The partnership went on for several years. Wherever Peninnah went, she took along records and tapes to sell or give as gifts. The whole experience proved to be one of her greatest delights. Many of the professional storytellers she became friendly with at guild meetings, festivals or conferences went to great lengths to promote themselves. They sent out flyers or postcards in mass mailings; they networked; they made a point to be at the right place at the right time to make contacts. That was the business. That was what you did to make a living as a storyteller. But like all things that are b'shert, somehow, Peninnah's work came to her by word of mouth, and her list of clients grew. She was invited to serve as storyteller-in-residence at the Jewish Museum, just a quarter of a mile from the Y. The first of its kind in the country and the oldest still in existence in the world, the Jewish Museum, circa 1908, is housed in the former mansion of the late philanthropist Felix M. Warburg. There Peninnah told stories once a month, using special exhibits or holidays as springboards for her stories.

She also presented workshops and performances at day schools and festivals, synagogues and universities. Then, in 1977, she was invited to the University of Rochester to present at the second Conference on Alternatives in Jewish Education, known as CAJE. It was there that she made a connection with the organization that lasted many decades. It was at a CAJE conference in the mid-1980s that Peninnah founded the Jewish Storytelling Network, a consortium of storytellers who supported each other and helped promote their work. For many years she led the group, along with such dear friends and devoted colleagues as Cherie Karo Schwartz, Bonnie Greenberg and Corinne Stavish, and she edited its Jewish Storytelling newsletter.

In 1984, Dr. Yael Zerubavel, who taught Jewish studies at Rutgers University in New Jersey, was planning a festival of Jewish arts at the famed City University of New York in Manhattan. A colleague suggested that Peninnah contact her, and from their first brainstorming conversation she went on to produce a Jewish storytelling conference-within-the-conference at Stern College. Among the fifty or so folklorists, musicologists and practitioners of various arts attending that day was Roslyn Bresnick-Perry, a sixty-something clothing designer born in Belarus. From the first story she told in public at the open mic event that Sunday, Bresnick-Perry went on over the next three decades to become a good friend and an internationally known storyteller in her own right.

When a conference presenter called her at home during the conference to cancel at the last minute due to a funeral, Peninnah sat at her kitchen table paralyzed, wondering what to do. At last she stirred herself enough to go to work. It was on the way that the perfect solution occurred to her. Rabbi Avi Weiss, a professor on the faculty of Jewish Studies at Stern who went on to become one of the most important rabbis in the nation, would be a wonderful addition to the conference. She hurried to the main office to find out his schedule, then waited outside his classroom until he dismissed the students. He was filling his briefcase with his class notes when she strode in, said hello, and made her request.

When she answered his question as to why she had invited him at the last minute, he thought for a minute, rubbing his chin. Then he said, "I wonder if you have someone who could do me a quick favor?"

She smiled. "Tell me. I'll do it myself."

"All right, I need you to get me the reddest, juiciest-looking apple you can find, as well as a knife and plate. And twenty *chumashim*." When she looked at him blankly, he laughed. "The apple is not to eat, I assure you! At least not right away. It's for a story I plan to tell."

"Ah, a story!" She clapped with delight. "Anything for a story! Also please, be sure to bring your class!" And off she went.

The story he told that day was "The Apple Tree's Discovery."

There was once a little apple tree that sat on a hill, gazing up at the winter night sky. How she wished she could have stars in her branches like the other, taller oak trees! Her own branches were just too small and bare. She begged God to give her stars as well, but to no avail. Then, when spring came, her branches grew leaves and fragrant blossoms. They were soft and vibrantly green, but still she bemoaned the fact that God had not gifted her with stars. Summer came, and she bore fruit. It was red and shiny, but not the same as stars. Why hadn't God given her stars in her branches? And then came autumn, and her first apple fell to the ground. (Here Rabbi Weiss placed the apple sidewise on the plate and sliced it in half.) It burst open and inside she saw the seeds, which looked for all the world (here he held up the halves of the apple to the crowd) like the points of a star. And she realized that she had in fact held stars inside her all along.

When she and her dear friend and former student Rachayl Eckstein Davis heard "The Apple Tree's Discovery" that afternoon, they looked at each other in awe. Although originally a Chinese parable, the Jewish variant that Rabbi Weiss had created touched them both so much that it became a signature story for each of them. Peninnah began to bring a ripe red apple and a small paring knife to concerts, in order to make the story come more alive. She went on to reprint it in her anthology *Chosen Tales*, sharing the byline with Rachayl. They eventually also published it as an illustrated book. And they told it wherever they went.

The Jewish storytelling festival was so successful that no one present wanted it to end. To maintain the spirit of sharing stories and teaching storytelling as an ongoing enterprise, Peninnah organized the Jewish Storytelling Center. The group was offered space at the Martin Steinberg Center at the American Jewish Congress on East 84th Street, and there it welcomed tellers and presenters, holding concerts and workshops. When the Center closed its doors, the JSC was at a loss, but only temporarily. Steve Siegel, a genealogist, archivist and librarian whom Peninnah had met when she worked with Laura Simms, now headed the Y's library. He invited the JSC members to meet and present their programs there—he even printed the newsletter. It was at the library that she met her good friend and colleague Gerry Fierst, who went on to collaborate with her on many projects over the years. The Y library was JSC's home until it too closed in 2013.

With the help of Dean Karen Bacon at Stern and a willing and burgeoning cadre of volunteers, Peninnah was able to organize two subsequent storytelling festivals at Stern College. Through it all, as she performed, taught, researched and built her repertoire, Laura Simms' words still stung: "You tell the Jewish stories, and I'll take the rest of the world." The two women didn't have anything to do with each other for quite some time. Then, little by little over the years, Peninnah came to realize what she had at first thought was simply impossible: Simms was right. In fact, far from being insulting, Laura had given her a wonderful gift. Who she was, what she breathed, ate, slept, yes, and told, was Jewish. She still told world folktales on occasion, but she found that even when she told African tales, or folktales from other places, she searched for variants in the Jewish tradition. She wasn't just a storyteller. She was a Jewish storyteller. After that, Peninnah and Laura slowly grew close again. She even hosted her friend's wedding at her Yorktown home.

In the summer of 1984, they were having lunch together at a bistro on the Upper West Side when Peninnah suddenly asked, "What can you tell me about the National Storytelling Festival in Jonesborough, Laura? How can I get invited as a featured performer like you?"

Simms took a sip of coffee, flipped her long dark hair behind her shoulders and leaned back in her chair. "Look, I've been doing this for years," she said. "Have a little patience. It will happen. It just takes time."

Peninnah briefly shut her eyes. I may not be as experienced as she is, she thought, but I can do this. I know I can. I'm just going to have to do it myself.

The Jonesborough festival was always held the first weekend of October. Peninnah decided to book a flight to Johnson City, Tennessee, the closest airport to Jonesborough. She had no idea what to expect, but she had booked a hotel in the small city and took a bus to the nearby town where the festival had been held since the early seventies. Each year, thousands of tourists descended on Jonesborough for the festival, and yet somehow it still retained its charming intimacy. She heard many innovative, captivating performers, including a Jewish storyteller from the Boston area named Doug Lipman, who shared some Chasidic folktales along with tales from around the world.

At the end of the first day, she felt overwhelmed at the wealth of talent. Exhausted, she returned to her hotel, where she met a couple in the lobby and started talking about how wonderful the festival was. They agreed to meet for breakfast at eight the next morning and ride the bus together back to Jonesborough. When she fell into bed that night, she was afraid she'd be awake with excitement for hours. Instead, the intensity of the day sent her to sleep in minutes.

Peninnah appeared at the hotel restaurant promptly at eight the next morning, but the couple she had agreed to meet wasn't there. She sat alone at a table for four, drinking coffee and looking around. Had she forgotten what they looked like? But there were no other twosomes in the restaurant, just a round table with six very refined-looking older women.

When the waitress came to her table with a refill, Peninnah told her she would wait just a few more minutes to order. It was then that one of the women turned to her.

"You're waiting for someone?"

"Yes, and unfortunately they're late. I've got to get to the Festival. Are you here for that too?"

"Of course. Are you a storyteller, if I may ask?"

"Yes I am. My name is Peninnah Schram. I'm a storyteller from New York."

"Really!" another woman asked. "Tell me, do you earn your living from storytelling?"

Peninnah pursed her lips. "It's not my living," she said simply. "It's my life."

The women laughed appreciatively. Then the first one said, "Well, tell us a story then!"

It was the first thing in the morning, she hadn't eaten breakfast, and she was sitting in a hotel restaurant. But Peninnah never missed an opportunity to tell a story. She stood up and related the Russian-Jewish folktale of "The Innkeeper's Wise Daughter," which she was just then working on.

An innkeeper and tailor argue about who is more wise. They take their case to the local nobleman, who gives them three riddles to solve in order to determine who is wiser: What is the quickest thing in existence, what is the fattest, and what is the sweetest? The innkeeper's daughter, who is very clever, solves the riddles for him, saying that the quickest is thought, the fattest is the earth, and the sweetest is sleep.

When the innkeeper admits to the nobleman that it was his daughter who supplied the answers, the nobleman wants to test her. He tells her father to have her hatch a dozen eggs in three days. The daughter, realizing that the eggs are hard-boiled, tells her father that in response, he should take boiled beans to the nobleman and ask him to plant them.

The nobleman is so impressed by the young woman's wisdom that he wants to meet her, but tells her father that she must arrive dressed and not dressed, not riding or walking, not hungry or full, and with a gift that is not a gift. She appears wearing a fishing net, half-leaning on a goat, eating a couple of almonds, and bearing two pigeons that fly away before the nobleman takes possession, thus fulfilling all his requirements.

The two are soon married, but the nobleman first makes one condition: His new wife must never interfere with his business, or she will be banished. In exchange, she stipulates that if he does banish her for interfering, she must be allowed to take with her the thing from his household that she holds most dear. He is so taken with her that he readily agrees to her demand.

The young wife soon gains a reputation for wisdom. One day, a peasant comes to see her, complaining that her husband has decreed that a foal born to his horse under his neighbor's wagon belongs to the neighbor. The innkeeper's daughter replies, "Let the nobleman see you fishing in a well. When he scoffs at you, tell him that it's as crazy to think somebody can catch fish in a well as it is to think a wagon can give birth to a horse."

Not long afterward, the nobleman does happen to laugh at the peasant's fishing in the well. On hearing the man's response, the nobleman recognizes his wife's reasoning and demands that she leave the house for interfering with his judgment. He does agree, however, to honor his side of the bargain and let her take the thing that is dearest to her.

That evening, the wife plies her husband with wine, until he falls into a deep slumber. When he awakens the next morning, he finds himself in her father's inn.

"What is the meaning of this?" he sputters.

Her reply: "We had an agreement. I took the thing that was dearest to me in the house."

Unable to hide his laughter or his love, the nobleman forgives her, and the two live in peace and harmony till the end of their days.

Just as the women at the next table were applauding Peninnah's performance, her new friends arrived, apologizing profusely for being twenty minutes late.

"No problem!" she said. "Let me introduce you to some lovely people."

The six women had finished eating. When they rose to say their goodbyes, the one who had asked her to tell the story leaned over to Peninnah and said, "Will you give me your phone number? I'm going to talk to Jay O'Callahan about you."

She had never heard the name, but why not? "Thank you," she said, handing the woman her card without quite knowing why. "It was lovely to meet you."

Not long after the Festival, she received a phone call from Jimmy Neil Smith, a Festival founder. He told her that Julia Ann Richardson, the woman who had asked her to tell a story at that fateful breakfast, was one of the major sponsors of the Festival and had raved about her restaurant performance. Because of that, he was inviting her to perform the following year.

The next year and several times after that, Peninnah performed in Jonesborough. She often housed with the sole Jewish family in town, having been told that she would "be more comfortable there." They were so hospitable and became such good friends that she stayed with them whenever she returned to town over the years. Once she roomed alone and had to purchase kosher hot dogs, the only meat she could find to eat, from miles away. And when she performed at the local library, she had the feeling that the crowd of Southerners was maybe, just maybe, looking for her Jewish horns. But no matter. Everyone was as nice and welcoming as could be.

At that first Festival performance, she led the audience through the story about the Chasid who paid a hundred rubles to learn two melodies. Throughout the weekend, audience members approached her on the street to compliment her work and tell her they kept hearing the tune over and over in their heads.

"Give me fifty rubles," she joked, "and I'll be happy to get it out of your mind."

In a tiny town in northeast Tennessee, Peninnah Schram had found her second tribe.

TWENTY
The Joy of Teaching

"Kichibah mukkeleh. Kichibah saggistir danlo!"

It was the first morning of the new semester at Stern College for Women, and Peninnah had walked into her customary classroom from her office two doors down just at the moment class was to start. At the sound of the odd syllables and the sight of the pretty, delicate-looking professor, twenty-five young mouths stopped chatting; twenty-five pairs of young eyes, squinting in confusion, watched her face.

"Chickegigig?" Peninnah asked, her smile broadening as she leaned closer to a tow-headed young woman in the first row of desks. "Compesori lokeesha."

Hebrew or Yiddish, it wasn't. Several students in the back began to giggle.

"Chickegigichik?" she asked, raising her eyebrows in surprise. "Korzoi amstid?"

At that moment she spotted a young woman standing in the doorway as though frozen in place. Peninnah paused, and the student said, "Oh, I must be in the wrong class. I thought this was Speech."

One of the seated students called out, "You're in the right place!"

The newcomer entered the room and made her way to the closest desk, all the while glancing around at the others.

"Plano, anchiboro!" Peninnah motioned for the student who had spoken to stand, which she proceeded to do. Then the professor turned back to the whole room and repeated the nonsense syllables in different commanding tones while motioning the class to rise. In ones and twos, they did so.

She smiled, gave a slight nod of her head, and they sat, nearly in unison.

"Okay!" she said. Her throaty laughter seemed to radiate all the way from her long earrings and colorful beads past her patterned jacket and the skirt skimming the tops of her tall boots.

"Now, can someone tell me what was that about?"

A pale sophomore, her heavy, dark-framed glasses filling half her face, waved her hand.

"Yes? Tell us, what is your name?"

"Sarah."

"Sarah. What do you think, Sarah? What were we doing there? Remember, there are no wrong answers. Just answers for other questions."

The student twisted a lock of her dark hair. "Was that Japanese?"

Peninnah shook her head. "I wish I spoke Japanese that well," she said with a grin. "I wish I spoke it at all!" She scanned the room. "Anybody else?"

A heavyset freshman in a bulky white sweater raised her hand. Without waiting to be acknowledged, she said, "Just random syllables! You weren't saying anything at all!"

"What's your name?"

"Abigail."

"Well, Abigail, are you accusing me, Professor Schram, of speaking nonsense?" The student froze a bit at her teacher's serious expression, but then, to her obvious relief, Peninnah burst out laughing. "You're right, it was nonsense! I wasn't saying anything. But what was I communicating?"

Someone called out, "You wanted us to stand and sit?"

"Yes! Who said that?"

"Kara!"

"Thank you, Kara! But how did you know?"

The student, who sat hunched forward in her seat, simply shrugged.

"I have a wonderful book," Peninnah said, "called *Put Your Mother on the Ceiling*. Isn't that a great title?" A few heads bobbed. "It's a book about creativity. And this book suggests to try not to anticipate what happens next, either when listening to someone or when preparing your own speech. In other words, the author—his name is Richard de Mille—he encourages us to be open to the possibilities of new and surprising things. Sooo," here she paused to hold their attention, "you knew that I was telling you to sit when you were standing up why?"

"Because we were already standing," Sarah said. "We expected that next you would want us to sit back down."

Peninnah beamed at her. "Ah, but then you are thinking ahead, anticipating what will logically come next. But what if I were to ask you instead to run in a circle? If you are going to anticipate anything in this class, as in life, I hope you will anticipate a surprise.

"But there's at least one more thing that exercise demonstrated." She scanned the room. "Anybody? Going once, going twice! No? Well, what if we consider communication, even storytelling, as not simply words? You will find in this class that we use much more than words to give a speech. We communicate with our whole being. For example, we humans communicate volumes through body language, through gestures and expressions. We will learn about that, as well as how to use our voices as musical instruments to be more effective." She had been standing at the front of the room; now she hoisted herself up on the heavy wooden desk again the blackboard.

"I have another question for you. How many people can tell me what kind of tree in this part of the country has gigantic white blossoms?" She was greeted by a canvas of blank faces. "Nobody? They are magnolia trees, and come spring, they gift us with large white blossoms! They are absolutely stunning! I encourage you to look around your world, to be observant. And that's saying something to Stern students!" Several of them chuckled at the pun.

"You will learn that there is so much out there that you realize, not just beautiful people but even—beautiful magnolia trees!" She looked at the startled stares; gradually each one melted before her broad smile.

"So tell me, did you like that exercise?"

A young woman in the front row raised her hand, and Peninnah nodded in her direction.

"It was funny. It was fun. To try to figure out what you were doing." She paused. "I'm Susan, by the way."

Peninnah nodded. "Good! Did you notice, Susan, that I didn't say anything, and you knew exactly what I was saying? Anyway, I'm so glad to hear that you thought it was fun. I want you to have fun in this class. For one thing, fun makes us feel good, and when we feel good, we learn better. That doesn't mean you'll be kidding around and laughing when you give a serious speech. But I really hope you will enjoy researching and talking about whatever topics you choose to focus on."

She took a breath and looked around the room once again. "Now. I'm going to take attendance, give you a few general guidelines, and then, if anyone has any thoughts, reflections, experiences you'd like to share with the class, you'll have some time to do so."

After class, she returned to her office. One or two of the students handed over a form for her to sign or had a question for her to answer. One of them, to her amusement, simply seemed unable to leave her side, making small talk and repeating questions Peninnah had just answered.

And then, all at once, she was completely alone. As she turned to a box of books to unpack, a thought popped into her head: I felt it at Iona, but now I'm sure: I was born to do this.

She had loved the stage, but teaching was something altogether more fulfilling. This was being truly, authentically herself—the lover of learning and knowledge—while helping young people become more authentically themselves, whatever that might be. This was leaving a legacy, not precisely the kind she hoped to give to her own children, but something that belonged to the world. When she had stood in front of the room, minutes earlier, she had felt her energy and attention flow into every one of them. And theirs back to her. And yes, she often thought, teaching is a form of performance.

She was a realist; after all, she'd taught before. As the semester wore on, young people could occasionally be rude; they could be oblivious to what was expected of them. But so could older people. She thought of her mother's saying: "Don't spit in the river; there may come a time to drink." All she could do was behave as though they were the people she wanted them to be. And more often than not, that was how they behaved, as well.

Which isn't to say she was a pushover. In fact, she had a well-earned reputation as a tough grader. Still, at the end of the semester she'd find love notes at the end of the A students' papers, which made her smile every time she thought of them. She remained in touch with these star students, writing them recommendations for graduate schools and teaching jobs of their own, reviewing their books, even co-authoring with them. She also derived a great deal of pleasure from the students who improved, those who had learned basically from scratch to create a coherent outline or deliver a flowing speech. They made her the happiest of all.

The big table was laden with wines, cakes and fruits; the soft music vaguely ethnic. Bottles of wine sat huddled together on the kitchen counter; the aroma of coffee wafted through the rooms. Peninnah had done everything she could think of to keep conversation not only flowing, but convivial. A dozen or so well-dressed Stern colleagues and friends milled around, filling their plates, cups and glasses. The mood was festive, yet subdued. On a high-back, comfortable chair in the middle of the room sat Isaac Bashevis Singer, the guest of honor.

It was a Sunday afternoon in 1972. As the men and women settled themselves in chairs around the great writer, they began to ask him about his work. What was his process? Did he prefer writing novels or short stories? What was his favorite of his many published works? Why did this-or-that character engage in this-or-that behavior?

"I'd rather not discuss my stories," he said, raising his hands as if to push away the questions. "I just want to relax on a nice Sunday afternoon, enjoying our lovely hostess's hospitality." He raised his glass to her, and they all did the same.

At one point, the talk turned to the new book by Alex Comfort called *The Joy of Sex*.

"You know it?" one of the women asked Singer. "It just came out. Non-fiction, about sexual practices."

"Are you sure about that?" someone asked. "I mean that it's non-fiction?"

Singer stroked his chin. "It's a good question. But I'm curious," he said, turning to the woman who had just spoken. "You mean to say you think this is a work of fiction?"

"Of course," she said. "I mean really. People don't suddenly become contortionists in the bedroom. The illustrations are laughable."

The woman who had mentioned it to Singer in the first place looked down, smiled, and shook her head.

"And what do you say?" he asked her.

"I say it takes all kinds of people, all kinds of bodies, all kinds of behavior to make a world. Of course people do these things!"

A professor of French literature leaned forward in his chair.

"Mr. Singer," he said, "Excuse me, but since we have this amazing opportunity to meet you, I think we've got better things to talk about with you. I would really like to ask you about the character of—"

But Singer didn't look in the man's direction. "And what do you say to that?" he asked the first woman, his eyes wide behind his dark-framed glasses. "Do you not agree?"

The gathering went on for a couple of hours, and the poor French professor never did get his question answered. But everyone, including Singer, who asked much more than he answered, seemed to have a wonderful time. For Peninnah, it had not been simply a party. It was her way of bringing together smart people and their ideas outside the walls of academia and into the community, which already looked to become a lifelong pursuit.

One fine spring morning some afterward, Peninnah stopped on her way into work to stand by the magnolia trees not far from the building. For several minutes she studied the broad, shiny leaves and breathed in the fragrance of the blossoms. Dean Mirsky had summoned her to a one-on-one meeting at 10 a.m. She was sure there was nothing wrong; not only was she a popular professor, but he was also the kind of colleague who would stop her in the hall and invite her informally into his office to chat if there was anything wrong Still, she knew something was afoot.

"Peninnah, so good to see you!" He rose from his desk chair when she entered and leaned forward to shake her hand. "Please, have a seat."

"It's good to see you too," she said, easing herself into the chair across from him. She inhaled deeply, trying to calm the butterflies circling her stomach. What on earth was she so nervous about?

"Peninnah," he said, "how long have you been teaching Speech for us now? Three years?"

She thought: If something were wrong, he would have my file on his desk. "Yes, I started in the fall of '69."

"And from all accounts, you've been doing a great job. Sterling evaluations."

"*Baruch* ha*Shem*!" Thank God!

"But I think we are wasting your talents here."

She held her breath. What was this?

"I've been thinking; I'd like you to consider offering a Jewish storytelling class here at Stern. What do you say?"

Muscles she hadn't known she had, much less that she was clenching them, released throughout her body.

"Oh how wonderful! What a great idea!"

"How soon can you start? Will you be ready for next semester?"

"Next semester?" She laughed. "I could start tomorrow!"

Peninnah taught Jewish storytelling at Stern College for the next forty-two years. Young women from that first class and others after them grew into storytellers and writers, educators and artists, with whom she would correspond and meet and work. One student who had gone on to become an editor requested a photo of the two of them with a book to which Peninnah had contributed a blurb for the back cover. Others told her years later that hers was their favorite class of their college careers.

And the magnolia trees continued to flower, every spring.

TWENTY-ONE

The Station That Speaks Your Language

The soaring melody seemed to dance around her head in streams of color and light, substance and texture. Peninnah felt transported, both spiritually and physically, by the rich voice and delicate instrumentation. She leaned back in her seat, and the walls of the theater melted. It was as though the music were lifting her up to the rafters and beyond.

Paul Kwartin had kept his word. When the friendly guest whom Peninnah had met at the Griswold Hotel the summer before moving to New York presented his 92nd Street Y concert of the sixteenth-century composer Salomone Rossi, he left her passes to the concert at the box office. When a client gave him tickets for the Lincoln Center Chamber Society and he couldn't make it, he passed them along to her. At those performances and the occasional others he invited her to over the years, she marveled at the scope and talent of both the performers and the compositions. This nephew of a world-renowned cantor had opened a new world for her, and she was grateful for it.

Time passed, and their contact was sporadic. Kwartin became a minor celebrity in town as the host of his own Jewish music show on WEVD radio. In those days, every New York City Jew who knew the difference between a bagel and a bialy was familiar with the station named after the well-known socialist activist Eugene V. Debs. It was run at the time by the Jewish paper the *Forward*, and at one point had broadcast primarily in Yiddish, in addition to its programming in Italian, Polish and other languages of the city's immigrant populations.

One afternoon in 1973, she was sitting marking papers in her office at Stern when the telephone rang.

Her mind still on the student essay before her, she said, "Hello, Peninnah Schram, how can I help you?"

141

"How are you, Peninnah Schram?" At the sound of the familiar voice on the other end of the line, she put down her pen and smiled.

"Baruch haShem. All is good, Paul. So nice to hear from you! How are things with you?"

"Fine, fine. Listen, your name came up in a conversation I had with Joel Plavin, the general manager here at WEVD. We were talking about maybe doing a series of Jewish stories for children on the radio. And of course I thought of you, my favorite Jewish storyteller! What do you say?"

"What do I say?" She felt her face flush with excitement. "I say when do I start?"

"Well, the first step is to meet the director and go over some ideas. I'll set up an appointment for you. When are you free to come down?"

Her first thought was: When am I not?

The title for the series came to her on the ride home that same evening. She remembered how Elie Wiesel occasionally started the stories he told during his lectures at the 92nd Street Y with the line, "Let us tell tales." She loved that. Then she thought of the series of radio plays she had heard as a child, "Let's Pretend," in which the young listeners, herself included, would take their places on an imaginary magic carpet and fly away—with a sound-effect *whoosh*—to the time and place in which the tale took place, then return safely back home again at the end of the show. Unfortunately the combined phrase, "Let Us Tell Tales," made her think of salad. What about "Let's Tell Tales"?

She met the director and told him her suggested title, as well as some of her other ideas. Several stories every week, according to a set theme. Segues and introductions, in which she'd tell a little about the source of the story, the motifs or recurring elements, a connection to Jewish ritual or an upcoming holiday. She also made it clear that she wanted to begin and end with music, as well as having it interwoven throughout certain stories. He was amenable to everything. They decided on a half-hour program, which would run for thirteen weeks. He told her it would air Friday afternoons at four p.m. She liked that. The thought of children huddled around the radio listening to her stories and staying out from underfoot while their mothers prepared for Shabbes was, to use one of her favorite words, delicious.

And so she began, sitting at a table in the studio with her typed text of the story, which she had carefully prepared with music cues underlined in red, and a microphone before her, keeping an eye on the sound engineer through a little window to make sure all was well on his end. Unlike when she had read for the blind, she needed to speak slowly enough for people to absorb the content. But just as when she performed, she had to be aware of rate, pitch, volume and pauses. Pauses that were just long enough, but not so long that people got restless and checked their watches or, God forbid, their radio dials.

One evening after a recording session, she stopped as usual to say good-bye and thank you to the engineer.

"Tell me, Mrs. Schram," he said, "how do you find your stories?"

She leaned against the sound booth, not having realized until that moment how tired she was. But this was a subject she loved, and she was delighted that the young man was interested.

"Well, I go through anthologies of Jewish folktales and legends," she said. "Sometimes I'm looking for stories I heard as a child; sometimes I find new ones. For every twenty I look at, maybe I find one that really speaks to me. You know, they say the story has to choose the storyteller; the storyteller doesn't choose the story."

He nodded thoughtfully. "Cool. And then do you write a script?"

"I only rewrite something if a sentence doesn't sound smooth when I read it aloud. Many of these old folktale collections are written in a sort of stilted, archaic language. Certainly not as you or I would speak them—which is pretty ironic, when you think about it, since they originally came from the oral tradition!"

"What's your story for next week, then?"

"Oh, next week is from the Talmud. It's a story about King Solomon and the demon king Ashmedai. You'll love it!" When she saw he was interested, she leaned forward. "Solomon wants to build the Temple, you see. But he's forbidden to use iron, because that's what weapons are made of. What to do? Then he hears about a *shamir*, a kind of worm that can cut through stone. But the only way he can get it is from this king of the demons. So he sends a young man through the desert to bring Ashmedai back to Jerusalem, so he can find out how to get hold of the worm. Great story—" she winked, "and all absolutely true! At least my children think so!"

The sound engineer chuckled. "You know," he said suddenly, "when you do your show, just like now, I feel like you're talking directly to me. I mean that as a compliment, of course," he added quickly. "You sound so natural. That's unusual for someone who's so new at this."

She felt her face grow red. "I take it as a compliment! Thank you so much. That's what I'm aiming for."

"How do you do it?

"It's simple, really. I used to love the old radio shows; that was my imaginary world as a child—that and books, of course. And I always remember Jimmy Durante saying, 'Goodnight, Mrs. Calabash, wherever you are' before signing off. It always sounded like he was talking to a real person. So I made up my mind to sound like that, too."

"Yeah, but how?"

"Promise not to tell the other on-air personalities?" She winked. "I'm just kidding. I decided that the microphone on the table is my friend, someone I like. I don't mean his name is Mike; I mean I imagine I'm talking to a close friend instead of a piece of electronics."

"Well, I gotta hand it to you, Mrs. Schram. You're a natural! You know what? For my money, you're one of the few people out there doing real radio."

She certainly didn't always feel like a natural. She still stumbled from time to time, and the engineer would have to ask her to start again. But as usual she was a quick study, and with her experience reading for the blind and telling stories to audiences, it honestly didn't feel like much of a stretch.

For her theme music she chose a melody by her favorite Chasidic singer, Ben Zion Shenker, which always put her in the storytelling mood. She also wanted to add musical cues, to highlight emotion, or to evoke certain kinds of settings. It turned out that the station's music director, Zalmen Mlotek, was the son of the Yiddish cultural icons Chana and Joseph Mlotek, whom she had met years before. She found that she could simply tell Zalmen what she needed the music for—a Sfardic or Eastern European story, perhaps—and he would work his magic.

After a while she got still more creative and asked if she could bring in an occasional guest. For one particular story, she wanted a voice with a very special timbre, but where did she know actors in New York? More importantly, how would she find actors she could afford?

She called her friend Maram, whom she had met years before when the two would take their toddlers to the neighborhood playground.

"Maram," she said, after they had exchanged a few pleasantries. "I could use you on the radio, if you're up for it."

"Sure!"

"Oh, and you're still in that acting class, right?" she asked.

"Don't tell me. What kind of voice do you need?"

She laughed. "You know me so well! Deep. I'm doing a King Solomon story, and I need a strong bass voice for the king of the demons."

There was a brief pause, so brief that Peninnah didn't even have a chance to sip her coffee.

"I know just the guy. Fabulous voice. Really resonant. I'll have him call you."

"Wow, you're amazing! Have you ever thought of moonlighting as a casting director?"

Marilyn laughed. "He's not the best-looking guy, though. Crazy tall and a bit nerdy."

"A face for radio is fine!" They agreed that Maram would ask her fellow student after class the following week, and that if he were game, the two would appear together in the segment.

The young, dark-haired man who showed up with Marilyn was gangly, with large, brown eyes. Although not exactly brusque, his manner was business-like. But his voice was sublime, and Peninnah was thrilled. As he rose to leave that evening, she told him how grateful she was that he'd agreed to help out.

"No problem," he said, towering above her. "I'm just happy to have the credit."

"Oh, of course, Jeff," she said as he turned to leave. "What did you say your last name was again?"

"Goldblum."

"Well, good luck, Jeff Goldblum," she said, picking up her script. "You've really got something there. I hope you make it as an actor!"

After the initial thirteen weeks of the series were over, WEVD repeated them. Then the station manager asked for an all-new second series to celebrate the nation's bicentennial. Paul Kwartin was delighted, and Peninnah was over the moon. This time, she decided to prepare literature on the theme of immigration, including a chapter or two from Sholem Aleichem's last, unfinished novel, *Motl the Cantor's Son*, subtitled "The Writings of an Orphaned Boy." It was the story of a young child who comes to New York in the early years of the century and is amazed by not only what he sees—skyscrapers like mountains looming high into the sky, roaring subways and the majestic Statue of Liberty—but also the unfamiliar language and customs.

Peninnah had racked her brain for the perfect title to the theme. When she thought of it at last, she was positively ebullient.

The next morning, she popped her head into the station manager's office.

"Good morning, Peninnah," he said, when she identified herself. "How are you?"

"Got tzu dankn," she replied, entering the room and taking a seat across from him. "Thank God, all is good. And you? Are you well?"

"Come on," he said with a laugh. "You look like the cat who swallowed the canary. What's the news?"

She shook her head. "Nothing much. Just that—I thought of a title! What would you say to calling the new show 'A Bundle of Rainbows'? Think about it." She could feel herself speaking faster in excitement, a train with no stops in sight. "The immigrants came here carrying peklach containing all their worldly goods, the clothing, jewelry, money, candlesticks—all of it. And they brought with them something else, too. They carried a rainbow of hope for a better life in America, like when Noah saw God's rainbow after the flood." When she saw from his face he needed no convincing, she stopped speaking and merely grinned.

Peninnah sat in the studio, content in the knowledge that she had prepared well, going so far as to mark the soundman's script with all the cues in red pencil. And right on cue, there came a snippet of a Yiddish melody that Zalmen Mlotek had chosen to set the scene. Then she read from the book:

"In America, there's a custom: you moofe. That is, you pack up from one apartment to the next. From one street to the next. From one biznes to the next. Everybody has to moofe. If you don't moofe of your own free will, then they make it so you have to."

Most Monday mornings she rode up in the elevator at Stern College with a colleague, a black-hatted, bearded Lubavitcher rabbi named Alter Metzger, who was a professor of religious studies. She was glad they shared a similar schedule; she always enjoyed his company on their brief vertical journeys.

One icy Monday morning, after greeting her as usual, the rabbi said, "Oh, Mrs. Schram, the stories you tell on your radio program! I sit with my children before Shabbes, and we are breathless to learn the end of the tales! Do you listen with your children as well?"

She nodded. "Oh thank you! That's so good to hear! Yes, I sit with my son and daughter in the living room, and we enjoy it together. I have to admit, it makes me *kvell*."

"As well it should." Here the man paused. "But then in the winter the sun sets so early, and we have to turn off the radio. My children insisted I ask you, how did last Friday's story end?"

She was so surprised and gratified that at first she stumbled on her words. Then she asked him how far he and his children had gotten in the story and she briefly supplied the rest. When she reached her floor, she said good-bye and walked down the hall toward her office. That is, she arrived at her office, so she figured she must have walked there. All she could remember was the man's compliment.

Thirty-five years later, she met Rabbi Metzger's family at a party at Stern celebrating his new book. At one point his eldest son, who had become the director of the Lubavitch Center in New York, appeared beside her.

"I have to tell you, Professor Schram, I am so glad to finally meet you. I have been a big fan almost my entire life. My siblings and I loved your stories on the radio!" She smiled, mumbled something by way of thanks, but could see he had more to say.

"I remember one story in particular," he said, "although for the life of me I can't recall the name. I remember there were three brothers who separated for ten years to discover who could return home with the most unusual gift. One bought a magic glass through which he could see all over the kingdom. The second bought a magic carpet. And the third a magic pomegranate. . . ."

This prominent community leader proceeded to stand there, drink in hand, and recount the entire story, scene for scene, as if he had lived it every day for the three-and-a-half decades since she had told it on the air. When he had finished, his eyes retained a faraway look. Whether he was still sitting at his parents' radio or at the sickbed of the princess in the story, Peninnah didn't know. But it was several seconds more before his consciousness returned to the room, to the party, and to her.

"So how did I do?" he asked. When he saw her beaming face he added, "I don't remember the name of the story though."

"It's called 'The Magic Pomegranate.' It's in one of my books."

"You know, Professor Schram, you taught me a lot about giving from that story."

"And Rabbi Metzger, you've taught me a lot about giving from that story, too."

His brows knit in confusion. "What do you mean?"

"Well," she said, "when I was recording that program, I would receive mail, and people would tell me they appreciated this or that story. But you remembered almost verbatim something I told thirty-five years ago!" She shook her head in disbelief. "You taught me that you never know who's going to pick up your gift, and what it's going to mean to them. As an educator, that's one of the most important lessons I could ever receive. I can't thank you enough."

Her final recording session at WEVD had come to an end, and Peninnah was thanking the engineer when she noticed the pile of reel-to-reel tapes from her shows stacked willy-nilly in a corner of the booth.

"Tell me," she asked the young man, "where do you store these?"

"Oh," he said, with a wave of his hand. "We record over them."

She shook her head in disbelief. He might as well have said he was painting over the Mona Lisa. Those tapes, after all, were *her* Mona Lisas.

"You mean you're going to tape over my voice?"

He sighed. "We have to, Mrs. Schram. It's nothing personal. Do you know how expensive these things are?"

"No, I really don't. Is it possible to buy them from the station?"

He counted the reels and did a few calculations on a pad. "You realize that's two hundred bucks!"

"Okay, save them for me, please. I'm going to buy them."

"Sure, but what are you going to do with them?" he asked.

"I don't know. Maybe they'll sit on a shelf in my apartment for years. But I can't let them go."

In fact, the reels sat on her shelf for twenty-five years. Then she learned of the National Jewish Archives of Broadcasting, housed at the Jewish Museum in New York City. In 1997, she donated the reels, along with the scripts.

Unfortunately, she still owes Jeff Goldblum a dollar in royalties.

TWENTY-TWO

In Print

She opened to the first page of the volume on the counter, ran her fingers down the sparkling white pages, and leaned down to breathe in the familiar scent of a brand new book. Peninnah was thoroughly enjoying her browse around the bookstalls at the CAJE conference marketplace. It wasn't just that particular setting, although being at a CAJE event always made her happy. Whenever she happened to be around books, especially on Jewish subjects, she felt a special kind of peace. As long as she could remember, books had been her greatest friends and teachers, healers and nurturers. They were her world.

When she felt someone come up alongside her, she looked up. Her eyes instinctively fell onto the woman's nametag. It read Judyth Groner, and it indicated that she was one of the owners of the well-known Jewish children's publishing company Kar-Ben, whose products Peninnah was examining.

"See anything you like?" Groner asked casually.

"Everything!" she replied. "I'm a storyteller, and I'm always on the lookout for new material."

"I know," the woman said. She had a lovely smile that started in her eyes and spread down her entire face. "You're Peninnah Schram. I was in your session this morning, and I'm wild over your story 'The Big Sukkah.'"

Peninnah put up a warning finger in jest. "Not my story. As a publisher, you know how careful we have to be about giving credit where credit is due! It's by the Yiddish writer Avraham Reisin. I just retold it." In the story, a poor man with many children is humiliated that he doesn't have enough room in his cottage for his extended family to change their minds, as the saying goes. He longs to invite them over to reciprocate for their generosity all year long. But in advance of the eight-day holiday of

Sukkot, he realizes he can build a *sukkah* that covers the vacant lot beside his house, and he joyfully hosts his entire family.

"Well you did a stunning job with it," the woman said. She paused. "Look, I know this is a little abrupt, but have you ever done a book of your own?"

Peninnah blinked. "Funny you should say that. I just signed a contract to do an anthology for Arthur Kurzweil at Jason Aronson."

"Oh that's a long-term project," said the publisher, shaking her head. "This will be much more fun. I'd love you to do just that story as a book for us, if you're interested."

"Am I interested?" Peninnah nodded. "When I love a story, I want the world to hear it—and tell it. If this becomes a book, I would shout it to the mountaintops!"

The publisher laughed. "In that case, let's talk before the conference is over."

It was the summer of 1985. As had become her habit, Peninnah attended the CAJE conference, this time at Northern Illinois University, to catch up with old friends and colleagues, meet new ones, and bask in the warm, welcoming atmosphere of Jewish culture and learning.

When she sat down with Judyth Groner over coffee later that weekend, they discussed the book project in more detail. Over the next few months, she signed a contract and focused her attention on getting the story just right. For the illustrator, she recommended her friend Jacqueline Kahane. She knew that although the book was to be designed using only yellow, black and white, Kahane would be able to make the shtetl scenes sing.

The Big Sukkah appeared in mid-1986. At the CAJE conference that year, held at the University of Maryland, Groner handed Peninnah the book. She held it up, looked at the cover with her name on it and that of her dear friend, turned the pages she now knew so well, closed the book and once again stared at the cover. She was so proud and pleased, it was as though she had given birth all over again. And when she returned home, she wrote to Judyth and her partner Madeline Wikler to thank them, noting the tremendous responsibility she felt that came with being an author.

At the same time, she was working night and day on her anthology, which felt to her sometimes like gestating the literary equivalent of quintuplets.

Peninnah had met Arthur Kurzweil years earlier, at the third CAJE conference in Irvine, California, in 1978. They were standing in line next to each other at the dinner buffet, and they started chatting. When she told him she was a storyteller and he told her that he was editor-in-chief for the publisher Jason Aronson's Judaica section, she had a feeling they would have a lot to say to one another. After the conference ended, they happened, as luck would have it, to be seated next to each other on the flight back to New York. And when they soon learned there would be a two-hour delay during which they could not leave the plane, she had a feeling their friendship was sealed. They talked non-stop for the whole time, exchanging "small world" and "Jewish geography" stories, discovering mutual friends and sharing memories of their personal and professional lives.

The two maintained a friendship over the years, and during one conversation, he suggested she start thinking about a book of stories for older children and adults.

She didn't miss a beat. "As a matter of fact, I've been thinking I'd like to compile an anthology of other people's retellings of Jewish folktales," she said.

He shook his head. "You're a storyteller. I want you to tell the stories your way."

She hummed a little of the signature Sinatra song, and they both laughed. "My way hasn't worked so well in the past," she said.

His brow furrowed. "What do you mean?"

"Just that over the years I've submitted stories to publishers, and they've always complained that they're too oral, too much like people talk, and like a storyteller might tell a story in the oral tradition—not the literary kind of language they were looking for. I've gotten several rejections due to that."

"I think I understand what you mean."

"Well, *I* didn't! I've never thought of myself as a writer, and I'm really not interested in writing literary short stories. I want these stories to read like I'm actually telling them on the stage, so that readers hear them in their hearts and feel like they can retell them. I'm only interested in doing a book if I can tell the stories the way I hear them in my head."

His response was as immediate as hers had been when he first brought up the subject. "Peninnah," he said, his eyes dancing, "that's just what I want, too!"

She was so delighted she could have kissed him.

Life has a habit of getting in the way, but sometimes it's all for the best. It wasn't until another CAJE conference, this time in 1984, that Kurzweil made her a serious proposal to write a book. By then she had a bigger repertoire, hundreds of stories to choose from. She had yards of books of Jewish folktales at her disposal in her home, her office, and at the Stern library. She had the stories she had loved since childhood. And she was always collecting more.

In early 1985, she sent a few of her retellings of stories to Arthur with introductory commentary. He was delighted. Three months later they signed a contract, and she began to work in earnest, all the while continuing to collect stories. Her first stop was the Israel Folklore Archives, introduced to her by the folklorist Howard Schwartz. The Archives were the masterpiece of Israeli folklorist Dov Noy back in 1955, created under the auspices of the Museum of Ethnology and Folklore in Haifa. They contained thousands of traditional stories collected in Israel from members of Jewish communities throughout the world, arranged according to tale type and motif, along with the name and origin of the person who had contributed the tale. Because each story was in Hebrew, her daughter Rebecca, living in Israel, offered to translate many of them for her.

For Peninnah, accessing that treasure trove was like opening a door into an enchanted castle. Her excitement grew with every hour of work she put into the project. She used some of the tales that were translated into English, some that Rebecca translated for her, and others that she had heard from her father: the Elijah stories, of course, and others from the Bible and Talmud. Then she started writing, both her variants of the stories and introductions that included the source, the symbols and concepts, tale types and motifs, and other information—much like her hero, Ruth Rubin the folksinger and ethnomusicologist, had done with her songs. She wrote longhand, on dozens of legal pads, sitting on the sofa at home. Then she had them typed before submitting a few at a time to Arthur.

When he received the first batch, he gave her a call.

"The stories are terrific," he said. Then he paused a beat or two longer than she'd expected.

"Arthur, please. I'm waiting for the other shoe to drop."

He sighed. "Look, don't get me wrong. The introductions are terrific. Like the one for 'The Magic Pomegranate.' It's great the way you explain that you changed the apple in the story to a pomegranate because it symbolizes fertility and plenty. And where do you find material like that King Solomon's crown was supposedly copied from the pomegranate's crown?" It was a rhetorical question, she knew, so she said nothing. "I love that kind of thing."

"But."

"But it doesn't work in the book. I'm telling you, you can't break up the rhythm of the stories with all that detail, like sources and motifs. It kills the flow. Put it into endnotes at the back of the book, like everybody else does."

Her stomach sank. She thought of how she had included Ruth Rubin's story of "The Nigun," and of how she had modeled her work on Rubin's.

"This is a storyteller's book, Arthur. Storytellers need this information. And if some readers aren't interested in the background, they can skip it. It's important that I put the story in context, as I do when I introduce a story in my programs." She took a breath. "Look, Ruth Rubin and Elie Wiesel introduce a song or a story that way. And if it's good enough for them, it's good enough for me."

"Peninnah, look, you know your business, I know mine. You're making a big mistake."

She was so used to giving in to someone in a position of authority that she surprised herself with her reply.

"Again, it's important to me to put the story in context before the reader turns to the story itself. And besides, it's my mistake to make, Arthur." She knew this wasn't entirely the case. The publishing house was backing her with its money, and Arthur with his reputation.

To her relief, he left the statement alone, only to attack on another front.

"And then there's the way you've laid out the type! The book will come out to two thousand pages!"

Within the stories she had used all kinds of typographical tricks: boldface, capital letters, or no caps at all. Sometimes the print looked more like that of a poem than a story, with spaces of different lengths to indicate breath or a pause that indicates emotion, much like the rest symbol in a musical composition. Or words run together without spaces at all, to indicate the rhythm.

"I want to show the orality in a visual way," she said simply. "Remember, I'm not a literary writer. I'm a storyteller. You knew that when you signed the contract. To be fair, you knew that when you met me."

To her relief, Arthur dropped the subject.

As it happened, not long after this conversation, Peninnah attended a dinner party. When she learned that one of the guests was a neurolinguist, she made a point of seeking him out and explaining her typography problem to him.

The man listened politely, and then he shook his head.

"I'm sorry to tell you this," he said, shoving his hands into his pockets, "but your publisher is right. People learn how to decode writing at a very young age, and they learn it in a linear way. You design your book the way you're describing it, and their eyes will fight with their brains. They'll grow tired and stop reading."

She called Arthur the next day and told him what the professor had said. She went on to say that she would use the typographical effect very sparingly, in only a few places.

"But I must maintain the introductions," she said. "On that I can't give in."

He sighed. "How many stories do we have by now?" he asked her. "I've lost count."

"Sixty."

"Okay," he said, clapping his hands with an air of finality. "I think we nearly have enough."

Hanging up the phone, she was glad that she hadn't given in to Arthur's arguments. This was her baby, the culmination of her years of reading, listening to and telling stories. This was her book, and she didn't expect to ever do another. This was what she had to give to the world, and it had to be done just right.

"Why don't you title the book after one of your Elijah stories?" a friend asked one evening after dinner, emerging from the kitchen with two glasses of wine.

She had been sitting on the couch most of the day, a legal pad on her lap, crossing off possible titles for the book as soon as she wrote them. Now she took a sip of the drink that had been handed to her and set it on a coaster on the coffee table.

"Thanks," she said. "For the wine, not the idea, unfortunately. Jason Aronson has a policy about titles. They have to reflect the contents of the book, as opposed to, say, taking the same title of a single story and then adding a subtitle. You're good with words. What do you think?"

"I don't know, how about 'An Ark of Jewish Tales'?"

"Not bad, but, I'd like to convey the idea that the stories are transmitted through time."

"Hmm." Her friend stretched out her legs and took a long swallow from her own glass. "Maybe 'Tales of Our Bubbes'?"

In another day or two, she had an epiphany: *Jewish Stories One Generation Tells Another*. No subtitle necessary.

As the process continued, Peninnah felt as though she were not just writing, but also eating and sleeping the book. The work completely consumed her on an intellectual, emotional, even a physical level, as she tried every evening to relax her eyes and shake off writer's cramp. Then one morning, it hit her on a spiritual level, as well. She woke up thinking about her father, about the way he davened the Hineni prayer on the High Holidays, pleading with God to accept his prayers as a shaliach tzibor. That prayer always stayed with her, how he sobbed at the seriousness of his request and the weight of his responsibility, how it seemed like the fate of the world hung in the balance.

The prayer had always haunted her, and that morning, opening her eyes to her sunny bedroom, she thought of what the word Hineini meant: Here I am, as in *Breishit*, the first book of the Tana*ch*, when God asks Adam where he is. God knows everything, she reflected, as she always did when she heard the prayer. But he needs Adam to be fully present and accountable, ready for whatever lies ahead. And so she set out to create her own storyteller's prayer, based on the model of Chasidic storytellers, saying Hineni, here I am.

Feeling reverential and heartfelt, hoping to mold the personal with a sense of community, she began her prayer with the words, "*Rebono shel olam*, God of the Universe, listen to my heart and my voice as I stand before you, wanting to tell our story." This would become her storyteller's prayer. It would become her guide for life, reminding her of her responsibility as a Jewish storyteller.

Arthur immediately pronounced it perfect, and she was delighted.

She was sitting at her desk at Stern poring over her manuscript one afternoon after classes when Arthur called. He wanted a prominent person to supply a foreword for the book. Who should it be?

She had no idea. She threw out a few names, but he wasn't interested.

Suddenly he said, "Wait, how about Elie Wiesel?"

Elie Wiesel had recently won the Nobel Peace Prize as a noted activist, author and lecturer on the Holocaust. She had met him the previous decade quite by chance in the midst of a normal workday at Stern College, when she happened to walk into the main office for something, and the Dean's office door was ajar.

"Peninnah!" Dean Mirsky had called out. "Come here, please! There's someone I want you to meet." She stepped in and saw a slight, wiry man in his mid-forties, with wispy dark hair and a pale, lined face.

"Elie Wiesel, this is Peninnah Schram."

He extended his hand, and when he took hers, she nearly felt the bones crunch at the strength of his handshake. But the thrill that went through her had nothing to do with the pressure. It was the way he looked at her, as though he were drinking her in. It was the way he said, "Ah, Peninnah," as though they were already old, dear friends.

She began to attend his annual lecture series at the 92nd Street Y, and in the next three decades, she missed very few. Every time he saw her at the reception afterward, he would greet her with those same words, "Ah, Peninnah," sometimes shaking her hand, at other times kissing her in the European style, on both cheeks.

She was hesitant to disturb the great man, but Arthur insisted, saying, "It's not many authors who have a close tie to Elie Wiesel. And I happen to be a friend of his, too."

To her surprise, when she called, Wiesel picked up immediately.

"Professor Wiesel, it's Peninnah Schram from Stern College. The storyteller. We met in Dean Mirsky's office recently. How are you?"

"Ah, Peninnah! So good to hear from you. What can I do for you?"

When she told him, he replied that he would be delighted to write the foreword, as soon as she sent him the galleys. She told him when that would be, thanked him and hung up. She called Arthur right away.

"So it's a yes, I gather?" he said, in lieu of hello.

"It's a yes," she said. "I can't believe it."

There was a small silence. "Peninnah, are you crying?"

She reached for her handkerchief. "Arthur, it's a yes!"

Weeks later, Wiesel called to tell her he was being sent to Poland for a UN meeting, so he was unable to write the foreword. She tried not to sound too disappointed, and in truth, she wasn't. She was devastated.

She was just about to say thank-you and hang up when he said, "But I have an idea. I've got an essay that was published in a magazine, it's called "A Storyteller's Prayer," about Rabbi Abraham Joshua Heschel of

Apt, who you undoubtedly know was a great teller of tall tales. What do you think?"

The coincidence, she thought, was too amazing to contemplate. Especially since he knew nothing about the prayer that she herself had written. She thanked him profusely. The following week she received the essay, just as Wiesel had promised. It would be a perfect segue to her own Storyteller's Prayer.

Peninnah sent Arthur more and more stories and commentary, five or ten in a package. Each time, she received a note from him acknowledging receipt, and thanking her. In June 1986, he wrote about the stories, "Am I getting boring when I say that they are superb? You have such a gift, such an ear for how a sentence, a paragraph, and a story must sound. This book is going to be a treasure."

Then came the day she received the laid-out text in the form of galleys. As she pored over them, she felt a pang. To her dismay, she realized that the book was not complete. She needed to add more folkloric details to the commentaries, in order to situate the stories within the classification system of world folktales. Never having had a class in folklore, she was teaching herself a new framework for understanding narrative.

Arthur said fine, but in order to meet his deadline, she had less than a week to integrate the material. She consulted the appropriate references and called upon a folklorist friend to help complete the work. Five days should have been more than enough time, but this was no ordinary week. Rebecca was getting married. In Israel.

Peninnah arrived at the airport for her overnight flight to Tel Aviv. As soon as she was settled in her seat, she flipped down the tray table and fanned out the galleys and notes around her. For nearly the entire eleven-hour flight, she penned her additions into the printed text. On the return trip, with a newly married daughter and completed manuscript behind her, she felt exhausted, but exhilarated.

That was in May. Two months later, Rebecca and her new husband Emile paid a visit to Peninnah in Yorktown, where she was now living, for a wedding reception for the dozens of friends and relatives who hadn't been able to get to Israel. The party flowed throughout the backyard, onto the paved driveway, the stone stairs, the flower garden and the wisteria arbor. The caterer set up tables in the carport, and they hired a trio to play chamber music, as well as the traditional *horah*. It was a beautiful summer day, the sky cloudless and bright.

When Arthur Kurzweill walked into the yard, she could see he had something in his hand. Peninnah walked over to him, expecting to tell him where to put the gift. Then she saw what it was he was holding. The first book off the presses, a rich, blue jacket around a hefty, five hundred-page volume. She reached for it and could barely hold on without losing her grip. Peninnah looked down at the book, then back up at her editor with tears in her eyes.

By the time they put out the paperback edition, she was a pro at the publishing game. And when Jason Aronson published her next book, *Eight Tales for Eight Nights: Stories for Chanukah*, in 1990, she was well into her next after that, *Tales of Elijah the Prophet*, with a foreword by Dov Noy.

TWENTY-THREE
Strengthen Yourself

Peninnah sat at the vanity in the synagogue's little dressing room, staring at her large eyes, her newly reddened lips. She had to admit she looked glamorous with a little more makeup than usual. A friend had told her she was positively incandescent. But did she look like a bride? She certainly didn't feel like one. Except for the jitters, that is. She held up a quivering hand, marveling at it as though it belonged to someone else. Until now, her feet had been squarely set on the ground. So what was this? Nerves. She would have thought getting married again would be easier than the first time around, but in fact, it was anything but.

When she walked down the aisle for the second time, in June 1974, her mother's arm was interlinked in hers, and the five children of the bride and groom watched their approach from the front of the sanctuary. About seventy-five guests sat in the pews, half the number that had attended her first wedding sixteen years earlier. She carried an opulent bouquet that offset the silky rainbow pastels of the dress she had bought at B. Altman's for the occasion. The groom's pale-blue suit was perfect for June, but she had nearly thrown a fit when she saw his tie. It was a pastel plaid and completely inappropriate for the occasion, she had told him that morning. Only after he explained that he had had no idea what her gown looked like and wanted to be sure not to clash did she relent—and soon realize that actually it was perfect.

It wasn't that she meant to draw comparisons; she simply couldn't help herself. When she had married Irv, her father was alive, and Judaism had permeated every aspect of the event. This time, although the rabbi conducted a Jewish service in a synagogue, the atmosphere couldn't have been more different. When she had married Irv, she was a young woman blissfully in love. It wasn't that she didn't love Jerry; he was a fine man. They shared the same values. He would make a good husband and father. But she was not really in love. Not like she had once been.

They had met half a year earlier, on a brisk winter evening in 1973, at the iconic Russian Tea Room on West 57th Street. He was a blind date, one of a number of men she had been fixed up with since Irv's death. Some were more interesting than others: a passionate dancer, a man who sent two dozen roses the morning after they met, an orthodontist. No one had quite fit.

The restaurant was beyond her means, but she had always liked the idea that its founders were former members of the Russian Imperial Ballet, and that it was still a meeting place for celebrities. From the décor to the menu, it had a certain class that married tradition and modernity in a way that appealed to her. She knew that over the years, it had catered to the tastes of celebrities as wide-ranging as Arthur Rubinstein and Tallulah Bankhead.

At the thought of the actress, her mind jumped to the joke she was telling when she met Irv, which felt like half a lifetime before. She thought of sharing it with Jerry, looked at the fit, balding stranger sitting across from her, and dismissed the idea with a quick shake of her head. Her date looked up from his blintzes, his eyebrows raised in curiosity. But she said nothing.

Jerry was five years older, a widowed optometrist with three teenaged children. They'd been introduced by a friend at the Society for the Advancement of Judaism, the well-known Reconstructionist synagogue on the Upper West Side. She learned that he had a passion for climatology and was a fairly serious swimmer. He also had a lovely home in Yorktown, he told her, less than an hour from the city.

The Tea Room date went well, and when he dropped her off at her Manhattan apartment that evening, he said he'd like to see her again. He began to make the drive in from Westchester on a regular basis for theater and movie dates. She knew almost immediately that she could never be in love with him as she had with Irv, but she soon grew to like and respect him.

After a few weeks of dating, he said at dinner one night, "What would you say, hypothetically, if I were to ask you to marry me?"

She reached for her water glass, took a sip, and placed it down carefully beside her plate.

"I'm not ruling it out," she said, looking into his blue eyes. "But I can't make a commitment at this point. I'd need to get to know you a little better."

He waited two months; then he proposed. This time, she said yes.

Jerry was an intelligent man, and supportive of her work, providing useful criticism on her manuscripts and good suggestions for book titles. He formed a close relationship with her children, especially with Mordechai, who she felt needed a mature man in his life. Sometimes she thought Jerry had more to say to Rebecca than he did to his own children. In turn, his daughter interviewed Peninnah for a class project and wrote about how beautiful and interesting she was. He was less religiously observant than she, but he did get into the spirit, building such a wonderful sukkah on the deck of the house that every fall they'd throw an Open Sukkah Party.

The chicken that Shabbes evening was tender, and seasoned perfectly, if she did say so herself. Jerry was helping himself to a second portion when he said, "Oh, I almost forgot. How would you like a few more Jewish folktale books to add to your collection?"

She sipped her wine. "Well, I only have about a thousand, so I guess I could use a few more to complete my collection. Whose are they?"

"Molly Picon's."

She stared at him. "What?"

"Didn't I tell you she sometimes comes to the office?"

"No, dear, I think I would have remembered if one of the most famous Yiddish actresses of all time was a patient of yours. Did you know I saw her in 'Milk and Honey' about ten years ago? I took my father. Not exactly his cup of tea, but she was unforgettable. And that great old movie 'Yiddle With His Fiddle' where she dressed up as a fiddler. . . . " Her voice trailed off as she pictured some of the scenes from the film.

Jerry swallowed a bite of chicken and said, "Well, anyway, she has a cottage in Mahopac, and she comes into the office now and then when she's around. So today she was asking what's new, and I told her we were married last year. Naturally she asked about you, and I said you were a storyteller. She got very excited and wants to give you some books before she closes up her cottage. Her husband died recently, and she doesn't want to keep the house anymore."

"Oh Jerry, I can't believe it! What a little ball of fire she was onstage!" She paused. "So sad she lost her husband. I remember reading about that in the paper."

It was just a twenty-minute drive from Yorktown to Mahopac. Peninnah gazed out at the buds sprouting on the early spring trees, their branches raised into the velvet blue sky as if conducting invisible birds.

"She was in the movie of 'Fiddler on the Roof,' wasn't she, Jerry? I think she played Yente."

"Mmmm."

The cottage was like something out of a postcard, she thought, charming and well kept. Molly Picon came to the door to welcome them. She was even tinier than Peninnah had expected, but her warmth and energy, all the more impressive for a woman in her late seventies, more than made up for her small stature. Before leading them inside, she showed them the swimming pool, which was pure shtick. At the shallow end, the height was replaced with the word *"Oy."* The next milestone was *"Oy vey,"* and at the deep end, someone had painted *"Gevalt."*

"Come in, come in," the star said at last, beckoning them to the door. "Take a look at the books while I go get us some iced tea."

An entire wall of the main room was filled floor to ceiling with nothing but books of all colors, shapes and sizes. Peninnah and Jerry just stared. When Picon returned with the tea she said, "Now, now, don't be shy. Here, let me show you a few things." She reached for a ladder, climbed up in double time, and commenced to pull books from the shelves and hand them to her two guests.

"Here are some folktales, ooh, and here are stories by Peretz and Sholem Aleichem. You like them, yes?"

"I love them!" But contrary to her words, Peninnah shook her head. "Really, Miss Picon, I'll only take a few."

"Bubbele, it's Molly, please! And that *Legends of the Jews* by Ginzberg—you can't just take a few; there are seven of them! Three volumes of *Mimekor Yisrael*; you know that classic, I'm sure."

"Yes, of course!"

The lady of the house kept pulling out books and handing them to Jerry long after Peninnah had collapsed in wonder on the couch. She opened one of the folktale anthologies when she saw an inscription and gasped. It was made out to the actor Jacob Kalich, who had been married to her hostess.

"Oh, Molly, this one is inscribed from the author to your husband! I can't take it! We are so sorry for your loss!"

She shrugged. "Thank you. But what do you suppose he's going to do with them where he is? Trust me, you are doing us both a mitzvah."

After loading several dozen books and chatting a bit more, Peninnah and Jerry said their good-byes.

"Miss Picon," Peninnah began, taking the older woman's hand. "I mean Molly. I don't know how to express what an honor it was to meet you. And these books! A treasure. I really can't thank you enough."

The great actress looked at the two of them and smiled. "Just do me a favor, will you? Take care of each other." She winked at Jerry. "It's not easy to find a good optometrist, you know!"

Mama was fading. It was hard for Peninnah to see her on her visits to New London, so diminished had her energy become. Her mother's old saying, which she had often used with a sigh in reference to her father, now echoed in her brain: *Vos kumt fun a mensch.* What happens to a person.

When Papa had endured his last illness years earlier, her mother had nursed him around the clock, preparing for him special teas and chicken soup, bathing him and keeping him as comfortable as she could. It had been hard on her, but true to form, she never complained. After his death, she went on with her apartment house rentals. She wouldn't downsize. Refusing to throw out a thing of Papa's, she said, as always, "Don't throw anything out; it will come in handy!"

She was in many ways still her usual stoic self, practical and realistic, not given to the dreamy sensitivity of her intuitive, creative husband. She was not an artist; neither was she an idealistic Zionist. She was an American businesswoman: all *tachlis*, substance. She was blunt. She didn't sugarcoat; she embraced the rough edges and dealt with them, one by one, in her efficient way.

From time to time Peninnah would try to engage her in conversation about the old days, asking her about her hometown of Lepl in White Russia. She brought up a story she had heard in her youth about one of her mother's exotic dresses that she wore to shul. Mama's brother Irving had supposedly lifted an elegant gown from a train carrying the deposed Tsarina's wardrobe, and that dress was apparently so luxurious and full it had been turned into three outfits: one for her, one for her mother, and the third for her sister. But her mother was no longer interested in old stories; more and more she inhabited the here and now.

Mama grew thin, refusing to follow her own advice to mourners to keep up their strength. (Shtark zekh, she always said. Strengthen your-self.) And yet, somehow she did have strength, although from whence it came, her daughter had no idea. Peninnah worried about her elderly mother's safety in that big Victorian house on Channing Street, but again and again Mama refused to relocate to a smaller home, one that would have been easier to manage. The stairway and rooms, the decorative objects and furniture—these were the trappings of her castle. She sat on her porch in the nice weather, proudly surveying her small empire. Only in rare moments would she confide to her daughter how lonely she was. *Alein vi a shtein*. Alone like a stone.

In 1978, Mama was admitted to the hospital. Peninnah made the two-hour drive from Yorktown to New London every second day after work, as she had already done for some time. Her mother was in the hospital about a week when she climbed into the car with the feeling that something was terribly wrong. It started in the pit of her stomach and radiated up her chest to her throat, then kept on rising. Her head was pounding by the time she reached the hospital room and saw Joe sitting in a chair by the bed.

"You just missed her," he said in a matter-of-fact tone. No hello, no emotion, and certainly no hug. "Come on, let's go to the office and take care of the paperwork."

"Give me five minutes with her," she said tersely. All her life her mother had wanted them to get along, and now that she was gone they were still fighting.

"Come *on*!" he said, waving her away. "It's late. Let's get out of here. She sure won't know you're here."

"I said five minutes!" She heard her voice take on the tone she only used with her brother, and she was grateful that he walked into the hall without another word. She wanted to photograph Mama in her mind. She wanted to mourn not only Mama, but also her own life in New London, her life as a daughter.

As soon as she arrived back at her mother's house, she called Jerry. He picked up on the first ring.

"My mother is dead," she said dully. "I missed her by minutes. Same as with my father."

"Oh no, I'm sorry," he said. "She was quite a woman."

"I'll need you to come tomorrow, of course. To bring the children. With something appropriate for them to wear. And a black dress for me."

"Of course. I'll be there soon as I can."

One thing about Jerry, she could always count on him. He arrived late the next afternoon, with the children, subdued and affectionate, in tow. In the midst of the funeral preparations, which had to be made as swiftly as possible, she was grateful that she had her own family to think about besides her mother, her children to feed and put to bed.

When she and Jerry bedded down for the night, she turned to him.

"I was thinking. Did I ever show you the photo of me when I was about twelve, wearing a lace shawl over my head and posing exactly like she did in a photo of her at that age?" He nodded. "Everyone always said I looked like her, but I never saw it."

"She had a beautiful face, like you. A unique style. Like you. She was an original. Also like you. Her own person."

She smiled. Then she whispered, "Now I'm nobody's little girl."

"I'm here, Peninnah. I'll always be here. Just don't ever leave me. You know I too have had so much death in my life."

After that there was a silence, as there often was with Jerry. It wasn't particularly uncomfortable, but she couldn't bear silence just now. She began to chatter.

"I've been so busy with my career," she said, easing herself from his arms to reach for a tissue from the nightstand. "That day Maram gave Rebecca a children's tape recorder, you remember? Maybe that was before your time? Anyway, I took it to Mama to record her memories, but it broke. I was going to buy a real recorder, but I never got around to it. I never even recorded her or wrote down her life story."

"She knew you were busy. And she was so proud of you, of all you accomplished."

In the midst of the tears trailing down her cheeks, she managed a smile. "As long as I was a good wife and mother first, of course."

He stroked her cheek. "Of course."

Joe hadn't changed much over the years, Peninnah reflected. He insisted that the children not stay for shiva. It was, he said, either them or him.

How could he not be at his mother's shiva? In a gesture of accommodation she immediately regretted, she sent her family home after just a few days. Jerry was, she often told her friends, a good helpmeet, supportive and steadfast. And the children were her life.

On one of Peninnah's trips back to New London to go through her mother's things, she and Joe, who still spoke as little as possible, went together to her mother's lawyer to discuss her will. Not wanting to have anything more to do with him now that their parents were gone, she decided to sell her brother her half of the house, for less, she soon realized, than it was worth. Joe went on to sell the house to a doctor, who sold it to the Jewish Federation several years later. When she read in the local Jewish paper that Federation had held a ceremony to affix their mezuzah, she wept with joy. Perfect. Absolutely perfect.

Meanwhile, her teaching was going well. She regularly performed at festivals, spoke at conferences and published in academic journals. She greeted every morning wondering what new professional pleasure the day would bring. And Jerry was right there to toast every book, every promotion. The years passed, and they found their rhythm.

Early one evening in 1990, Peninnah picked up the phone to hear Elie Wiesel's voice. He was calling, he said, to invite her to give a talk to his graduate seminar at Boston University on the Power of Story. She didn't have to consult her calendar to say yes. He explained whom to talk to about working out the flight and car service expenses. When she hung up the phone, she turned to Jerry.

"You'll never guess who just invited me to teach his graduate seminar at Boston University."

"Umm, Elie Wiesel?"

"You heard me!"

"That's an amazing honor, Peninnah."

"Do you—do you want to come with me?"

He thought a moment, then shook his head. "You know I'd love to, but I think this is something you should do on your own. This is your world, not mine."

When the car service delivered her at the university building where the class was held, she was anxious to get started. A staff person was waiting to escort her to the great man's private suite of offices. She vaguely wondered why, when he was certainly out of town. But there he was, waiting for her.

At the unexpected sight of him, she felt a little faint. "Professor Wiesel, how are you?"

"Ah, Peninnah." He gave her a warm hug and kissed her twice on both cheeks. "I'm so happy to see you! How was the flight?"

"It was wonderful, thank you! I'm delighted to see you. I was sure you'd be away, and I was here as the pinch-hitter."

He laughed. "Let's go over to the classroom. We don't have much time."

Listening to his opening remarks, she was glad that she had started the tape before her own talk began. He introduced her to the forty or so graduate students, sitting informally around several tables, with the words:

"This book," he said, holding up *Jewish Stories One Generation Tells Another*, is equivalent to a doctoral thesis. It contains many stories of brave, courageous, active men and women, and brilliant commentary about them. And here is the brave, courageous, active woman who researched and wrote it. Ladies and gentleman, please welcome Professor Peninnah Schram."

"Thank you," she said nervously when the applause subsided. She silently berated herself to stop shaking. It happened more often than she cared to admit, this feeling of not being good enough. You are not shy little Penny Manchester from New London, she told herself. You are a college professor. A colleague of Elie Wiesel's. You deserve those things he said about you. You have earned your reputation.

"And thank you, Professor Wiesel." She looked at him, and he smiled. To the class, she said, "There's an anecdote about a Chasid who would visit his rebbe in a distant country just to watch him tie his shoelaces. To tell you the truth," here she turned to her friend, seated next to where she stood, "I would have come just to watch Elie Wiesel tie his shoelaces."

At that, Wiesel stretched out his left leg and pulled up his trousers a few inches to reveal shiny brown loafers. The class broke into laughter.

Within the space of a very few words, her nervousness melted away. For the next ninety minutes, she forgot all about shy little Penny Manchester from New London. She was Professor Peninnah Schram, teaching about cante fables, the stories that contained songs. Wiesel was seated beside her, watching with a thoughtful expression, and she could feel him drinking in her words. Never had she experienced someone who could listen like that.

Hours later she flew home to New York with mixed emotions: as sad that it was over as she was relieved that it had gone so well. When she reached the house, she was so energized at the success of her trip that she relived every moment of it for her family until late into the evening. It had been, she told them, one of the greatest experiences of her life.

As Peninnah's star continued to rise, Jerry never ceased to applaud her. He dutifully drove her to bookings in the tri-state area and sold her books and recordings without complaint. At the same time, he began to find himself less and less interested in remaining in the background, whether at her professional events or at dinner parties, where guests were invariably more interested in her teaching and storytelling than in his optometry or amateur climatology. Finally, when he was considering retirement, he announced his desire to rusticate on the land he owned in Vermont, and to spend the winters relaxing in Florida. He also had a hankering to travel to the Galapagos Islands.

She wanted no part of it.

"Look, Jerry, I like a long walk as well as the next New Yorker," she said slowly. "But roughing it is not my idea of a good time. I prefer a comfortable bed, not a sleeping bag in a tent, or a bunk bed in a cottage in the woods. Neither are long, lazy days at the beach my fantasy. And the Galapagos? Really? You knew when you married me that I was a city girl, Jerry. Sure I would go to Paris anytime, but not on a boat. As you may recall, I get seasick. Remember that short ride from Cancun to Cozumel when I lost my lunch?"

Not meeting her gaze, he began to pace the living room floor, while she sat ramrod straight on the couch.

At last he said, "You were born in New London, Connecticut, for God sakes! Not midtown Manhattan!"

She shook her head. "I'm not ready for that retirement life yet, if I ever will be. I want to keep doing what I'm doing, teaching at Stern, where I hope to become full professor some day, and performing, writing books. Besides, Rebecca lives in Israel now. If I travel out of the country for anything apart from work, that's where I want to be."

"Now let me get this straight," he said. He had stopped his pacing to reach down and flip through a magazine; now he tossed it in the general direction of the coffee table and glared down at her.

"You're choosing between your career and your kids on one hand and me on the other." He turned away from her and looked out onto the deck. "In point of fact, you've already made your choice."

She didn't respond for several minutes. Then she said, "You know, we've been going on our separate paths for years, and it's been okay. Not ideal, but it worked for us. But now you're asking me to give up my path to join yours, all on your terms. We've never talked about what was going on. But it looks as though we're at a fork in the road.

Nothing more was said between them on the subject for weeks. Then one evening on the ride home from picking her up at the train station, he pulled the car over to the side of the road and told her he wanted a divorce.

She felt her stomach heave, but all she could say was, "Oh."

They drove the rest of the way home in silence. Once in the house, he pulled together his pajamas, pillow and a blanket and went off to sleep in the den. For her part, she lay awake all night, not knowing what she was feeling. Rage? He had known who and what she was when he married her. Pain? How could he appear to so easily go on with his life without her? Anger? Yes, she was angry that she would once again be without a life partner. She had never planned to live her life alone. She heard her mother's voice. What happens to a person.

Still, she told herself, sometime before dawn, this was also something of a gift. *I am getting my life back.* She could now go to Israel to visit her daughter and her family at a moment's notice, without feeling guilty for abandoning her husband. And she knew that their children would always be a part of both their lives. That was the most important thing. As she was to say to family and friends, it had been a good run.

Jerry didn't move out; the house on the hill with the wonderful view was his, after all, and she accepted the arrangement without complaint. Fortunately, she had never let go of the apartment in New York that she had shared with Irv, in part so that she could stay overnight when she needed to be in the city, in part because it was rent-controlled so extremely cheap, and in part so that Mordechai could live there when he graduated college and lived in the city. Now, she happily moved back fulltime to the neighborhood she had known as a young wife and mother. In a short time, it felt like home again. It was 1997, nearly the dawn of a new millennium. At sixty-two, her future was hers to invent.

The last time she saw Jerry was at a family wedding in December 2018. They barely spoke, but he did walk over to her at the dinner to tell her how wonderful she looked, and how beautifully she had told the story under the chuppah. He died of leukemia less than a year later, at age eighty-eight.

TWENTY-FOUR

Here I Am

Peninnah leaned back in her seat and let the speaker's precise, clipped tones wash over her. She was as entranced by his manner as by his subject. Although her presence at the event was in fact a mitzvah for a colleague, she truly loved attending talks like this. She was always astounded at how much there was to know in the world, how well read and well traveled some people were. How many experiences there were to enjoy, how much more there was to know. She knew she would never stop learning.

Merkin Concert Hall on West 67th Street is not as well known as Lincoln Center, but what it lacks in brand name appeal, it makes up for in intimacy and acoustics. That evening in 1990, she attended a presentation on Turkish Jews, delivered by a fellow YU professor. Sitting in the balcony scanning her program before the lecture began, she was pleasantly surprised to find that during the second half of the evening there was to be a performance by a classical guitarist and bass-baritone named Gerard Edery.

She read a little about Edery during intermission. Born in Casablanca and raised in Paris and New York City, he had a sterling reputation both for performance and composition, particularly for his interpretations of his Sephardic musical heritage.

She found the music to be a delightful mix of Ladino and Jewish rhythm and melody. In the lobby afterward, as the performer sold and signed his CDs, she got a closer look at his 6'4" frame, shaved head and handsome, olive-skinned face. Passing him on the way to the door, she said, "Mr. Edery, I just wanted to tell you that you have two magnificent instruments there in your voice and your guitar. That was an absolutely magnetic performance. Thank you so much!"

"Thank you!" he replied. She could tell from his face that he was both tired and exhilarated after the show, and she could certainly relate. "That's so nice of you to say. May I ask who you are? Are you a performer as well?"

"My name is Peninnah Schram. I'm a storyteller."

In an instant the lines of fatigue vanished, as though a veil had been lifted from his face.

"A storyteller! I've always wanted to work with a storyteller! A professional performer? On stage?"

She shrugged. "Well, if you consider a professional someone who's performed at the Pete Seeger festivals, as well as others in four states, the Limmud conferences and conferences all over the world, who founded a Jewish Storytelling Center at the 92nd Street Y. . . ."

He started to laugh. She felt as though the waiting fans encircling him had melted away, and they two were alone in the hall.

"Yes, I guess that sort of makes you a professional. Hey, are you telling stories anywhere nearby where I can come see you perform?"

Her eyes shone. "As a matter of fact, I'll be appearing on West 70th, at Congregation Shearith Israel, in two weeks. And of course I'll be telling Sephardic folktales."

"It's a date," he said, reaching for her hand. "I'm going to come and hear you. Who knows? Maybe we can work together."

She must have written her number on the brochure she handed him, along with the day and time and location of the event, but she didn't recall. All that remained with her as she emerged onto the noisy street was the feeling of wonderment and anticipation. Wouldn't that be amazing if it worked out?

Shearith Israel, founded by Portuguese and Spanish settlers in 1654, is considered the first Jewish congregation in North America. Its current, neoclassical-style building on Central Park West, built in 1897, boasts Tiffany glass windows and showcases a wealth of ritual objects. It was a wonderful place to work, and her show that day, sponsored by the synagogue's Sephardic Center, went particularly well; the crowd response was dazzling. Afterward, Gerard Edery waited for her to finish chatting with a few friends. When at last they stood alone, he said, "I love the way you tell stories. Let's figure out a program we can do together."

This time, it was she who was tired and exhilarated. "It would be a pleasure," she said simply. "Let's talk tomorrow." When they said their good-byes, she felt her heart thundering in her chest. She thought: This is a miracle!

And so they made an appointment by telephone to meet. Over tea, he asked her about the stories he had heard her tell, and then about the organized storytelling world. She told him about the National Association for the Preservation and Perpetuation of Storytelling, known as NAPPS, and its National Storytelling Festival. She talked about Laura

Simms, Roslyn Bresnick-Perry, Gioia Timpanelli, Diane Wolkstein, and the other tellers at the New York Storytelling Center. She told him about her own Jewish Storytelling Center and the Jewish Storytelling Network at CAJE. Through it all, he watched her as though transfixed, as though she had taken him down a rabbit hole into a new and mysterious world.

Soon they began to brainstorm, to interweave their repertoires and their instruments like braiding dough into challah. They called themselves the Minstrel and the Storyteller, and when they were ready, they were booked without delay at Shearith Israel, followed by venues in the greater New York City tri-state area, at CAJE conferences in various states, as well as venues in Michigan, Texas, and Colorado. Later, they put out a CD. Perhaps the pinnacle of their collaboration, however, was in Berlin, when they performed at the Jewish Cultural Festival, the *Judische Kulturtage*, both at Rykestrasse Synagogue, and the Jewish Museum, where they were joined by Arabic storyteller Maha Alussi. The crowds stomped their feet, giving standing ovations and demanding encores. The events were so momentous for the community that Peninnah was interviewed in three local newspapers.

One morning in 1995, she picked up the jangling telephone and uttered a small "Oh!" when she heard who was on the other end. It was the director of the Covenant Foundation, informing her that she had won the highest honor in Jewish education, the prestigious Covenant Award.

"This is the very heart of our work," the woman said. She also said something about heritage, continuity, identity, and large cash prizes to her, to an organization of her choice, and to Stern College. Peninnah dutifully wrote it all down; she knew she couldn't have repeated it afterward without her notes to save her life.

When she hung up the receiver, tears spilled down her cheeks. She closed her eyes very tightly and said a prayer of thanks. She thought of her parents, of what it would have meant to them to see this, and of what she owed them for helping to make it possible. She called her daughter in Israel.

"Mom? We just talked yesterday! Are you okay?"

"Am I okay? I will never be anything but okay for the rest of my life!" She was still holding the piece of paper she had used to take notes from the conversation. "I won the Covenant Award! Remember I told you I'd been nominated? Well I won it! I won it! Oh honey, I can't believe it! This Covenant Foundation gives only three of these awards for outstanding educator every year. And I'm a recipient as a storyteller-educator. As a storyteller!"

"That's terrific! And of course you should believe it. Who else should they give it to, I ask you?"

"Well, you've got a point there. I mean, after all, I *am* the only Jewish educator in the world, that's true." She laughed. "So now I've got a gala to go to. I think I'll buy a new dress. Oh, so much to do!"

In the time between the phone call and the gala, she read the letters of support that people had sent the Foundation. The lines danced in her head:

Her friend and editor Arthur Kurzweil had told the committee, "Peninnah Schram has almost single-handedly revived an active tradition of Jewish storytelling in our generation. . . ." Her dear storyteller friend Gerry Fierst wrote, "For twenty years she has spread Jewish culture, encouraged Jewish education, and made Jewish storytelling integral to our family and communal lives. . . ." Colleague and friend Carolyn Starman Hessel of the Jewish Book Council wrote, "At a time when the unique culture of the groups within the Jewish community is fading, Peninnah is passing on their stories to future generations. . . ."

She read the words over and over, till she had nearly memorized them, so touched was she by the sentiments. It was Elie Wiesel's letter, however, that floored her:

"Last year we were privileged to have Peninnah visit our class, 'The Power of the Story.' My students did not stop talking about her and her stories. They had been assigned to read her book, but I don't think they knew how inspired they would be by her active participation in the class. Her presence was deeply felt by all of us. . . ."

By the time she rose to speak at the event, she was intoxicated, not by the wine, although that was in abundance, but by the praise. As she spoke, she could almost see her kvelling parents in front of her. She told the group:

"I know that with these Jewish stories I have been nourished and nurtured in my understanding of people and the wisdom of Judaism. And so I hope to enrich others with these stories.

"Several years ago I realized that before I tell stories I needed to have a prayer, much like the cantors and the Chasidim who pray before their prayers. I must remember why I am telling these stories, so that I can become ready to tell the stories, and also to prepare my audience to listen and receive the stories. . . . .

"One of the most awesome prologue prayers is the Hineni, the prayer the cantor chants before the main service on Rosh Hashanah and Yom Kippur. For me the Hineni evokes special associations because my father was a cantor. I see him, in my memory's eye, standing in the doorway at the rear of the synagogue, Ahavath Chesed, in New London, Connecticut, waiting to enter. He was waiting for the congregation to sense his presence, to become ready to hear his opening prayer, Hineni —'Here I stand'—in which he would ask God to consider him worthy and to accept his prayers and to accept him as a messenger who sends up the prayers of the people. . . . And so, too, did we all chant with him and call out, Hineni."

Peninnah had started to attend Kabbalat Shabbat services at the nearly two-hundred-year-old Congregation B'nai Jeshurun on West 88th Street in the late nineties. "BJ," as it was known, was within walking distance from her house, and her son, who had by then become a cantor like his grandfather, occasionally davened with Rabbi Rolando Matalon at the bimah. After her divorce in 1997, when she moved back to West End Avenue full time, Peninnah became a member.

Over the years, the rabbi asked her to do a storytelling presentation or a talk about the oral tradition, or she herself would attend classes. He asked her to create a video of her retelling of the story of the Biblical Peninnah and Channah for Rosh Hashanah, when the story is read in the synagogue. She and Gerard Edery performed at BJ as well, along with Edery's ensemble, presenting a full concert of stories interwoven with music and songs in the splendidly appointed Byzantine/Moorish BJ sanctuary. That was in November, 2001. Her life, it seemed, had come full circle.

As her reputation grew and her skills deepened, Peninnah found that she was becoming more and more entwined in the lives and careers of her students, and that they were fast becoming colleagues, in large part due to her efforts. She had an extravagantly talented student named Amy who "majored in Schram," having taken every course she taught. Peninnah served as her friend and mentor for decades after, assisting with her women's theater group and attending her wedding. She taught Naftali, a young man at the Yeshiva University graduate school, whose father was chief rabbi of Turkey and who was studying to be a rabbi himself at Yeshiva University. He went on to contribute "Haberes Buenos," a story of his grandmother's for her anthology *Chosen Tales*. And there was another graduate student named Eliezer, who was so moved by a lesson of hers about how folktales are transposed from place to place that it led him to write "The Untouched Oil" for the same book.

In addition, she was honored more and more by her peers. Along with the Covenant Award from the Covenant Foundation, the national storytelling organization gave her the Regional Leadership Award, the Circle of Excellence Award, and the Talking Leaves Award for her numerous publications. Then, at age sixty-nine, she received the organization's Lifetime Achievement Award.

At that ceremony, she looked out at the smiling faces of colleagues and friends, and said:

"You know, I often put lipstick on without a mirror. People are surprised to realize that I know where my lips are without a mirror. In fact, a woman who saw me do it once even gave me her Italian leather lipstick/mirror case to keep.

"But perhaps the question is not where my lips are—because if I don't know after all these years—but rather, where am I, which is, by the way, a similar question to the one God asks of Adam in the Garden in Genesis 3:9: Where are you?

"When you think about it, that's actually the first question in the world directed to a human being: Where are you? Where are we? Where's our mouth? Where's our heart? How do we use our words?

"And we best find the answers to these questions, and so many more, through our stories."

The crowd, as they say, went wild.

TWENTY-FIVE

Ever After

The wind had whipped up unexpectedly that morning, and for once, Peninnah hadn't dressed for the weather. Making her way to the subway at West 86th Street, she hugged her arms for warmth, struggling to balance the strap of her big leather bag more securely on her shoulder. Twice she nearly turned back for her heavier coat, but she chided herself: the station was just a block and a half from her apartment.

Outside Penn Station she stood shivering for five minutes until the crosstown bus stopped at the corner of West 34th Street and Seventh Avenue. She preferred the bus to the train; she was always interested in watching the people sprinting down the busy streets, so intent on arriving at their myriad destinations. Relationships, dreams, responsibilities: these, she knew, are the stuff of life.

At Lexington Avenue, she made her way to the front of the bus, stepped onto the sidewalk and walked one block to the Stern building on West 35th. She called out a hearty hello to the security guards at the downstairs elevators and to the secretary in the department office. By the time she reached her office, she was thoroughly chilled. She dropped her bag on her desk and went in search of the day's third cup of coffee.

Returning to her office from the cafeteria, she lifted the Styrofoam cup to her lips and sipped the scalding liquid. She closed her eyes and a thought came to her, not for the first time. *I am in my seventies. Maybe I should retire and make room for a younger person to take my place?* As if to try out the idea, she stood up and carried the mug two doors down to her empty classroom. *What if today were my last day teaching here?* The sudden rush of anxiety at the thought was nearly overpowering. She considered sitting down, but didn't want an early-arriving student to find her in that state. Instead she returned to her office and shut the door for a few minutes until she had composed herself.

"One more year," she whispered to the bookcase, the computer monitor, the graded papers. "I love it so much, and I know I'm still doing what I came here for."

Then, in 2014, the administration made the proverbial offer that was too good to refuse. They were giving new retirees extra money and extra medical insurance. She was going to be eighty in December. There was no good reason she could think of not to take it.

Peninnah wasn't the sole honoree at the retirement party. A couple of other faculty members in their seventies and eighties also took advantage of the generous offer. The event was held in a large common room in one of the apartment houses that Yeshiva University used as dorms. Attending with her son, daughter-in-law and three-year-old grandson, she felt tremendous *nachas* as she introduced them to her colleagues.

After the hors d'oeuvres and drinks were passed around, Dean Bacon said a few words in honor of the three faculty members who were being celebrated, then invited each of the honorees to speak. When it was Peninnah's turn, she prayed that she would get through her ten minutes without tears.

"When my beloved husband Irv died in the winter of 1967," she said, "I didn't want to go anywhere. That fall, I began teaching at Iona College in New Rochelle, and it was all I could do to go to work, take care of my two children and put one foot in front of the other." She paused. *I can do this.*

"Then I received a wedding invitation. You know how much a new widow looks forward to attending a wedding?" The crowd nodded; several people clicked their tongues in empathy. "I didn't want to go in the worst way! But I told myself, this is a mitzvah, celebrating the wedding of two young people. You need to be there.

"And that's where I met Dr. Abraham Tauber, at the wedding, through a mutual friend. He set up an interview with Dean Isaac Bacon. We had a wonderful interview, however I wanted to remain at Iona a second year. Then Dr. Tauber set up an appointment for me to meet Dean Mirsky—and the rest is history. When I became a faculty member at Stern College in 1969, Dr. Tauber's daughter June Golden was my colleague and office mate, and we became good friends. When Karen Bacon became Dean in 1977, she was very supportive of my storytelling course and gave us the support to organize three storytelling festivals, co-sponsored with the 92nd Street Y Jewish Storytelling Center. I've been grateful for her enthusiasm and support all these years.

"Now, forty-five years later, I am leaving Stern. I ask myself, where did the time go? And more importantly, what would I be doing if I hadn't performed that mitzvah? Thank you, all of you, for celebrating us elders today. I know I speak for the other retirees when I say, it was our sincere honor to work here."

As the start of the next semester approached, she was keenly aware of the calendar. The feeling of not having to go to work that first morning was strange. Throughout the first year of her retirement, she was in touch with the College quite a bit, but each year, a little less. She presented annual workshops for the honors education majors, after which she would step into the Dean's office to say hello to Dean Bacon, to the secretaries who had been so good to her, to some of the others in the administrative office suite, to the librarians, whom she always acknowledged for their assistance in her books. Every time she visited, she was greeted with smiles and hugs. She was delighted even when the security guards still remembered her when she stopped for a chat.

But there was so much storytelling work to do! So many invitations and requests to co-author, to contribute, to edit. A *Festschrift*—essays by a number of scholars written about her work—in her honor. Teaching in the new Maggid-Educator training program to support new Jewish storytellers. CAJE and New CAJE conferences, either in person or virtually. Requests from former students or rabbis or casual acquaintances for help locating a particular story. Invitations to teach a class from one of the faculty members of the Azrieli Graduate School of Jewish Education & Administration at Yeshiva University. At the end of some days, her fingers rested stiffly on her keyboard, but still she answered the mail, picked up the telephone, took the subway, or the plane, to perform, teach, present.

She continued to attend her beloved synagogue, B'nai Jeshurun. She increased her schedule of trips to Israel. She spoke on the telephone to friends and family every day. Sometimes she called her old Channing Street neighbor Katherine, her mind now too far gone to remember how they used to call themselves Linda and Lorraine when they played school.

And, far more often than she would ever expect, somebody who had seen her teach or perform twenty, thirty years earlier would look her up and ask her a question, invite her to present a program, or just want to bask in her aura. One day, she received an email from a young rabbi in Warsaw, asking her to recommend some of her stories for a series he planned to translate and record for Jewish children. She suggested half a dozen from her book *The Hungry Clothes*, including the popular Solomon story "This Too Shall Pass" and a lesser-known tale called "Remember." Another day, it was a letter from a man in Milwaukee who wanted to hire her after a co-worker told him about her performance from twenty-five years earlier. A woman she had met thirty years earlier in Montreal wrote for permission to tell a story of hers.

And there is more.

There are her children, Rebecca and Mordechai. Rebecca came to New York from Israel to stay with her while she recovered from each hip replacement. There are the grandchildren, Dorielle, Aaron and Ilan in

Israel, Tzahi and Simha in the States. There is an apartment and storage compartment full of memories, of her father's love letters to her mother, photos of her family and hundreds of books. A stack of letters to her from her father, and one from her mother. A professional photograph of her father in cantor's garb, and a few of her mother when she was young. Her parents' framed wedding portrait. Her mother's beads and clothing, the book of leaves Peninnah made as a child, classical music on the piano, the Fu Manchu costume she wore in a school play. Her father's menorah from Lithuania, with a bullet casing serving as a substitute *shammash* in place of the original, which had long since broken off. The reel-to-reel recording of her first wedding. The Teacher of the Year plaque from her students, on which they had engraved the words "Once upon a time there was a teacher. She was dearly beloved by all her students. She was as wise as she was beautiful." There was an outstanding senior faculty plaque from the College, and too many storytelling awards to count. Thank-you notes from lawyers writing that they still used what they learned in her class. A note from her beloved friend and colleague Cherie Karo Schwartz about the NewCAJE Renewing Initiative for Storytelling Education program, which she had created in Peninnah's honor. The cut-crystal Victorian lamp with the domed top that had sat on her parents' dining room table, reposing now on her mother's old Singer sewing machine. An Edison wind-up phonograph, with records half-an-inch thick. Her father's book, *Kol Rinah Utfilah*. A set of sterling silverware that her mother had brought from Russia. A pile of rubles. Her parents' passports and important papers. A box of 3x5" index cards, completely covered in Yiddish on both sides, which were her father's notes for his *divrei Torah*, his sermons, when he took the role of rabbi in his shul all those decades before.

There is also the legacy that no visitor can see: the love of Judaism, of stories, of excellence that her parents instilled in her and that has served her for eighty-six years. She is a pomegranate, brimming with the seeds of wisdom of everyone she has ever known and loved.

In a certain kingdom, the people maintained an unusual tradition for choosing a king when the old one died. The dead king's advisers released the Bird of Happiness. It flew around the heads of the country's men, and whomever it sat on was crowned king.

It so happened that a king died, and the ritual was performed as usual. This time, to the amusement and horror of the assembly, the bird alighted on the head of the court jester.

"You must put away your cap of bells, your drum and your foolish clothing," the advisers told him. "Now that you are king, you must wear this crown and these robes. And above all, you must remember that you are now the king, and not the jester."

The first thing the new king did was to arrange for a small shack to be built near the palace. One day, the people saw him disappear into the shack with his old jester's cap, drum and clothing. After a while he emerged, locked the door and returned to the palace.

This went on from time to time, till the advisers started to whisper. Finally the bravest of them asked, "Sire, what is it that you do in that shack?"

"I look at my jester's costume," he said. "To be a good king, I must always remember where I came from. I must remember where I came from, and who I am."

My Storyteller's Prayer

by Peninnah Schram

Rebono shel olam, God of the Universe, listen to my heart and my voice as I stand before you, wanting to tell our story.

Help me to understand and find the right feelings and words with which to transmit the tale.

Make my voice expressive and clear so that the collective wisdom of our people can reach the hearts of those who listen.

May I merit to hear well with my ears and heart.

Keep me from the jealousy of other tellers and from my jealousy of them so that we may be able to share and hear each other with open hearts.

Allow me to assume this responsibility as my forebears did before me—to continue to tell our stories.

Help me to choose my stories wisely and let my words live.

Make me worthy to be a storyteller of our Jewish people.

Glossary of Yiddish and Hebrew Terms

Note: "Y" indicates Yiddish; "H" indicates Hebrew. The "ch" sound is pronounced gutturally. Words that are spelled the same in Hebrew and Yiddish are usually pronounced differently. Also, the "ei" spelling indicates a long "a" as in "table." The "ay" spelling indicates a long "i" as in "life."

Alef-beis	Alphabet. In Hebrew, the "s" sound is replaced by a "t" sound. (Y)
Aliyah	Emigration to Israel; literally "going up" (H)
Atarah	Literally "crown." Ornament placed on the top of the Torah scroll or ornamental neckband on prayer shawl (H)
Baruch haShem	Literally "Thank God." Often said when asked, how are you? (H)
Bashert	Destined, or "meant to be" (Y)
Bimah	Large stage in a synagogue sanctuary from which a service is led (H, Y)
Bris	Ritual circumcision (Y)
Bubbe	Grandmother (Y)
Chazzan	Cantor (H)
Chazzen	Cantor (Y)
Chametz	Leavened bread, forbidden during the eight-day holiday of Passover (H, Y)
Chasidim	Members of an ultra-Orthodox Jewish sect that celebrate God through joyful song, dance and storytelling (H, Y)
Chuppah	Canopy under which the bride and groom stand at a Jewish wedding (H, Y)
Chutzpah	Nerve, gall (Y)
Daven	Pray (Y)

Der Fir Kashas	Literally, the Four Questions. Traditionally recited by the youngest child at the Passover Seder, they refer to specific practices during the ritual meal, throughout which they are answered. (Y)
Divrei Torah	Interpretations of the Torah portion read in the synagogue, usually on the Sabbath (H)
Dreidl	Top used in a game played for Chanukah, also a symbol of the holiday (H, Y)
Erev	The night before, as in the Sabbath or any holiday, which begins in the evening (H, Y)
Farchailke	Head scarf (Y)
Goldeneh keppele	Smart, literally "little golden head" (Y)
Gott tzu dankn	Thank God, literally "God be thanked" (Y)
Halacha	Jewish law (H, Y)
Ketubah	Traditional Jewish marriage contract (H)
Kibitz	To chat, or to offer unsolicited advice (Y)
Kiddush	Blessing over wine (H, Y)
Kind mayne	My child (Y)
Kindele	Little child (Y)
Kinder	Children (Y)
Kittel	White robe worn by the rabbi or cantor for special synagogue services, such as Rosh Hashanah and Yom Kippur (Y)
Kneidlach	A mixture of matzoh meal and eggs rolled into balls and simmered in water or chicken broth. Plural of kneidl (Y)
Kol ha kavod	Literally "all the honor." Said when a person accomplishes something worthwhile (H)
Kvell	To be immensely proud and joyful (Y)
Latkes	Potato pancakes (Y)
L'chayim	Traditional Jewish toast, literally "to life" (H, Y)
Litvak	Lithuanian (Y)
Lokh in kop	Hole in the head, as in, "I need that like a hole in the head." (Y)
Lubavitch	An ultra-Orthodox sect of Hasidic Judaism (H, Y)

Mamzer	Bastard (Y)
Mazel tov	Congratulations, literally "good luck" (H, Y)
Matzoh	Unleavened bread, traditionally eaten during the holiday of Passover (H, Y)
Meidelah	Little girl (Y)
Mayn	My (Y)
Mensch	Literally, a person. Can connote an honorable, decent person (Y)
Midrash	Homiletic commentary (H, Y)
Mishpacha	Family (H, Y)
Mitnagdim	These Eastern European Jewish "opponents" of the Chasidic movement in the eighteenth and nineteenth centuries believed in serving God through serious study rather than joyful song and dance. (H, Y) In Yiddish, the "t" sound is substituted with an "s"
Mitzvah	Good deed. Plural Mitzvot. In Yiddish, the second "t" sound is substituted with an "s" (H, Y)
Mohel	Ritual circumciser (H, Y)
Neshome	Soul (H, Y)
Nigun	Traditional tune, often accompanied by nonsense lyrics like bim-bim-bam (H, Y)
Nosh	Snack, or to snack (Y) Nove bransiche, ehre plansiche, pastechl, katchke, tzuganke, goldene kepele, new recruit, little airplane, little shepherd, goose, gypsy, golden head (Y) (List of pet names Papa called Peninnah, usually running them together as one)
Nu	So or well, as in, "Well?" (Y)
oy gevalt	Literally, "oh, violence!" An expletive connoting fear or astonishment (Y)
oy vey	An expletive connoting frustration or dismay (Y)
Peklach	Bundles, as in packages (Y)
Pesach	The eight-day spring holiday of Passover, commemorating the exodus of the Hebrews from Egypt (H, Y)
Purim	The spring holiday in which Jews dress up in costume, celebrating the rescue of the Jews of Persia from slaughter (H, Y)
Schlep	Carry or drag (Y)

Schlepper	A worthless or stupid person (Y)
Schmaltz	Fat (Y)
Scholom	Peace (H, Y)
Seder	Ritual meal marking the first and second nights of the Passover holiday (H, Y)
Sephardic	Referring to Jews of Spanish, Portuguese, Arab, Turkish and West Asian origins (H)
Shabbes	Sabbath (Y).
Shaliach tzibor	Messenger of the people (H)
Shechtn	To slaughter (Y)
Sheina punnum	Pretty face (Y)
Shidduch	Match leading to marriage (Y)
Shlechtn	Bad (Y)
Shoah	The Holocaust (H, Y)
Shochet or Shachet	Ritual butcher (H, Y)
Sholom	Peace (H, Y)
Shtele	Position, as a job (Y)
Shtetl	A small village in Eastern Europe in which resided a large proportion of Jews (Y)
Shul	Synagogue (Y)
Shpilkes	Agitation, antsiness; literally "pins," as in "on pins and needles"
Sukkah	An open-air room built to celebrate the festival of Sukkot (H, Y)
Tallis	Prayer shawl with special symbolic fringes on the four corners (H, Y) In Hebrew, the "s" sound is replaced by a "t" sound.
Tanach	The canonical collection of Hebrew Scriptures. The word is an acronym for "Torah" (Law), "Nevi'im" (Prophets) and "Ketubim" (Writings). (H)
Tochis	Buttocks (Y)
Tzugankele	Little gypsy (Y)
Tzu schechtn	To butcher (Y)
Yarmulke	Skullcap (Y)

Yiddishkayt   Jewish cultural knowledge (Y)

Yom tovim   Holidays; literally "good days" (H, Y)

Zeide   Grandfather (Y)

Selected Publications and Recordings by Peninnah Schram

Oren, Miriam, and Peninnah Schram, 2004. *A Tree in the Garden*. Raleigh, NC: Nora House.

Sasso, Sandy Eisenberg, and Peninnah Schram, 2015. *Jewish Stories of Love and Marriage: Folktales, Legends and Letters*. Lanham, MD: Rowman & Littlefield.

Schram, Penninah. 1986. *The Big Sukkah*. Minneapolis: Kar-Ben.

———, 2000. *The Chanukah Blessing*. New York: UAHC Press.

———, ed., 1995. *Chosen Tales: Stories Told by Jewish Storytellers*. Lanham, MD: Jason Aronson.

———, 2010. *El Rei Dels Captaires i Altres Contes Hebreus*. Barcelona, Spain: Editorial Vicens Vives.

———, 2010. *El Rey De Los Mendigos y Otros Cuentos Hebreos*. Barcelona, Spain: Editorial Vicens Vives.

———, 2005. "Elijah's Cup of Hope: Healing Through the Jewish Storytelling Tradition." *Storytelling, Self, Society: An Interdisciplinary Journal of Storytelling Studies* 2, no. 2 (Spring): 103–117.

———, 2008. *The Hungry Clothes and Other Jewish Folktales*. Edison, NJ: Sterling Publishing.

———, 1996. "Jewish Models: Adapting Folktales for Telling Aloud." In *Who Says? Essays on Pivotal Issues in Contemporary Storytelling*, edited by Carol Birch and Melissa A. Heckler, 64-90. Little Rock: August House.

———, 1987. *Jewish Stories One Generation Tells Another*. Lanham, MD: Jason Aronson.

———, 2007. *The Magic Pomegranate*. Minneapolis: Milbrook Press.

———, 2005. *The Purim Costume* URJ Press.

———, 2000. *Stories Within Stories: From The Jewish Oral Tradition*. Lanham, MD: Jason Aronson.

———, 1991. *Tales of Elijah the Prophet*. Lanham, MD: Jason Aronson.

———, 1998. *Ten Classic Jewish Children's Stories*. Pitspopany Press.

———, 2012, and Rachayl Eckstein Davis. *The Apple Tree's Discovery*. Minneapolis: Kar-Ben.

———, and Gerard Edery, 1999. *The Minstrel & the Storyteller* (Audio CD). New York: Sefarad Records.

———, and Steven A. Rosman, 1990. *Eight Tales for Eight Nights: Stories For Chanukah*. Lanham, MD: Jason Aronson.

About the Author

Caren Schnur Neile, Ph.D., MFA, has taught storytelling studies at Florida Atlantic University for more than two decades. A performance storyteller, she co-hosts The Public Storyteller on South Florida public radio WLRN, as well as numerous local storytelling events. She is a former Peace Corps volunteer, former chair of the National Storytelling Network, and has worked in six countries, including as a Fulbright Senior Specialist in Austria and Israel. A co-founding editor of the academic journal *Storytelling, Self, Society*, Dr. Neile has published widely, including a chapter in the *Oxford Handbook of American Folklore and Folk Life Studies*, an entry in the *Encyclopedia of Jewish-American Literature*, a biweekly column on storytelling for the *Florida Jewish Journal*, and the books *The Great American Story* and *Florida Lore*. Her latest book is *Only in Florida*.